The Letters of
Flannery O'Connor and Caroline Gordon

The Letters of
Flannery O'Connor
and
Caroline Gordon

Edited by Christine Flanagan

≈

The University of Georgia Press
Athens

Publication of this book was made possible, in part, by a generous gift
from the University of Georgia Press Friends Fund

Designed by Erin Kirk New
Set in Arno Pro
Printed and bound by Thomson-Shore, Inc.

The paper in this book meets the guidelines for permanence and
durability of the Committee on Production Guidelines for Book Longevity
of the Council on Library Resources.

Most University of Georgia Press titles are
available from popular e-book vendors.

Printed in the United States of America
18   19   20   21   22   C   5   4   3   2   1

Library of Congress Control Number: 2018018111
ISBN 9780820354088 (hardcover: alk. paper)
ISBN 9780820354071 (ebook)

With gratitude to Mom & Dad & Dave & David

Contents

Acknowledgments

One day, Professor Thomas Gavin at University of Rochester read aloud Flannery O'Connor's "Everything That Rises Must Converge"—and nothing was ever the same. Professor Gavin gave me Flannery O'Connor and Anton Chekhov and John Gardner. He taught me to *read* and gave me the courage to write. At Emerson College, Melanie Rae Thon showed me *how* to be a writer: how to unfurl yourself on the page, how generosity begets generosity, how quiet work culminates into a life well-spent. The letters of Caroline Gordon and Flannery O'Connor—filled with generous detail, astute analysis, and humble gratitude—have reminded me of my best teachers: those who value curiosity, attention to craft, joy in the classroom. Thank you.

Melanie Rae Thon's publication in a book edited by Frederick Busch, *Letters to a Fiction Writer* (W. W. Norton, 1999), introduced me to Caroline Gordon. There, among thirty-three letters, is Gordon's spellbinding 1951 letter to the young O'Connor. Since then, I have enjoyed visits to Georgia College and State University: attending O'Connor conferences, visiting the archives at her alma mater. In 2014, I was fortunate to attend the National Endowment for the Humanities Summer Institute, expertly facilitated by Bruce Gentry and Robert Donahoo, who encouraged me to continue this project. Nancy Davis Bray and the Ina Dillard Russell Library at Georgia College provided a research grant in 2016—along with over a decade of assistance on a number of O'Connor-related writing projects. The O'Connor community has been a tremendous source of support, including Carol Loeb Schloss, Bruce Henderson, Sue Whatley, Lindsey Alexander, Rhonda Armstrong, Ali Arant, Eric Bennett, Gina Caison, Jordan Cofer, David Davis, Doug Davis, Marie Lathers, Monica Miller, Dan Moran, Cassandra Nelson, George Piggford, James Potts, Jimmy Dean Smith, Alison Staudinger, Daniel Train, and Colleen Warren.

The pursuit of these letters—to unearth as many as possible—has been delightful detective work. The biographies of Caroline Gordon written by Nancylee Novell Jonza, Ann Waldron, and Veronica Makowsky provided invaluable insight. O'Connor biographers and scholars whose work provided assistance include Brad Gooch, Sarah Gordon, Jean Cash, Katherine Prown, and Paul Elie. The original documents—the letters—are available, however, because of the tremendous archival resources available at the Special Collections of the Ina Dillard Russell Library at Georgia College; the Special Collections of the Firestone Library at Princeton University; the Stuart A. Rose Manuscript, Archives, and Rare Book Library at Emory University; the Southern Historical Collection of the Louis Round Wilson Special Collections Library at University of North Carolina at Chapel Hill; and the Special Collections and University Archives at the Jean and Alexander Heard Library at Vanderbilt University. My thanks go to Sandra Bossert (Princeton), Kathy Shoemaker (Emory), Teresa Gray and Rachel Koch (Vanderbilt), and Kristin Leaman (Indiana University). Jim Cummings of the J. W. England Library at USciences helped throughout a research sabbatical, generously provided by University of the Sciences.

I am indebted to the literary executors of Caroline Gordon and Flannery O'Connor, who made it possible to share this master class. Caroline Wood Fallon shared memories of her grandmother and supported this work without hesitation. Material from the published and unpublished writings of Caroline Gordon is used with the permission of Caroline Wood Fallon; I hope this book brings an appreciation of Caroline Gordon to a new generation of readers and writers. Flannery O'Connor, meanwhile, finds new audiences all the time—in popular culture, church book clubs, college classrooms, and more. Thanks to the Mary Flannery O'Connor Charitable Trust for allowing the use of published and unpublished writings of Flannery O'Connor. The invisible hero of this book is Sally Fitzgerald. Material from the unpublished writings of Sally Fitzgerald is used with the permission of Ughetta Fitzgerald.

Carol Flanagan and Georgeanne McVay provided astute feedback over several drafts of this book. At University of the Sciences, Kevin Murphy, Barbara Byrne, and Suzanne Murphy provided essential support. Thanks also to my colleagues who supported the various stages of this work: Phyllis Blumberg, Jeff Brown, Laura Caccioppoli, Shaylea Caccioppoli, Martin Carrion, Leah Comeau, Elaina Corrato, Ruth Crispin, Mike Dockray, Annemarie Flanagan, Joan Franks, Casey Granic, Brenna Holland, Peter Hoffer, Warren Hope,

Laurie Kirszner, Steve Metraux, Cliff Robinson, Sarah Robinson, Kim Robson, Roy Robson, Sam Talcott, and David Traxel. From the very beginning, Bob Boughner was a champion. Cindy Hong arrived when I needed help in the final stages of completing this manuscript. Reinforcement, beginning to end, came from Larry Boylan, Margo Brousseau, Laurie Fladd, and Marissa Feinsilver.

Thank you to the staff at University of Georgia Press: Walter Biggins, David Des Jardines, Ana Jimenez-Moreno, and Bethany Snead. Thomas Roche and C. J. Bartunek are the ideal editors: insightful, wise, clear, and kind. Thank you.

Finally, I am grateful to my family: they are the ones who received and answered my earliest letters, and the ones who continue to provide unqualified and unwavering support.

Selected Works by Flannery O'Connor and Caroline Gordon

Flannery O'Connor

Wise Blood. New York: Harcourt, Brace, 1952.

A Good Man Is Hard to Find. New York: Harcourt, Brace, 1955.

The Violent Bear It Away. New York: Farrar, Straus, and Cudahy, 1960.

Everything That Rises Must Converge. New York: Farrar, Straus, and Giroux, 1965.

Mystery and Manners: Occasional Prose. Edited by Sally Fitzgerald and Robert Fitzgerald. New York: Farrar, Straus, and Giroux, 1969.

The Complete Stories. New York: Farrar, Straus, and Giroux, 1971.

The Habit of Being: Letters of Flannery O'Connor. Edited by Sally Fitzgerald. New York: Farrar, Straus, and Giroux, 1979.

The Presence of Grace and Other Book Reviews. Compiled by Leo J. Zuber. Edited by Carter W. Martin. Athens: University of Georgia Press, 1983.

Flannery O'Connor: Collected Works. Edited by Sally Fitzgerald. New York: Library of America, 1988.

Flannery O'Connor: The Cartoons. Seattle: Fantagraphics, 2012.

A Prayer Journal. Edited by William Sessions. New York: Farrar, Straus, and Giroux, 2013.

Caroline Gordon

Penhally. New York: Scribner's, 1931.

Aleck Maury, Sportsman. New York: Scribner's, 1934.

None Shall Look Back. New York: Scribner's, 1937.

The Garden of Adonis. New York: Scribner's, 1937.

Green Centuries. New York: Scribner's, 1941.

The Women on the Porch. New York: Scribner's, 1944.

The Forest of the South. New York: Scribner's, 1945.

The House of Fiction: An Anthology of the Short Story with Commentary by Caroline Gordon and Allen Tate. New York: Scribner's, 1950; second edition published in 1960 by Charles Scribner's Sons.

The Strange Children. New York: Scribner's, 1951.

The Malefactors. New York: Harcourt, Brace, 1956.

How to Read a Novel. New York: Viking, 1957.

Old Red and Other Stories. New York: Scribner's, 1963.

A Good Soldier: A Key to the Novels of Ford Madox Ford. Davis: University of California Library, 1963.

The Glory of Hera. Garden City, NY: Doubleday, 1972.

The Collected Stories of Caroline Gordon. New York: Farrar, Straus, and Giroux, 1981.

Editor's Note

Salutations and closings have been removed from the letters to prevent unnecessary repetition and to conserve space. Return addresses are included only for the first letter at each location.

Idiosyncratic spelling from the original letters has been retained. Otherwise, obvious typographical or minor errors have been silently corrected.

These letters are unabridged and transcribed from original documents. Brackets indicate editorial insertions.

The Letters of
Flannery O'Connor and Caroline Gordon

Introduction

Flannery O'Connor was twenty-six years old, anxiously awaiting acceptance of her first novel, when a stranger read her work. "I'm glad you gave me Flannery O'Connor's novel to read," Caroline Gordon told the mutual friend who introduced them. "This girl is a real novelist." As the well-regarded author of eight books of fiction, Gordon could offer opinions that carried weight. Over the next thirteen years, letter by letter, a complex relationship between the two women would evolve. Born a generation apart, Gordon and O'Connor never assumed the roles of mother and daughter, never shared the intimacy of confidantes, never celebrated equal professional acclaim. Gordon's encouragement could uplift the young writer as easily as her critiques could alienate. Nonetheless, the women maintained a steadfast connection until O'Connor's untimely death at thirty-nine. Until now, their artistic and personal exchanges—most boxed away for decades—have been unavailable to the scholars and biographers who might best appreciate this timeless correspondence.

Flannery O'Connor's initial encounter with Caroline Gordon would seem, at first, to be a quiet moment in an otherwise tumultuous time for the young writer. At twenty-two, O'Connor had won the 1947 Rinehart-Iowa Award: $750 and first option for Rinehart Publishing to acquire her novel-in-progress, *Wise Blood*. Two years later, hoping to sign a contract and receive an advance from the publisher, O'Connor submitted nine chapters and an outline. The response made her bristle. Rinehart editor John Selby vaguely suggested that they "work with her" to "change the direction" of the book. O'Connor objected to the criticism; three of the novel's chapters had been published in prestigious journals, after all. "I feel the objections they raise are connected with its virtues," O'Connor wrote to her agent, "and the thought of working with them specifically to correct these lacks they mention is repulsive to me." Furthermore, she predicted that John Selby, who treated her like a "slightly dim-witted Camp Fire Girl," would not want the finished novel "if left to my fiendish care."

O'Connor lived with her friends Sally and Robert Fitzgerald* in Ridgefield, Connecticut, as she worked slowly and steadily to complete her novel, which featured Hazel Motes, a backwoods World War II veteran and self-appointed preacher for his Church Without Christ. A year later, in 1950, O'Connor untangled her commitment with Rinehart and signed a provisional contract with Harcourt, Brace. She moved home to Milledgeville, Georgia, survived her first serious health crisis, and—at last—sent the finished novel to her editor at Harcourt in early March 1951.

"So far as I am concerned," O'Connor told her agent, "this is the last draft of the book." To Robert Giroux, her new editor at Harcourt, Brace, O'Connor wrote, "I'm still open to suggestions about improving it and will welcome any you have."

Giroux did not respond.

Giroux had seen the published excerpts of *Wise Blood*; he had remained patient while O'Connor extracted herself from her original publisher's contract. But months passed, and O'Connor worried. Behind the scenes, Giroux worried, too. By some accounts, *Wise Blood* was "the most shocking book" the publisher had ever read, populated by con-artists, heretics, prostitutes—even a shrunken mummy. As she would later recall, Sally Fitzgerald learned that at Harcourt, Brace, "Someone, or more than one, was evidently withholding agreement. Still, there was no outright rejection, so someone else was evidently standing firm. This was of course Robert Giroux, who was determined that the novel should not be turned down. That there was a struggle in progress was perfectly clear to us [the Fitzgeralds] in Ridgefield, as well, although Flannery was not told of the telephone call from Giroux to Robert Fitzgerald, requesting a supporting opinion."

Robert Fitzgerald had an idea. He asked O'Connor's permission to send her book to a friend: fellow Catholic, accomplished novelist, and experienced teacher of creative writing Caroline Gordon. O'Connor agreed.

Caroline Gordon's immediate reaction was enthusiastic ("she is already a rare phenomenon: a Catholic novelist with a real dramatic sense, one who relies more on her technique than her piety") and constructive ("a touch here and

---

* Robert Fitzgerald was a poet and translator of Greek literature, including the works of Euripides, Sophocles, and Homer. After O'Connor's death, Robert served as her literary executor; both Robert and Sally Fitzgerald would edit O'Connor's letters and essays for posthumous publication.

there and a re-writing of two key scenes which she has muffed would do wonders"). Gordon mailed an extended critique to Robert Fitzgerald and Fitzgerald
sent her recommendations to Giroux. Fortified by the opinions of Fitzgerald
and Gordon, Giroux, finally, told O'Connor that Harcourt would publish the
novel. He forwarded Gordon's comments, along with his own, to O'Connor
and urged her to review Gordon's "extraordinary" suggestions.

With that, the "master class" began.

≈

Caroline Gordon is not widely read or taught today. Even during her life, she
was more often identified as the wife of poet Allen Tate than as a successful
novelist in her own right. But by the mid-1950s, when her friendship with
O'Connor deepened, Gordon was at the height of her career. She had completed eight novels and one short-story collection; had earned a National Book
Award nomination alongside William Faulkner, Truman Capote, and J. D.
Salinger (1952); had won a Guggenheim award (1932); had received a second
prize in the O. Henry Prize Stories (1934); had written an introduction to a
new American edition of Flaubert's *Madame Bovary* (1950); and had published
(with Tate) *House of Fiction* (1950), a short-story anthology taught in literature
and creative writing programs. Maxwell Perkins—editor to Ernest Hemingway,
F. Scott Fitzgerald, and Thomas Wolfe—had been Gordon's editor for twenty
years, until his death in 1947. Gordon's achievements had won her a rare place
in the overwhelmingly male literary establishment.

From an early age, Carolyn Gordon (b. 1895)—later Caroline—showed a
remarkable intellect and work ethic. In 1905, at age ten, she attended her parents' classical preparatory school for boys in Clarksville, Tennessee. Gordon
relished her studies in Greek and Latin. She read Virgil and Shakespeare at
school; at the family home in Woodstock, Kentucky, she heard endless tales
about her Meriwether ancestors and the glory of the old South. In 1912, only
sixteen, Gordon entered Bethany College ably prepared to skip first- and sec-
ond-year Greek. She graduated with a BA in classical studies in 1916, taught for
two years, then worked as a journalist for nearly a decade.

This long apprenticeship served her well, not least because it clarified that
her aspirations transcended nonfiction. By the fall of 1922, Gordon woke regularly at 4:00 a.m. to write fiction before heading off to the *Chattanooga News*.
"Carolyn approached her task with single-minded dedication," wrote biographer

Nancylee Novell Jonza in *The Underground Stream: The Life and Art of Caroline Gordon* (1995). Gordon had a wealth of writing and publishing experience by the time she was twenty-eight, when she met Vanderbilt poet and co-founder of the *Fugitive* Allen Tate. Gordon moved to Greenwich Village, found a job at a newspaper syndicate, became pregnant, and quickly married Tate in May 1925.

A breakthrough occurred two years later in New York, when Gordon became a secretary to novelist Ford Madox Ford, who occasionally dictated his work to her in his undergarments. Author of *The Good Soldier* (1915) and the *Parade's End* tetralogy (1924–28), Ford was a friend of Henry James, Stephen Crane, James Joyce, and Joseph Conrad. Eventually, during an extended stay in Paris, Gordon decided to show Ford her novel-in-progress, which would become *Penhally*. Ford approved so enthusiastically, she recalled, that he "took me by the scruff of the neck about three weeks before I left, set me down in his apartment every morning at eleven o'clock and forced me to dictate at least five thousand words, not all in one morning, to him. If I complained that it was hard to work with everything so hurried and Christmas presents to buy he observed 'You have no passion for your art. It is unfortunate' in such a sinister way that I would reel forth sentences in a sort of panic." Ford would become Gordon's effusive advocate, calling *Penhally* (1931) "the best constructed novel that modern America has produced."

Caroline Gordon and Allen Tate lived among literati in New York, Paris, and Rome. Their friends included Hart Crane, E. E. Cummings, Malcolm Cowley, Dorothy Day, Katherine Anne Porter, and F. Scott Fitzgerald. In Paris, they celebrated Thanksgiving with the Hemingways. Allen Tate was especially close with his Vanderbilt and *Fugitive* brethren John Crowe Ransom, Andrew Lytle, and Robert Penn Warren (who had been Tate's college roommate). When they moved back to Clarksville, Tennessee, the Tates' home, "Benfolly," served as a writing retreat for their friends. (Pulitzer Prize–winning poet Robert Lowell once famously lived in a tent on their front lawn.) Gordon was both hostess and writer, with "one hand on the kitchen stove and one on the typewriter," as she put it.

After publishing five novels and one short-story collection, Gordon found a new passion: the Catholic faith. She was baptized in December 1947, when she was fifty-two years old. "It's like suddenly being given authority to believe all the things you've surmised," she said. Her vocation as a writer had prepared the ground for this late-life conversion to Catholicism. Gordon explained,

I was converted, I suppose, mostly by reading the Gospels. I was reading the Gospel of St. Mark last summer, out at Robber Rocks, and all of a sudden the words that had been in my memory all my life were saying something I'd never heard before. I think I have been converted partly by my own work, too. I have lived most of my life on the evidence of things not seen—what else is writing a novel but that?—and my work has progressed slowly and steadily in one direction. At a certain point I found the Church squarely in the path. I couldn't jump over and wouldn't go around it, so had to go into it.

In 1949, the Tates met the French Catholic theologian Jacques Maritain, who was considered the most influential Catholic philosopher on either side of the Atlantic. His book *Art and Scholasticism* (1920) had been translated into English in 1930. Maritain was teaching at Princeton and living near the Tates in New Jersey. When Allen Tate followed Gordon into the Catholic Church, Jacques Maritain and his wife Raïssa served as Allen's godparents. A lasting friendship followed, and Gordon quoted Maritain in her epigraph to *The Malefactors*.* After its publication, Gordon felt that Maritain was one of the few who understood the technical achievement of her novel.

Alongside her own writing, Gordon began to provide encouragement and editorial suggestion to other writers, remembering, always, Ford Madox Ford's generosity. Twenty-one years after his death, Gordon wrote, "I do not believe that any imaginative writer who possessed a vestige of talent ever came your way without being the better for it. I am told that when you died [. . .] one corner of your rented desk was piled high with the manuscripts of young fiction writers, some of whom, unknown at the time, have since attained fame."

Gordon's own desk soon became legendary: stacked with manuscripts of young writers and, nearby, a ready pen set to deliver the same fulsome—and sometimes ruthless—support Ford had once offered her.

≈

When Ford first took Gordon by the scruff of the neck, Mary Flannery O'Connor (b. 1925) was four years old in Savannah, Georgia. O'Connor's home with her parents, Regina and Edward, had a bathtub for storytelling and a back yard for

* Their correspondence is published in *Exiles and Fugitives: The Letters of Jacques and Raïssa Maritain, Allen Tate, and Caroline Gordon*, ed. John M. Dunaway (Baton Rouge: Louisiana State University Press, 1992).

chickens; next door was Cousin Katie Semmes and her electric car. O'Connor could leave her house and walk the perimeter of Lafayette Square to reach any place that was important. One block north, the towering spires of the Cathedral of St. John the Baptist rose into the sky, marking the seat of Georgia's Roman Catholic community and the O'Connors' spiritual home. Her school, St. Vincent Grammar School, stood between home and church. On the far side of Lafayette Square, O'Connor played the piano at the Girl Scouts Headquarters and wrote her first newspaper article, about the troop, published in a 1935 issue of the *Savannah Morning News*. O'Connor's family moved to Atlanta briefly before settling in Milledgeville, Georgia, when O'Connor was thirteen. Her father had been diagnosed with systemic lupus erythematosus, an autoimmune disease that would take his life just before O'Connor's sixteenth birthday.

One year later, at seventeen, O'Connor entered Georgia State College for Women in Milledgeville. She finished her BA in social science in three years, earned recognition for her art and editorial cartoons, and enrolled in the University of Iowa's Graduate School of Journalism. After a semester, she transferred into the Writers' Workshop, home to aspiring fiction writers and poets taught by Paul Engle, Andrew Lytle, Robie Macauley, and Robert Penn Warren. (Visiting poet Allen Tate later said that he registered no impression of O'Connor whatsoever.) At Iowa, O'Connor read Caroline Gordon's fiction for the first time. "'Old Red' was the making of me as a short story writer," O'Connor later told Gordon. "I think I learned from it what you can do with a symbol once you get a hold of it."

In graduate school, O'Connor wondered whether her art aligned with her faith. Her *Prayer Journal*, produced during her Iowa apprenticeship, was her attempt to "reconcile her Catholic piety with the strictures of literary modernism and the nasty characters, violent episodes, spicy idiom, and low jokes she was drawn to write about," wrote Paul Elie. In the journal, O'Connor prayed, "Please let Christian principles permeate my writing, and please let there be enough of my writing (published) for Christian principles to permeate." While at Iowa, she attended daily mass at St. Mary's Catholic Church and consulted a priest about her writing. Was her subject matter . . . *scandalous*? "He gave me one of those ten cent pamphlets that they are never without," O'Connor later told Gordon, "and said I didn't have to write for fifteen year old girls."

In the summer of 1948, O'Connor left Iowa and went to Yaddo, the Saratoga Springs artists' colony. That year, she wrote, "What first stuns the young writer emerging from college is that there is no clear-cut road for him to travel on. He must chop a path in the wilderness of his own soul; a disheartening process, lifelong and lonesome." At Yaddo, O'Connor met Robert Lowell, who wrote to Caroline Gordon, "There's a girl here named Flannery O'Connor, an admirer of yours, a Catholic and probably a good writer, who is looking for a teaching job. Is there anything at Columbia?" (No response survives, if any existed.)

At Yaddo, Jacques Maritain's *Art and Scholasticism* served as "a thunderclap to O'Connor," wrote biographer Brad Gooch. Maritain believed that "Everything, sacred and profane, belongs" in Christian art. The whole of man, for Maritain, encompassed good *and* evil; to plumb the nature of evil was a Christian exercise, not a heretical pursuit. O'Connor's most iconic stories, written well after her introduction to Maritain and Gordon, are certainly not written for fifteen-year-old girls. In one, a grandfather kills his beloved granddaughter by smashing her head against a rock. In another, a hardworking Polish émigré has his spine crushed by a tractor; three characters stand beside and do nothing. And, famously, another: a family car trip ends when two children, their parents, and their grandmother are murdered on the side of a country road.

"It has puzzled some of her readers and annoyed the Catholic church," wrote Alice Walker in an essay about O'Connor, "that in her stories not only does good not triumph, it is not usually present." It would be some years before O'Connor could articulate the theoretical underpinning for her characters' extreme circumstances:

> The novelist with Christian concerns will find in modern life distortions which are repugnant to him, and his problem will be to make these appear as distortions to an audience which is used to seeing them as natural; and he may well be forced to take ever more violent means to get his vision across to this hostile audience. When you can assume that your audience holds the same beliefs you do, you can relax a little and use more normal ways of talking to it; when you have to assume that it does not, then you have to make your vision apparent by shock—to the hard of hearing you shout, and for the almost blind you draw large and startling figures.

Jacques Maritain was perhaps the first to articulate for O'Connor the spiritual and artistic dilemma she would confront for the rest of her career: that Christian art is "doubly difficult—difficulty squared" because "the whole life of the age is far removed from Christ."

O'Connor's work would never puzzle Caroline Gordon, who had easily synthesized her early classical education with the Gospels. For her, Catholic writers like Flannery O'Connor and Walker Percy were "people who don't have to spend time trying to figure out what moral order prevails in the universe." Technique and faith became synonymous for Gordon. When Gordon responded to O'Connor's story, "A Good Man Is Hard to Find," she wrote,

> The story, on the whole does not have enough "composition of scene" to borrow a phrase from St. Ignatius of Loyola. It is not well enough located in time and place. Remember that the Lord made the world before He made Adam and Eve. Events take place in time and space. [. . .] I particularly miss landscape after The Misfit comes on the scene. One wonders how the grandmother is able to keep her mind on her conversation with him when Bailey goes off in the woods with the two boys.

Gordon's 1947 conversion to Catholicism and, coincidentally, O'Connor's 1947 visit to an Iowa priest had facilitated a similar realization: Catholic writing need not consist of pious "pablum" or sanctimonious anecdotes. Some readers have struggled to reconcile O'Connor's violent content with her image as a Southern woman who delighted in raising swans and peacocks and as a devout Catholic who attended daily mass throughout her adult years. However, Christian dogma, O'Connor understood, "frees the storyteller to observe. It is not a set of rules which fixes what he sees in the world. It affects his writing primarily by guaranteeing his respect for mystery." To a large measure, this shared axiom—that Christian faith expanded one's artistic capacity—allowed Gordon and O'Connor to transcend any generational differences or personality clashes they might encounter over their thirteen-year friendship. After O'Connor's death, Gordon said of her, "[S]he dismisses the popular notion that the Catholic Church acts as a 'restraint on the creativity of the Catholic writer' and maintains that, on the contrary, Christian dogma is an 'instrument for penetrating reality.'"

~

When O'Connor and Gordon met in person in June 1952, a full year after Gordon first read *Wise Blood*, they knew a number of important things about one another. They shared close friends (the Fitzgeralds, the Lowells) and they shared a moral and artistic compass. Less obvious was the unique isolation of pursuing their art in a literary landscape not always welcoming to women. Rosemary Magee, editor of *Friendship and Sympathy: Communities of Southern Women Writers* (1992), described women such as Gordon and O'Connor as "defined by a set of intertwining circles—communities not contained by time or space, without the comforts of a shared college campus or the hospitality of a literary establishment." Women authors faced competing demands; Gordon taught at more than twenty different colleges and writers' conferences throughout her career, but she was also a mother and housewife. She sewed her own dresses. She gardened and cleaned and cooked and painted. In a letter to friend Ward Dorrance,* Gordon wrote:

> [W]hile I am a woman I am also a freak. The work I do is not suitable for a woman. It is unsexing. I speak with real conviction here. I don't write "the womanly" novel. I write the same kind of novel a man would write, only it is ten times harder for me to write it than it would be for a man who had the same degree of talent. Dr. Johnson was right: a woman at intellectual labour is always a dog walking on its hind legs. When you add to that the task of running a house, serving dinner that seems to have been prepared by an excellent cook, and all the while trying to be a good hostess—which means trying to make every man in the room have a good time—oh well, I am inclin[ed] to self-pity now and I don't deserve any pity at all, for I have a good time in this life. But I *do* have a lot on my hands. I bite off more than I can chew all the time.

Flannery O'Connor was never expected to manage a household or serve as dinner hostess; as an adult, she was diagnosed with lupus, the debilitating disease that had killed her father. The cycle of her illness meant that remissions and flares alternated. As her immune system attacked healthy tissues, joints, and organs, the painful flares and difficult treatments damaged the systems of her body irrevocably.

O'Connor's illness redirected the writer's life she had envisioned while a student at Iowa. O'Connor's mother, Regina, provided care and stability at Andalusia, the family's 500-acre dairy farm. O'Connor lived in a first-floor bedroom and could work each morning, uninterrupted. Her life was not wholly isolated; friends, editors, and even strangers felt free to visit. O'Connor and her mother attended church daily at Sacred Heart and ate lunch at Milledgeville's Sanford House. But in November 1951, O'Connor wrote to Gordon, "There is no one around here who knows anything at all about fiction (every story is

---

* Ward Allison Dorràance, a fellow writer and longtime friend of Gordon, became a correspondent of O'Connor's in the year before her death. Dorrance corresponded with several of the most prominent Southern writers of the mid-twentieth century, including Eudora Welty, Andrew Lytle, and Erskine Caldwell.

'your article' or 'your cute piece') or much about any kind of writing for that
matter." Gordon's correspondence opened passage to a literary community that
the young O'Connor yearned to inhabit. O'Connor's achievements—a master's
degree, prestigious publications, and invitations to travel and lecture—eventually elevated her among the hierarchy of accomplished writers. But, as Magee
has noted, "[E]ven college-educated women did not have easy and regular ac-
cess to one another or to an open literary community; they were part of that
world yet apart from it." Within the content of her letters, Gordon illustrated
what was possible for a woman writer. By mid-career, O'Connor would follow
Gordon into the lecture circuit, speaking (and earning an income) at many of
the same universities in the South and Midwest as Gordon had.

The O'Connor-Gordon correspondence never provides explicit instruction,
however, on how a Southern woman writer could navigate through the predom-
inantly male literary scene. Neither are the letters an exchange of pleasantries or
insipid compliments. Gordon critiqued O'Connor's writing with clarity, precision, and thoughtful analyses that echoed her critical essays and class lectures.
She was direct: she told O'Connor that she lacked a "classical education" and
couldn't "even write a complex sentence." Again and again, Gordon repeated,
O'Connor violated the omniscient narrator's perspective with her colloquial
tone: "You can't go straight into the Presence talking Georgia." Or, "You may
have a fondness for the word 'Squinch' but it doesn't like you—as the ladies
who can't eat cucumbers put it. I wish you would pluck it out of your vocabulary." In a discussion of "The Enduring Chill" that extended over three letters,
Gordon described O'Connor's writing as "flatfooted" nine times when object-
ing to various technical choices. And later, after they had known one another
for over a decade: "I know I sound damn didactic," Gordon wrote. "The point I
am trying to make is that a carelessly used participle is like the first drink to an
alcoholic. You use one and you'll use another."

O'Connor was not a fragile student. She received Gordon's criticism with
equal parts patience, gratitude, frustration, and humor. "She takes great pains
and is very generous with her criticism," O'Connor mused. "Is highly energetic
and violently enthusiastic. When I am around her, I feel like her illiterate grandmother." O'Connor acknowledged to many that Gordon had "taught me considerable." By the time O'Connor had finished the introduction to *A Memoir of Mary
Ann* (1961), though, her patience had thinned. "I see anew her limitations," she
wrote to a friend. "She will sacrifice life to dead form, or anything to grammar."

For those unfamiliar with Caroline Gordon's work and achievement, these letters provide a vivid entrance into her singular expertise: her knowledge of craft, her nuanced understanding of O'Connor's vision, and her uncanny ability to pinpoint opportunities for revision. O'Connor certainly recognized Gordon's pedagogical acumen, even though she had read only selections from Gordon's prolific body of work. When she finally read Gordon's "Summer Dust" in 1956, O'Connor acknowledged her craftsmanship:

> You read it and then you have to sit back and let your mind blend it together—like those pictures that you have to get so far away from before they come together. She is a great student of Flaubert and is great on getting things there so concretely that they can't possibly escape—note how that horse goes through that gate, the sun on the neck and then on the girl's leg and then she turns and watches it slide off his rump. That is real masterly doing, and nobody does it any better than Caroline. You walk through her stories like you are walking in a complete real world. And watch how the meaning comes from the things themselves and not from her imposing anything. Right when you finish reading that story, you don't think you've read anything, but the more you think about it the more it grows.

≈

This compilation of letters is the unfinished project of Sally Fitzgerald, who first saw many of these letters fifteen years after O'Connor's death—and, regrettably, after she had completed editing O'Connor's collected letters for *The Habit of Being*. Gordon's letters to O'Connor were typical of Gordon's correspondence in general: the length, tone, and density of content occurs in letters to various other recipients. But the letters that arrived in Milledgeville were unlike any others O'Connor herself received. Sally Fitzgerald's discovery of these letters was made possible by one factor: both O'Connor and Gordon were her own close friends.

Sally Fitzgerald and Caroline Gordon met through their husbands, who were both accomplished poets and academics. Robert Fitzgerald taught with Allen Tate at the Indiana School of Letters, and in the spring of 1951, the Fitzgeralds (also devout Catholics) had asked Allen Tate to be their child's godfather. The Fitzgeralds and Tates crossed paths with some regularity, even in their far-flung adventures. "The Fitzgeralds have arrived in Milan," Gordon wrote to O'Connor from Rome in October 1953. "We are dying to see them."

Sally Fitzgerald first met Flannery O'Connor in February 1949, when Robert Lowell brought O'Connor to the Fitzgeralds' apartment in New York. Sally remembered O'Connor's blue corduroys and her stooped, awkward gait. The following summer, the Fitzgeralds offered O'Connor a cheap garage apartment at their new home in Ridgefield, Connecticut, in exchange for afternoon babysitting. Sally, Robert, and their children quickly became "adopted kin," said O'Connor. Each morning they attended church and each evening they shared dinner and conversation. O'Connor stayed with the Fitzgeralds for the remainder of 1949. Twice more she would enjoy extended stays in their Connecticut home, working on her writing and spending afternoons helping Sally with the children. Flannery became godmother to their third child.

In May 1949, O'Connor saw a doctor for an ache she thought was appendicitis. Then, in late 1950, when O'Connor felt stiffness and joint pain, a Connecticut doctor suggested a diagnosis of rheumatoid arthritis. O'Connor returned to Milledgeville that December, quite ill. By February 1951—the ten-year anniversary of Edward O'Connor's death—Regina O'Connor told Sally in confidence that Flannery also had lupus. Flannery O'Connor continued to believe her illness was rheumatoid arthritis until Sally revealed the truth in the summer of 1952, a year after the definitive diagnosis.

In her will, Flannery O'Connor appointed Robert Fitzgerald her literary executor. He helped release *Everything That Rises Must Converge* (1965) after O'Connor's 1964 death and *The Complete Stories* in 1971, the latter of which won the National Book Award. Together, Sally and Robert Fitzgerald prepared O'Connor's prose writings in *Mystery and Manners: Occasional Prose* (1969). And Sally, finally, edited O'Connor's collected letters, *The Habit of Being: Letters of Flannery O'Connor* (1979), which was recognized with the National Book Critics Circle Special Award. Sally Fitzgerald became "the preeminent O'Connor scholar," said Sarah Gordon, former editor of the *Flannery O'Connor Bulletin*. "She made O'Connor much more available to us as a human being, particularly in the letters."

Sally Fitzgerald sifted through the letters between O'Connor and more than fifty correspondents to edit *The Habit of Being* (1979). On several occasions, Fitzgerald and other correspondents (like Ashley Brown, Gordon's first literary executor) articulated a wish to protect Caroline Gordon from hurtful or embarrassing references to her marital problems with careful edits to O'Connor's letters. Nevertheless, of the nearly eight hundred letters published in *The*

Habit of Being, Sally Fitzgerald was able to locate and publish only three let-ters from O'Connor to Caroline Gordon. Despite this, Gordon is mentioned by O'Connor in more than *one hundred* of the letters.

Sally Fitzgerald had already completed *The Habit of Being* when she learned that a major cache of letters between O'Connor and Gordon existed—and had been withheld—during her efforts to collect O'Connor's letters. Gordon's letters and O'Connor's carbons of her own letters had been in Regina O'Connor's house since O'Connor's death. Publicly, Fitzgerald said that Regina might not have known she held the letters, or she repeated Gordon's claim that a graduate student failed to re-turn O'Connor's letters to Gordon. Privately, Fitzgerald expressed anger and frus-tration: although Regina profited from *Habit,* she did not provide Fitzgerald *any* of the letters that were in her possession. Regina certainly knew about Gordon's let-ters. In May 1965, on the day that O'Connor's posthumous collection *Everything That Rises Must Converge* was published, Regina wrote to Gordon expressing her gratitude. She had come across a letter written by Flannery, she said, that reminded her how much Flannery had appreciated Gordon's help.

Fitzgerald knew, of course, that Gordon had offered O'Connor reliable and thorough criticism. During the fifteen years of O'Connor's publishing career, the Fitzgeralds were the only ones who consistently received the same drafts that O'Connor sent Gordon; and now, with many of Gordon's letters in hand, Fitzgerald saw more clearly the evolution of O'Connor's drafts to published sto-ries and novels. Without these letters, Sally Fitzgerald understood, all scholarly records about O'Connor would be missing crucial information. Fitzgerald tried to explain to Regina why her failure to provide Gordon's letters was a critical oversight. In response, Regina wondered, obtusely, if she should send Gordon some candy. Instead, she located a set of handkerchiefs—an unopened gift—and asked Fitzgerald to deliver them the next time she saw Gordon.

Sally Fitzgerald immediately published the first threads of the O'Connor-Gordon correspondence in the *Georgia Review* (Winter 1979) in "A Master Class: From the Correspondence of Caroline Gordon and Flannery O'Connor." ("A Master Class" contains material from the first three letters in this book.) Fitzgerald then obtained permission from Caroline Gordon for a new project: to publish a collection of O'Connor-Gordon letters. She also began to write an authorized O'Connor biography, "Mansions of the South."

Years passed. Though eagerly awaited by scholars, neither volume was com-pleted. Sally Fitzgerald died in June 2000. In 2008, when Emory University purchased Sally Fitzgerald's papers, scholars were at last able to see the material that Fitzgerald had so faithfully gathered. But more letters remained to be unearthed from the O'Connor-Gordon correspondence: in the Flannery O'Connor Papers at Georgia College and State University; in the Caroline Gordon Papers (and Ashley Brown Collection of Caroline Gordon) at Princeton University; in the Brainard and Frances Neel Cheney Papers at Vanderbilt University; in the Ashley Brown Collection at Emory University; in the Ward Dorrance Papers at University of North Carolina at Chapel Hill; and, more recently, in a 2014 Emory University acquisition from the Flannery O'Connor estate.

≈

Of the sixty-six letters contained in this volume, only six have ever been published in complete form. Some letters (most notably, the letters discussing "The Displaced Person" and "The Enduring Chill") show Gordon's detailed critiques over multiple drafts of a particular story. Scholars who have argued over how much credence O'Connor placed in Gordon's comments might now reexamine O'Connor manuscripts to evaluate the impact of Gordon's teaching, both on O'Connor's style and content.

Whatever scholars conclude about her influence, Gordon's admiration for O'Connor's work was genuine. Before the publication of *A Good Man Is Hard to Find*, Gordon wrote to O'Connor, "I think that this group of stories you've just done are among the finest that have been written by any American." "Revelation," she told O'Connor, was "perhaps your most profound so far." To Jacques Maritain, Gordon called O'Connor "the most gifted of the younger fiction writers."

O'Connor was equally appreciative. "I thank you the Lord knows for haranguing me twice on the same counts and at the expense of boring yourself stiff," O'Connor told Gordon in 1953. To a friend in 1957, she wrote, "Whenever I finish a story I send it to Caroline before I consider myself really through with it. She's taught me more than anybody." And in her final note to Caroline Gordon, in the quiet culmination of a master class totaling over sixty thousand words, Flannery O'Connor registered her final, understated offering of thanks: "You were good to take the time."

Part 1

Wise Blood
(May 1951–February 1953)

[H]is eyes were what held her attention longest. Their settings
were so deep that they seemed, to her, almost like passages leading
somewhere and she leaned halfway across the space that separated
the two seats, trying to see into them.—Flannery O'Connor, *Wise Blood*

You begin and end the book with his eyes. This is one of those places
that mustn't be hurried over. In fact, it might be well to do it twice,
that is, in two ways. Mrs. Hitchcock ought to spend more time over
his eyes so that the reader, looking over her shoulder, will also tarry
there long enough to realize that they are, indeed, very peculiar.
—Caroline Gordon to Flannery O'Connor, 13 November 1951

∾ In the spring of 1951, Caroline Gordon agreed to a favor. Yes, she told Robert Fitzgerald, she would read the work of a new young writer. Flannery O'Connor was twenty-six; a Catholic from Georgia; and her first novel, *Wise Blood*, was under consideration with Harcourt, Brace.

Gordon, fifty-five, had just completed her seventh novel, *The Strange Children*.

Caroline Gordon to Robert Fitzgerald

Undated [May 1951]

I'm glad you gave me Flannery O'Connor's novel to read. I'm quite excited about it. This girl is a real novelist. (I wish that I had had as firm a grasp on my subject matter when I was her age!) At any rate, she is already a rare phenomenon: a Catholic novelist with a real dramatic sense, one who relies more on her technique than her piety.

I hope that old GS [General Studies] 40 hasn't gone to my head, but I find myself wanting to make a few suggestions about this book.* I think that it has real objectivity, but I think, too, that certain technical imperfections deprive it of its proper frame of reference and actually limit its scope. I believe that a touch here and there and a re-writing of two key scenes which she has muffed would do wonders for the form. I feel so strongly about this that I am going to go ahead and make the suggestions I have in mind and you can pass them on to her or not, as you see fit. After all, I know her very slightly. She may find me presumptuous.

* In her 1979 essay "A Master Class: From the Correspondence of Caroline Gordon and Flannery O'Connor," Sally Fitzgerald noted, "If these preliminary suggestions were contained on a separate sheet sent with this letter, to be passed along to Flannery, they have not survived" (829). These comments have been located and now appear in the postscript to this letter.

17

But I am much interested in the book itself. Her general procedure seems to me sound. She is, of course, writing this kind of stuff people like to read nowadays: about freaks. Her book, like those of most of the younger writers, is full of freaks, but she does something with them that [Frederick] Buechner and [Truman] Capote and those boys seem to be incapable of doing. Truman's people all seem to me to belong in some good clinic. Her characters started out real folks but turned into freaks as the result of original sin.

She has one line of dialogue that I contemplate with envy: On page 142: "'Blind myself,' he said and went on into the house." You remember two lines of Ernest's [Hemingway] in *To Have and Have Not*: "Are those girls any good? . . . No, hon . . ." I always thought that those were the two fastest lines of dialogue that any of my contemporaries had written, but this "Blind myself" strikes me as being just as good. If this girl is capable of writing a line like that she is certainly capable of making the revisions this manuscript needs. I hope she won't think I'm being presumptuous in pointing them out.

We—all of us, including the prospective godfather [Allen Tate]—await news from you all. Do let us hear as soon as you can.

[postscript]

Dear Robert again:

As I said, Flannery may think me a terrible Meddlesome Mattie, but this manuscript seems to me to be crying out for a few revisions. Here are two I'd make off the bat. They concern the first and last scenes.

In the first place, I think that she has implicit here the sort of thing that really ought to be done in any novel: The first scene ought to foreshadow the last, ought, so to prepare us for the last that when we get there we think, "I knew it all along."

But in handling her last scene she has consulted her own convenience. There were certain pieces of information that she wanted to get in and she *crammed* them in, regardless of what form they took. The book ought to end on a more exalted note. Her last sentence doesn't *sound* good enough, high-toned enough. After all, she ought to have us well off the ground by this time. But she has what it needs to do the trick embedded in the paragraphs on page 141: the landlady's image of the blind man's head as containing a long, dark tunnel into which she hardly dares to look. The image is wonderful but is in the wrong place and therefore doesn't have its full effect. She ought to pull it out of that place where it's wasted and end on it: the landlady peering into this tunnel that to her is so mysterious. I think that if she does that, the shifting of the viewpoint to the landlady will be very effective. As it is, we realize that she does it just for convenience. I think, however, that the tunnel business will not work unless prepared for. It ought to be prepared for at the beginning of that chapter. The ground-work could be laid by having the landlady think of it as she sits rocking the cat on the porch. But the real ground-work ought to be laid in the first or second paragraph in the book, and again, I think it is already there and needs only to be brought out more.

Mrs. Wally Car Hitchcock* is a sort of precursor of the landlady. She ought, therefore, to do just what the landlady does: peer into Motes' eyes and find them almost as mysterious as the landlady will eventually find them. The tunnel of the eyes ought to be there in the beginning, only since it hasn't yet taken its ultimate form, we won't recognize it for what it is till we see it at the end of the book.

As it is, the fact that the book starts so abruptly limits its frame of reference off the bat. Makes it seem less imposing than it actually is. We ought to *see* Hazel Motes before we hear him say anything or before we are taken into his thoughts. That business about the black cat looking as if it would bite you doesn't work because it comes too soon in the action; she begins playing tricks with us before she has really got hold of us. The way Motes looks, particularly the way his eyes look, ought to be played up in the beginning. Her focus at the very beginning is too circumscribed, I think. Her spotlight ought to take in the whole car, maybe a landscape—certainly a landscape as seen through the window—before she settles it on Motes.

The second chapter ends with Hazel being driven up to Mrs. Watts' "friendly bed." The third chapter starts a whole new train of action. In fact, it is only in that chapter that the complication gets underway. It is certainly best to leave the amorous antics of Mrs. Watts and Hazel to the imagination. She [O'Connor] is following there the principle advocated by [Henry] James, [Charles] Baudelaire, and God—not I—know what other worthies,

---

* "Wally Bee Hitchcock" in the final draft of *Wise Blood*.

but I ask you, in the name of Uncle Henry [James] himself, I asks you, how can we imagine what goes on between Mrs. Watts and Hazel if you have never seen Mrs. Watts in the palpitant flesh? She is asking the reader to do the impossible. It seems to me that if that chapter ended with a glimpse of Mrs. Watts—in bed or out of it; she receives him in bed in the respective parts. Why not here? Anyhow if it ended with a *glimpse* of Mrs. Watts then she could safely leave the reader's imagination to chew on that savory morsel while she set the stage for the next act. But we are [drawn] away from Mrs. Watts before we really know her.* Consequently we [aren't] ready to fix our attention on Enoch and the preacher and the child.

I do not believe in that gorilla. This seems to me forced. It is unlikely that Enoch's father was inside the gorilla suit. I don't think he needs to be, anyway. Enoch is looking forward to the pleasure of insulting an ape. Won't the fact that the ape turns out to be a human be shock enough? It might look at him with the eyes of his father, in which once said eyes would have to be planted [earlier] in the story, but even that might be dangerous. It seems to me that having a man inside that suit is enough. Enoch's preoccupation is the abnormal, the mis-fit, the sub-human. Getting a human glance in an ape's eye ought to fix him.

I think she muffs one of her big scenes:

On [page] 127 Enoch sticks his head in the door of the room in which Sabbath and Hazel are living. Getting his head inside the door establishes the action is seen through his eyes. When she [O'Connor] says he saw "Motes lying on his cot" she puts a veil between the spectator and event, a veil which is not needed, I think. This is no time for psychic distance.

[As for one of] the most important scenes in the book. She muffs it by not giving it enough build up. The chapter [is an] anti-climax. It ought to end up with a vision of the off spring of the [relationship] between Haze and Sabbath: a dead homunculus. She doesn't render this dramatically. She tells us about it. Forces the note. I'm not sure she [can get away] with that speech of Sabbath's at all. At any rate, it [would be much] more dramatic to have Sabbath *acting* as if she had just become [a mother] and let the reader say to himself that [poor] baby than to attempt to put it over

---

* In this letter, the archival documents are partially illegible. The bracketed insertions that follow contain editorial inference.

by a forced, unnatural speech. [I'm not] sure, too, that the chapter ought to end on the baby and not [have the] business about Enoch tacked on. Chapters ought to end with bangs [not whimpers] as Uncle Tom has so aptly pointed out.*

I have one more recommendation to make. I think that Ms. O'Connor fails to realize that the omniscient narrator never speaks anything but Johnsonian English. He is too high-toned, too much like God, to speak of somebody "slurping up" a soda. He is *above* that kind of talk. She often lets the tone down just when it ought to be most exalted by using a colloquial rhythm or idiom or even some word like "just" or "right" or "though." That sort of thing will collapse or at least slacken the tone every time. I believe that the abrupt and ill-placed slackening of tone deprives the notion of its proper frame of reference and so makes it seem less imposing than it actually is. The substitution of a word here and there, or at least the omission of colloquial rhythms or idioms in places where the omniscient narrator is speaking would do wonders for the whole manuscript, it seems to me.

⌇ O'Connor received these suggestions in June and revised her novel that summer. On September 1, 1951, she told her agent to expect a new draft of *Wise Blood*, thanks to advice she'd incorporated from Robert Giroux and Caroline Gordon. "I think its a lot better but I may be mistaken and will have to be told," O'Connor wrote to Sally and Robert Fitzgerald. "[S]teel yourselfs to read the changed parts of that manuscript again."

In mid-October, O'Connor sent what she called "Opus Nauseous No. 1" to the Fitzgeralds and to Giroux. O'Connor asked the Fitzgeralds: Would Caroline Gordon mind reading it once more? And might she have Gordon's address so she could send thanks? O'Connor—who had been working on the novel since 1948—said that the revision process "was like spending the day eating a horse blanket."

That fall, Caroline Gordon moved to Minneapolis with her husband, poet Allen Tate, and accepted a teaching position at the College of St. Catherine. She also began work on her eighth novel, *The Malefactors*, revising the opening

---

* From T. S. Eliot, "The Hollow Men": "This is the way the world ends / Not with a bang but a whimper."

chapter four times. "The business of a fiction writer is," Gordon said, "in its humble way, the same as the Almighty's: incarnation—and it has to proceed at an even slower pace."

Caroline Gordon's first letter to Flannery O'Connor follows below.

Caroline Gordon to Flannery O'Connor

Undated [1951]
1801 University Avenue S.E.
Minneapolis, Minnesota

I am delighted to hear that you are feeling better and that you have finished your novel. As you know, I was much impressed by the novel in its original form. There are so few Catholic novelists who seem possessed of a literary conscience—not to mention skill—that I feel that your novel is very important. I shall be glad to read it whenever Robert [Fitzgerald] sends it. I am going to write to Robert Giroux, too, and tell him that I want to review the novel when it comes out and that I would like to do anything I can to help—though, of course, there is little that one can do, or needs to do to help a good novel.

I had a letter yesterday from Will Percy's nephew, Walker Percy, who lives at Covington, Louisiana. He says he has written a novel [The Charterhouse] which he guesses is "a Catholic novel, though it has no conversion or priests in it." I don't know that your paths are likely to cross, but if they ever should I imagine that you'd find it interesting to know each other. He has been in the Church about five years.

Allen and I are crazy about Minnesota. Everything is on such a grand scale, and the city itself is very handsome, with the Mississippi River, to my continual surprise, running right through it. Frank Lloyd Wright was here, all right. There are a lot of modern churches, Mother Cabrini's shaped like a Viking ship, St. Ignatius, shaped like a fish, and then there is one church that has a dialogue Mass. St. John Abbey, sixty miles away, is the largest Benedictine community in the world. Three hundred monks and three thousand acres of this fat black earth.

I am teaching a seminar in fiction at the College of St. Catherine. I have about twelve girls and, each week, an outer circle of auditors, alumnae and nuns. The presence of the nuns made me rather nervous at first, but I am getting used to them. They are sister[s] of St. Joseph of Carondelet, an order that was almost exterminated during the French Revolution—I believe they had to give up the habit and lived about in caves or sheltered by peasants—till the order was finally re-planted and six nuns were sent to St. Louis, Missouri, from which community nuns were sent here.

I shall await the manuscript with eagerness. Many thanks for sending it.

⌒ Once again, O'Connor sent the manuscript of *Wise Blood* to the Fitzgeralds, who delivered it to Gordon. O'Connor said that Gordon's critique—a nine-page, single-spaced letter—"certainly increased my education thereby."

Caroline Gordon to Flannery O'Connor

St. Didacus' Day, 1951 [November 13]

Your manuscript has come. I spent yesterday reading it. I think it is terrific! I know a good many young writers who think they are like Kafka. You are the only one I know who succeeds in doing a certain thing that he does. When I say that I am merely reaching out for some phrase that will partly convey my notion of your work. I do not mean that it is in any way derivative of Kafka. In fact, this book seems to me the most original book I have read in a long time. But you are like Kafka in providing a firm Naturalistic ground-work for your symbolism. In consequence, symbolic passages—and one of the things I admire about the book is the fact that all the passages are symbolic, like life itself—passages echo in the memory long after one has put the book down, go on exploding, as it were, depth on depth. As that old fool, E. M. Forster, would say: "You have more than one plane of action." (And what a contrast they are to the maunderings which he presents as *his* planes of action!)

Robert Fitzgerald reported to me something that you said that interested me very much, that your first novel was about freaks, but that your next book would be about folks. It is fashionable to write about freaks— Truman Capote and his followers write about little else. It astonishes— and amuses me—to find a writer like you using what is roughly the same kind of subject matter. But what a different use you put it to! Whenever I read any of the homosexual novels that are so popular nowadays I am reminded of something Chekhov said, that "he and she are the engine that makes fiction move." That strikes me as profoundly true. One can write about homosexuals if one shows them as differing from normal people, as Proust does, but when a writer gives us a world in which everybody is a freak it seems to me that he is doing little more than recording the progress of his disease.

But homosexuality, childishness, freakishness—in the end, I think it comes to *fatherlessness*—is rampant in the world today. And you are giving us a terrifying picture of the modern world, so your book is full of freaks. They seem to me, however, normal people who have been maimed or crippled and your main characters, Sabbath, Enoch and Haze, are all going about their Father's business, as best they can. It *is* a terrifying picture. I don't know any other contemporary who gets just such effects. [Jean] Genet achieves remarkable effects but for me they are all marred, finally, by his sentimentality. You are never sentimental.

I think that you have done a good job on the revision. I don't really see how you managed it. The Fitzgeralds told us that you have had a severe illness and are only recently out of the hospital. There comes a time for any manuscript when one must let it go with no more revisions. I think that having done the job you've done you could let this manuscript go with a good conscience. But I am going to make a few suggestions and comments. They are really suggestions for your future work, but I have to have something to pin them to, so I am going to take passages from Wise Blood as illustrations of the points I am trying to make. If I seem overly pedantic it is doubtless the result of teaching. When you are reading a manuscript for a fellow writer you can say "I like this" or "I don't like that" and he figures it out for himself, but if you are dealing with students you have to try to relate your reactions to some fundamental principle of the craft.

I admire tremendously the hard core of dramatic action in this book. I certainly wouldn't want it softened up in any way. I am convinced that one reason the book is so powerful is that it is so unflaggingly dramatic. But I think there are two principles involved which you might consider.

It is the fact that in this world nothing exists except in relation to something else. (I take it that being a Catholic you are not a Cartesian!) In geometry a straight line is the shortest distance between two points. Theology takes cognizance of a soul only in its relation to God; its relation to its fellow-men, in the end, helps to constitute its relations with God. It seems that it is the same way in fiction. You can't create in a vacuum. You have to imitate the Almighty and create a whole world—or an illusion of a whole word, if the simplest tale is to have any verisimilitude.

As I say, I admire the core of dramatic action in this book very much, but I think that the whole book would gain by not being so stripped, so bare, by surrounding the core of action with some contrasting material. Suppose we think of a scene in your novel as a scene in a play. Any scene in any play takes place on some sort of set. I feel that the sets in your play are quite wonderful but you never let us see them. A spotlight follows every move the characters make and throws an almost blinding radiance on them, but it is a little like the spotlight a burglar uses when he is cracking a safe; it illuminates a small circle and the rest of the stage is in darkness most of the time. Focusing the reader's attention completely on the action is one way to make things seem very dramatic, but I do not think that you can keep that up all of the time. It demands too much of the reader. He is just not capable of such rigorous attention. It would be better, I think, if you occasionally used a spotlight large enough to illuminate the corners of the room, for those corners have gone on existing all through the most dramatic moments.

What I am trying to say is that there are one or two devices used by many novelists which I think you would find helpful.

Often one can make an immediate scene more vivid by deliberately going outside it. A classical example is the scene in *Madame Bovary* in which Charles and Emma are alone together for the first time. Charles' senses are stirred by Emma, he is looking at her very intently. At the same time he hears a hen that has just laid an egg cackling in a hay mow in the courtyard. Going outside that scene somehow makes it leap to life. The very fact that the sound is distant makes the people in the room seem more real. Hart Crane uses the same device in a poem called "Paraphrase." A man is standing beside a bed looking down at the body of a dead woman and grieving for her death. His grief is made more real by "the crow's cavil" that he hears outside the window.

I think that this very device could be used very effectively in *Wise Blood*. Occasionally you get a powerful effect by having the landscape reflect the mood of the character, as in the scene where the sky is like a thin piece

of polished silver and the sun is sour-looking. But it seems to me monot-
onous to have the landscape continually reflecting their moods. In one
place I think you could get a much more dramatic effect by having it contrast with them. For instance, in the scene where Haze, Sabbath and Enoch
meet, I think that the landscape ought to actually play a part in the action,
as it does sometimes in Chekhov's stories. If the night sky were beautiful,
if the night were lyrical, the sordid roles the characters have to play would
seem even more sordid. After all, here are three young people trying to
do as best they can what they feel that they ought to do. Sabbath wants to
get married. Enoch wants to live a normal human life. Haze, who is a poet
and a prophet, wants to live his life out on a higher level. You convey that
admirably, I think, by emphasizing his fierce dedication to his ideals. But
the scene itself is too meagre for my taste. Your spotlight is focused too
relentlessly on the three characters.

There is another thing involved: the danger of making excessive demands on the reader. He is not very bright, you know, and the most intelligent person, when he is reading fiction, switches his intellect off and—if
the author does what he is trying to do—listens like a three or thirteen
year old child. The old Negro preacher's formula for a perfect sermon applies here: "First I tells 'em I'm going to tell 'em, then I tells 'em, then I
tell 'em I done told them." It takes much longer to take things in than we
realize. In our effort to keep the action from lagging we hurry the reader
over crucial moments. But anything that is very exciting can't be taken in
hurriedly. If somebody is killed in an automobile accident, people who
were involved in the accident or who merely witnessed it will be busy for
days afterwards piecing together a picture of what happened. They simply
couldn't take it all in at that time. When we are writing fiction we have to
give the reader ample time to take in what is happening, particularly if it
is very important. The best practice, I gather, is to do the thing twice. That
is, the effect is repeated, but is so varied that the reader thinks he is seeing
something else. Actually the second passage, while it interests the reader,
exists chiefly to keep him there in that spot until he has taken in what the
author wants him to take in. Stephen Crane uses this device often and to
perfection in *The Red Badge of Courage*.

Yeats puts it another way. He says that in poetry every tense line ought
to be set off, that is, ought to be preceded and followed by what he calls "a
numb line." He is constantly doing this in "[In Memory of] Major Robert

Gregory." His numb lines do not slow up the action. They make it more powerful.

I am going to take an example from *Wise Blood*, page 140. The place where the patrolman has just pushed the car—the pulpit!—over the embankment.

The paragraph: "Them that don't need a car, don't need a license" etc. is admirably concise. But I think you need another stroke or two in the next paragraph. I don't see Haze plainly enough. The chief thing I have learned from Flaubert is that it takes at least three strokes, three activated sensuous details to convince us of the existence of any object. I want to know how Haze's face looked then. His knees bending and his sitting down on the edge of the embankment is fine, but it is not enough for me.

Also I want to know how the patrolman looked when he said, "Could I give you a lift to where you was going?" If we are to believe that anything happened we must be able to visualize the action. The minute we are unable to visualize it we quit believing in it. Very often a scene in which two people figure will be unconvincing because it is lopsided. The writer furnishes us the data which will enable us to visualize the main character but he doesn't give us the data that we must have to visualize the subordinate character. But he is there, taking up just as much space as the main character, and I think that he must be presented with just as much care. If, for instance, the main character is doing all the talking, the reader's attention must be directed to the subordinate character at regular intervals. The fact that he isn't talking must be dramatized almost as much as the fact that the other man is talking—or you will get a one-sided affair. This whole passage is too hurried for me. It needs more sensuous detail and more numb lines. I want again to see how Haze's face looked when he said he wasn't going anywhere, and again I want to know how the patrolman looked or at least what position his body assumed when he said, "You hadn't planned to go anywheres?" A few, a very few more strokes would do wonders for that passage.

There is another thing that I think the book needs: a preparation for the title. Henry James says that at the beginning of every book "a stout stake" must be driven in for the current of the action to swirl against. This stout stake is a preparation for what is to come. Sometimes the writer prepares the reader by giving him a part of what is to happen. Sometimes he conveys the knowledge symbolically, sometimes he does it by certain cadences, as in *A Farewell to Arms*, when at the beginning the narrator says "The leaves fell early that year"—another way of saying "My love died young." At any rate, however it is done, the reader must be given enough to go on, so that, in the end, he will have that comfortable feeling that accompanies "I told you so!"

I don't think that your title is prepared for enough. And this brings me to a consideration of Chapter V. I think that there is too much statement in this chapter. This is the only part of the book where you rely on statement rather than rendition. I *think* it is because you are so uncomfortably aware of the difficulty of putting over Enoch's conviction that he has "wise blood." (It's a hellishly difficult problem!) I don't think you handle it quite right. You rather give your show away beforehand. That is, you tell us what Enoch did every day before you show him in the act of doing it. If you sum up what is going to happen before it happens the reader is not interested in it when it does happen. You tell us about his spying on the woman in the bathing suit beforehand. When he does spy on her it's not very dramatic. But suppose you had prepared a little for your wise blood in previous chapters, say when Enoch and Haze first meet. Enoch is impressed by Haze. It is Haze's idealism, his fierceness, his latent power that impresses Enoch. But suppose Enoch let drop a few words to the effect that he, too, has a secret power? Maybe several times. This would be a dramatic rendition of the effect Haze has on him, which, I think, would be all to the good. It would also be a preparation for what is to come. He would not reveal what his secret power was at the time, beyond using the phrase "Wise Blood," but the reader would be on the lookout to find out what it was. Then, you could start Chapter V with action. That is, you could show Enoch to us in action, and refer to his "wise blood," and could inform the reader that he did certain things every day after showing him in the act of doing them instead of killing our interest by telling us about them beforehand.

To sum up, there are three places in the book where I think a few strokes might make a lot of difference, this scene and the scene where the patrolman pushes the car over and the scene where Haze and Sabbath and Enoch first meet.

And one more thing: I think you are just a little too grim with Sabbath when she is nursing the mummy. I don't like the use of the word "smirk" there. It is almost as if the author were taking sides against her. I think it would be more dramatic if you were a little more compassionate towards her. After all, she is a young girl trying to lead a normal life and this is the nearest she'll ever come to having a baby—since she'll probably end in the Detention Home. At any rate, the situation is grim enough without the author's taking sides.

I will now—God help us both!—make a few, more detailed comments.

I think that you overdo the summing-up of Mrs. Hitchcock's remarks. You sum them up half a dozen times. This would be more effective if you alternated direct quotation occasionally. I think that perhaps her first remark ought to be [a] direct quotation. Reporting what she says there takes away from the immediacy of the scene and you are out to establish that.

You attempt to create Haze's eyes by two strokes. I don't think that it can be done. I have thought about this business of three strokes being necessary to create the illusion of life and I've come to the conclusion that it's related to our having five senses. A person can get along without one or more of his senses but once he's deprived of all of them he's dead. Two strokes is like a person who is deaf and dumb and blind and has, perhaps, lost his sense of touch to boot. He's hardly there.

Another thing. You begin and end the book with his eyes. This is one of those places that mustn't be hurried over. In fact, it might be well to do it twice, that is, in two ways. Mrs. Hitchcock ought to spend more time over his eyes so that the reader, looking over her shoulder, will also tarry there long enough to realize that they are, indeed, very peculiar.

Page 2 "Yellow rock head." You or I might say that a man had "a yellow rock head," but the omniscient narrator, who is speaking now, can't say that. He speaks and writes Johnsonian English.

2   "Moved on him" isn't very good. Not exact.

3   Flaubert made it a practise never to repeat the same word on one page unless it was a word like said or did, a colourless word. Those two "flats" bother me.

5   When Haze says, "I reckon you think you been redeemed," I think you ought to tell us what Mrs. H. said and how she looked. "Seemed confused" is too far away from the action, too much like reporting rather than rendering. We want direct action here.

6   I think you slip up a little on your viewpoint here. You haven't established the fact that we are seeing things through Haze's eyes and yet you use words he would have used: "the headman," for instance. I think it would be better to stick to the viewpoint of the omniscient narrator here.

6   Similarly, I think it would be better to say "the woman" Mrs. H. was talking to, rather than "the lady." The Om. Nar. would not call her lady. In his sight all women are equal.

7   "Squinched" is not good usage. The omniscient narrator doesn't ever use words like that.

7   "The knobs framing her face were like dark toadstools." In fiction "did" is always better than "was"—unless you are handling some state or condition so that mere being becomes a form of action. It seems to me that the toadstools ought to *frame* her face instead of just being.

9   Same thing goes for the sentence: "In his half-sleep he thought where he was lying was like a coffin." "Was" makes it less dramatic there. If I were doing it I'd say, "He thought that he was lying in a coffin." I'm not sure, though, that I'm right here. Maybe not.

13   "He had all the time he could want to be converted to nothing in" is another place where I think you hurry the reader too much. After all, his conversion to *nothing* is the crux of the book. You must give us time to take that in.

14   I don't like "The army had released him etc." You set the scene in one time then shift to another. Confusing. Why not, "When the army released him a hundred miles north of where he wanted to be, he went immediately etc."

14   I'd say "glare-blue" instead of "the glare-blue."

14   I wish we could see the house from the outside, the figure it cut on the landscape, before he goes inside. Again, you go too fast.

17   I need to see the inside of that toilet. The scene would be much more real if we could see what it was like before you begin telling us of his situation: "He had no place to go," for instance. The fact that you haven't set your stage properly, haven't showed us what the little room looked like, takes away from the drama of this scene, which otherwise would be one of your best.

18   You have not taken the trouble to create the driver of the cab. I think that if a man sells somebody a newspaper in a story that man must be rendered. That is, the reader must be given just enough details to enable him to visualize the man. Otherwise you will have what Ford Madox Ford used to maintain was the most dreadful ghost story he knew: the guest in the country house who decides he will smoke in the night and is pretty upset when an unseen hand hands him a match.

Anybody would be and anybody is when this happens. One gives a character like this a different kind of attention from the kind one gives important characters. Nevertheless, one must give him his due or he will take his revenge.

18   Here a device is needed that I think you had better get on to. It is dangerous, I think, to have a character emit more than three sentences in one speech. If he does you get an unlifelike effect. If he has to say more than that you ought to dramatize the fact that he is making quite a long speech. Ordinarily, one can improve dialogue tremendously by making three speeches out of every speech. Thus:

Haze: "Listen, I'm not a preacher."

Then, the driver either says something or doesn't say anything. In either case, the reader must learn how he received what Haze said.

Then we ought to know how Haze looked when he makes his next speech: "I don't believe in anything."

Again, we ought to know how the driver received that or what he said. Then Haze says, "I don't have to say it but once to nobody."

When speeches are run together in one paragraph the way you have Haze's remarks here, they muffle each other. Speeches need air around them—a liberal use of white space improves almost any dialogue. White space at the end of a paragraph gives a speech room to reverberate in and if you will clear the space for it, will reverberate every time.

I think you have improved the scene where Haze meets Mrs. Watts but I think it still goes too fast.

The first paragraph on that page surely should end with Haze's picking her foot up and moving it to one side. But you have tried to handle Mrs. Watts in the same paragraph. You can handle only one idea in any one paragraph, just as you can handle only one main idea in any one sentence. A paragraph, like a sentence, is a miniature story and like a story, must always have a climax, must stop on the important note.

I want to know how Mrs. Watts looked when she drawled "You hunting something?" The fact that I can't see her makes it hard for me to believe she said that. Also, I think that this is a place where you need white space. I'd break this up, like this:

Show how Mrs. W. looked, then have her say "You hunting something?"

Show how Haze receives this, then have him say "I'm no goddamn preacher."

Then show Mrs. Watts again and have her say something.

Then show him again and have him say, "I've come for the usual busi-ness." I think then that your ending would work, all right. But as it stands, this passage goes so fast and is, besides, so meager, that it isn't as convinc-ing as it might be.

24   The omniscient narrator doesn't use expressions like "green-peaish colour."

50   I believe that the name of the shrub is lobelia. At any rate, I don't think "obelia" is right.

59   "There were two black bears in the first one." Why "were"? Why not make it did instead? "In the first cage two black bears sat etc."

62   Your use of a colloquialism like "squinched" in the crucial scene when they see the mummy lowers the tone of the whole scene.

62   I think that you should let the woman come in the door instead of telling us that Haze saw her. It would be more dramatic.

64   I think that your statement that he began preaching that night is giving the show away. Show him in the *act* of beginning his preaching and let the reader be the one to say, "Oh, he began preaching that night." If you sum up what he does before he does it nobody wants to see him do it.

Also, if he is going to preach he's got to have somebody to preach to. "People" won't do it. You can't see, touch, taste, smell or hear "people" in general. You ought to create one, two or even three people who will stand for the rest of the crowd. But if he talks he's got to talk to somebody.

Also at the beginning of this chapter is a time when I'd like to know what kind of night it was. You go into your action too fast.

On page 67, you handle three or four ideas in one paragraph: Haze and the girl. Her father. His starting of his church. Won't work. That ought to be broken into several paragraphs, with, perhaps, a little more material worked in, a little amplification.

74   I think this scene ought to be broken up, too. For my students, I have fallen into the habit of making this sign [underlines phrase four times] for such a breaking up and all through this letter I've found myself wanting to make that sign.

Each remark he makes in this passage ought to be in a paragraph by itself, accompanied by a rendering of how he looked when he said it. Also you ought to interpolate paragraphs showing how she received his remarks. If you did that you'd get the feeling of tension between two people. As it is, it goes too fast to be very lifelike.

Well, that's enough of that! I *would* like to see you make some preparation for the title, "Wise Blood," and I'd like to see a little landscape, a little enlarging of the scene that night they all meet, and I'd also like to see a little slowing up at certain crucial places I've indicated, but aside from those few changes I don't think that it matters much whether you make any of the revisions I've suggested. I am really thinking more of the work you'll do in the future than of this present novel which seems to me a lot better than any of the novels we've been getting. But of course in writing fiction one can never stand still. Once you learn how to do one thing you have to start learning how to do something else and the devil of it is that you always have to be doing three or four things at a time.

I have taken illustrations for the points I want to take out of your book. I might almost as easily have taken them from my own most recent novel, *The Strange Children*. I am far enough away from it now to see some of the most glaring faults. One of them is the very thing I have been harping on all through this letter: hurrying over crucial moments too fast. My story purports to be the story of something that happened to a child and it is that story on one level of action, but it is also and chiefly, I think, a story of what happened to her father. In the first part of the story the child seems nearer to her mother. She goes to look at the waterfall with her mother but she looks at the stars with her father. Halfway through the book there is a shift of the emphasis from mother to father. When she falls off her pony it is her father who picks her up and at the last she is standing beside her father, with his arm around her. I told them, but I didn't tell them that I was going to tell them or that I had done told them. I should have forced the reader to linger long enough to realize that the emphasis was shifting from the mother to the father. As a result, few readers get it. But a few more strokes, a sort of holding up of the action long enough for the reader to be *made* to realize that something important was going on would have done the trick. Well, hindsight is always better than foresight.

You won't, of course, pay too much attention to anything I've said in this long letter. After all, it's just one novelist talking about the way she thinks things ought to be done. I may be quite wrong.

But my heartiest congratulations to you, at any rate. It's a wonderful book. I've written to Robert Giroux, expressing my admiration. My best wishes to you. I do hope that you continue to feel better.

Next morning:
I realize that in all this long letter I've said little about what I admire in the book. It is, first of all, I think, your ability to present action continually on more than one plane. Only writers of the first order can do that. Everything in your book exists as we all exist in life, mysteriously, in more than one dimension. When Haze runs the car over Solace Layfield he is murdering his own alter ego as well as Layfield. His Essex is not only a means of lo-comotion. It is a pulpit. When he finds out that Sabbath's father is blind he finds out much more than that. This goes on all through the book and yet you never succumb to the temptation to allegorize. I admire, too, very much, the selection of detail. You unerringly pick the one that will do the trick. And the dialogue is superb. But you will have gathered, by this time, that I am tremendously enthusiastic about the book. My heartiest con-gratulations on the achievement. It is considerable.

⟿ Flannery O'Connor's first letter to Caroline Gordon survives only in draft form.

Flannery O'Connor to Caroline Gordon

Undated [November 1951]
[Milledgeville, Georgia]
   Thank you so much for your letter and for wanting to help. I am afraid it will need all the help it can get. I never have, fortunately, expected to make any money out of it, but one thing that has concerned me is that it might be recognized by Catholics as an effort proper to a Catholic; not that I expect any sizable number of them who aren't kin to me to read it—reading is not necessary to salvation which may be why they don't do it—but I have enough trouble with the ones who are kin to me to know what could be expected. You can't shut them up before a thing comes out but you can look forward to a long mortified silence afterwards. I used to be concerned with writing a "Catholic" novel and all that but I think now I was only occupying

myself with fancy problems. If you are a Catholic you know so well what you believe, that you can forget about it and get on with the business of making the novel work. This is harder to do, knowing what you believe, but Catholic writers ought to be freer to concentrate on good writing than anybody else. They don't, and I wouldn't know why. When I first started my book, I was right young and very ignorant and I thought what I was doing was mighty powerful (it wasn't even intelligible at that point) and liable to corrupt anybody that read it and me too, so I visited a priest in Iowa City and very carefully explained the problem to him. He gave me one of those ten cent pamphlets that they are never without and said I didn't have to write for fifteen year old girls. The pamphlet was by some Jesuit who did reviewing. He seemed to think that *A Tree Grows in Brooklyn* was about as good as you could get. Somebody ought to blow the lid off.

Since your letter to Robert [Fitzgerald] this summer, I have been examining my conscience on the business of writing about freaks. I didn't start out with that intention or any other but I found that I couldn't sustain a whole character. Andrew Lytle saw a few of the early discarded chapters and said you keep out of that boy's mind, you'll get yourself messed up if you don't. It appeared to me to be good advice, but then the only way I seemed to be able to make clear what Haze was thinking was to have him do extreme things. I suppose what I needed to do then was make it plain that he was a freak in the philosophical order and not the kind that belonged in a clinic and I don't know if I've done that or not. This occurs to me now; nothing occurred to me while I was doing it.

I went to school to the Sisters of St. Joseph Carondelet in Savannah and liked them but I wouldn't much relish having a ring of them around my seminar; however, I don't think it would hurt them any to be there. I have always had a horror of Catholic girls' colleges. There seems to be a peculiar combination of money and piety and closed forms about them—this is all pure prejudice, I never attended one, and times may have changed. We have three of those sisters here, trying to start a school for the children. Two of them are former Baptists.

All these comments on writing and my writing have helped along my education considerably and I am certainly obliged to you. There is no one around here who knows anything at all about fiction (every story is "your article," or "your cute piece") or much about any kind of writing for that matter. Sidney Lanier and Daniel Whitehead Hickey are the Poets and Margaret Mitchell is the Writer. Amen. So it means a great deal to me to get these comments.

I had felt that the title wasn't anchored in the story but I hadn't known how to anchor it. I am about that now. It won't be a stout stake but it'll be something.

I had also felt that there were places that went too fast. The cause of this is laziness. I don't really like to write but I don't like to do anything else better; however it is easier to rewrite than do it for the first time and I mean to enlarge those places you've mentioned. I've been reading a lot of Conrad lately because he goes so slow and I had thought reading him might help that fault. There is not much danger of my imitating *him*.

The business about making the scenery more lyrical to contrast with their moods will be harder for me to do. I have always been afraid to try my hand at being lyrical for fear I would only be funny and not know it. I supposed this would be a healthy fear if I had any tendency to overdo in that direction. By this time working so long on the book I may have cultivated the ugly so that it has become a habit. I was much concerned this summer after your letter to Robt. to get everything out of that book that might sound like Truman Capote. I don't admire his writing. It reminds me of Yaddo. Mrs. [Elizabeth] Ames* thought he had about achieved perfection in the form of the short story. I read in the *Commonweal* that his last book was better than the first one. The reviewer quoted something from it with great admiration about private worlds never being vulgar. I can think up plenty of vulgar private ones myself.

≈ O'Connor sent further revisions of *Wise Blood* to editor Robert Giroux, defending the changes: "They were all suggested by Caroline." To friend Robie Macauley, O'Connor wrote, "You will be interested to know about Enoch's daddy. I had him inside that ape suit at first . . . and thought it was terribly funny but Caroline said No and she was right." While O'Connor waited for the book's final publication, she began working on new short stories, including "The World Is Almost Rotten" (later published as "The Life You Save May Be Your Own") and "A Late Encounter with the Enemy."

* Director of the artists' community Yaddo when O'Connor was in residence, 1948–49.

Flannery O'Connor to Caroline Gordon

17 April 1952

I have asked Bob Giroux to send you a copy of my book. I'm sure you are as sick of it as I am but I wanted you to have a copy. You can give it to some of the sisters who sit in on your lectures and they can see how they like Catholic novels with gorillas in them. I am very much obliged to you for letting them use your comment on the jacket. It will help.

After I'd made the changes you suggested I found that the book had already gone to press but I was able to get some of them in on the proofs. I am writing some stories now—trying to get the apes and rat-colored cars out of my head so I won't write the same novel over again—but they are not much.

I hope to see the Fitzgeralds in June if I am still well.

≈ During the winter and spring of 1952, Gordon had struggled while writing her novel *The Malefactors*. "I really do not think I can write another novel after this one," she said. Gordon's remedy was to engage in a pleasurable distraction: re-reading Henry James. Gordon believed that James's fiction contained religious undertones that no critic had yet explored. James's novella *The Figure in the Carpet*, for example, featured a novelist with a secret. Those who learned the secret eventually died without revealing it; the narrator attempted, but failed to uncover it. "The secret, I am convinced," Gordon wrote, "is *caritas*, Christian charity, *agape*, call it what you will." James's work, Gordon believed, beautifully illuminated this precept of charity, a fusion of love and compassion. "[I]t is not a secret to be told, primarily, but a secret to be lived," Gordon explained. James's exploration of *caritas*, she thought, could serve as a model for her own life and work.

Gordon regularly delivered public lectures alongside a full calendar of teaching and entertaining. That April, however, marked the beginning of an unusually demanding schedule of lectures that would continue throughout 1952. Speaking fees alleviated some of Gordon's financial distress; Allen Tate had, at this time, hidden outstanding debts totaling over two thousand dollars. Gordon learned about their dire circumstances when a check arrived: Tate had secretly sold land that Gordon had purchased years earlier. In the spring of 1952, they took in three boarders; Gordon even substituted for Allen Tate when his poor health rendered him incapable of fulfilling speaking obligations. Her correspondence with O'Connor often reflected the content of these lectures while masking her financial burdens and marital strains.

Gordon's 1952 lectures synthesized her ideas about religious faith, the writer's craft, and the communion of artists. In a Newman Center annual lecture at University of Minnesota titled "The Art and Mystery of Faith," Gordon said that the wholehearted pursuit of writing fiction was both sacred and communal: "[W]e are anxious to initiate anybody who shows talent into its art and mysteries. That is the way I feel about my own craft no matter how much I complain! I have been following it now for over twenty-five years, which means thinking about it during most of my waking moments and it still seems mysterious to me. [. . .] The writing of serious fiction is, in essence, a religious act. We are moved to imitate our Creator, to do as he did, and create a world." Gordon's ease and comfort with O'Connor, a young writer the age of her daughter, was likely a result of these shared convictions. "In life, as well as in the writing of novels," Gordon wrote, "faith is the key to the puzzle; the puzzle doesn't make any sense until you have the key."

Although O'Connor wouldn't send Gordon a new work of fiction for another year, the two women continued their correspondence.

Caroline Gordon to Flannery O'Connor

Undated [April 1952]

I am not going to be able to review your book, after all. I stupidly forgot to caution HB [Harcourt, Brace] about using my name as a blurb and am therefore ineligible to review the book, Francis Brown* tells me. I'm sorry. I am vain enough to think that I understand better what you're getting at than the next reviewer.

The sisters who sit in on my lectures will read it with great interest, I'm sure. They continue to astonish me. The other day, after I had finished giving my interpretation of Joyce's *Portrait*, which, to say the least, is not the interpretation that I was, so to speak, brought up on, one of them sighed softly and murmured: "That's what Sister Mariella Gable† has always said!"

---

* Editor of the *New York Times Book Review*.
† Catholic American writer, literary scholar, and English professor who championed Catholic fiction writers.

I am so glad to hear that you have been feeling well again. If you visit the Fitzgeralds in June maybe we'll see you. We hope to land in Princeton around the first of July.

Spring has come at last! All the ice is gone from the river. The sidewalks are at last clear of snow and ice and the grass is turning green. It seems to happen overnight here and a damned good idea it is. I don't think we could have stood much more of that other stuff.

I have been having a great time all winter reading and re-reading *The Golden Bowl*. If you take into consideration three facts: a) that it is the only one of James' novels that has a happy ending; b) that it is the only one in which a child is born to the hero and heroine; c) that it is the only one in which the hero and heroine are both Catholics. You don't see James turning into a Catholic but you see the book turning into something quite different from what [literary scholar] F. O. Matthiessen et al. would have you believe it is.

Allen appalled me when I had finished an essay on this subject by saying that I ought to expand the essay into a small book. The idea does fill me with horror—I can't write expository prose. However, the fact that nobody will be anxious to publish such a book will probably save me from having to write it.

Another book we have read this winter is R. W. Chambers, *Life of St. Thomas More*. It is simply terrific. Not having read it is for me a little like studying the Civil War from the Yankee point of view—you don't get much idea of what it was all about.

I hope the stories go well and we look forward to seeing you soon.

Flannery O'Connor to Caroline Gordon

2 May 1952

I'm sorry you won't be able to review the book but I am glad to have the comment on the jacket, where it will give pause. I thought you would be interested in [Evelyn] Waugh's comment which was as follows: "You want a favorable opinion to quote. The best I can say is: 'If this is really the unaided work of a young lady, it is a remarkable product.' End quote—It isn't the kind of book I like much, but it is good of its kind. It is lively and more imaginative than most modern books. Why are so many characters in recent American fiction sub-human? Kindest regards." Well, I am dee-termined there'll be no apes in the next one.

I have heard from Robie Macauley who liked it. He says his own novel has been accepted by Random House and will be published in November. I am very glad because I like him and what he writes. Today I had a letter from Cal [Robert Lowell]. They are in Salzburg and he is teaching at the American school there. The letter was very nice and very much like him but it makes me sad to think of the poor old boy.

I haven't worked my way up to *The Golden Bowl* yet, but I have just finished *The Portrait of a Lady*. The convent in that is the most awful I have ever read about. It beats the place where Julien Sorel was a seminarian. When the Mother Superior said she thought the child had been there long enough I thought I would jump out the window. This winter I read that book of Max Picard's *The Flight from God*. I was knocked out by that.

I do hope I will see you all this summer. I hope to get to Ridgefield [home of the Fitzgeralds] by taking it easy. I am about ninety-two years old in the matter of energy and will have to travel with the sterilizer and syringe and all such mess but I am looking forward to it.

‿ In the following letter, Gordon, for the first and only time during their correspondence, asks O'Connor's opinion on a piece she has written.

Caroline Gordon to Flannery O'Connor

Undated [May 1952]

The book [*Wise Blood*] arrived just after I wrote you. I think the end comes off marvelously. And that was a ticklish job, too. I have been holding my breath for fear I had been giving you a bum steer, but I really don't think so, now I see what you've made of my suggestion. It was all there implicit in the action, anyway, of course, just needed a little more bringing out.

Waugh's comment on your book is interesting. I don't really think that he is a novelist. His *Edmund Campion* is a beautiful thing, but *Helena* is amateurish, at times embarrassingly so.

I am enclosing the piece on James I have been laboring on all winter.*

---

* Caroline Gordon, "Mr. Verver, Our National Hero," *Sewanee Review* 63.1 (January–March 1955): 29–47. The early draft of this essay was titled "The Figure at the Window on the Carpet." Letters dated in early 1953 reveal that one version of Gordon's essay on Henry James included a discussion of *Wise Blood*. (See FO to CG, 29 January 1953.)

I'd like to know how it strikes you. I don't feel that James has been read yet. Certainly, when read from the Christian view-point he yields some results he hasn't yielded to any of the critics. I have a lot of other notions about his work that I couldn't get into the essay. It is strange, for instance, that so many of his big scenes take place in churches. Strange, on the other hand, that he will present a convent, say, in the most stereotyped way: the one Claire de Cintre retires to, in *The American*, for instance. Graham Greene, in a piece called "Henry James: An Aspect," says that the fact is that James was abysmally ignorant both of the dogma and the rites of the Catholic Church, though he was strongly attracted to it.

This house is in turmoil. Allen leaves Friday morning to fly first to Princeton where he will inspect little Carolyn Wood and other members of the family, then he'll take off for a cultural congress in Paris [Congress for Cultural Freedom], to be gone about three weeks in all. He's scared to death of flying, but not as scared as he used to be before he joined the Church. I told him I would pray all the time he was on the ocean. He said that was all right, but he'd like to have a few nuns' prayers, as well. He'd appreciate yours, too, no doubt, even if you aren't a professional. He doesn't seem to think that converts' prayers avail much.

We look forward to seeing you this summer. I do hope your health continues to improve.

[postscript]

Allen read the first paragraph of your book and said, "You can tell from that first paragraph that she is a real writer." It is such an original strong book I am delighted by it all over again. You've got something that none of the rest of them seem to have.

Flannery O'Connor to Caroline Gordon

12 May 1952

I was very pleased to be able to read this piece on James and I have read it a couple times by now and with wonder every time. Since my critical training, such as it was, took place in a lump at Iowa, I've always felt that it would be horribly gauche to voice any insights on a novel or poem that came via Catholic conviction. At the same time I've thought that if a thing is art, it has to take in enough to be catholic—at least with a little c—and that if it's that, it is penetrable by Catholic standards. But aesthetics is way over my head. I don't have enough of the proper kind of words. Anyway, as I read it I felt that this was surely the normal, natural way to react to Henry James; I mean the way God and Henry intended.

I get so sick of reading all this stuff about his "accident."* I am sure you mean to dismiss it once and for all when you say, "If he had been congenitally incapable of the marriage relation he would have written books different from the ones he wrote," but this statement confuses me. I'm not very subtle; to me, it puts the emphasis back where you intend to take it off. I think he could have been physically incapable of marriage and still have written the books he wrote because I don't think that that would have had anything to do with his talent or the Grace that he had to write them with. I guess you mean that if he had been morally or emotionally unfit for the marriage relation, he would have written different books, which I can readily see. Maybe I am being knocked over by a gnat here but I wish you would enlighten me. I arrive at the obvious only after lengthy research.

Most of the stories you used in it, I haven't read but I did find a copy of "The Great Good Place" and read it yesterday. I thought the vision was more one of Purgatory than of Heaven. It wouldn't have been much of a Heaven to a Catholic anyway. While he didn't suffer there, the young man who took his place was a suffering figure and wasn't there a kind of communion of saints atmosphere between them? Also, although the Brother called it the Great Want Met, it was only a great want for contemplation and regaining of the self—it wasn't the great want you think of as being satisfied in Heaven. The presence of God is in the place but it is experience only vaguely and never seen. Wasn't St. Catherine of Siena rewarded with self-knowledge in her visions of Purgatory, or rather when she felt she was actually there? I don't mean that James thought of the great good place as purgatory but only that Dane was probably not as far up as he thought he was, or James maybe thought he was.

I will certainly pray for Mr. Tate in the air but my opinion is contrary to his. I always thought converts' prayers availed more, else they wouldn't be

---

* Henry James did not explicitly identify the nature of a "horrid" injury that he suffered and mentioned in his autobiography. Many speculated that he had suffered testicular damage.

where they are and that born Catholics are only born Catholics because they would be too lazy to save themselves any other way. But maybe this only applies to the Irish.

I am certainly indebted to you for letting me see this piece and I think it ought to be a book. If Catholic novels are bad, current Catholic criticism is PURE SLOP or else it's stuck off in some convent where nobody can get his hands on it. Sr. Mariella Gable ought to disguise herself as Freudina Potts and undermine the *Partisan Review* from inside. She could send the whole place to the devil.

≈ O'Connor's novel was published on May 15, 1952, with Gordon's endorsement inside the front book jacket: "I was more impressed by *Wise Blood* than any novel I have read in a long time. Her picture of the modern world is literally terrifying. Kakfa is almost the only one of our contemporaries who has achieved such effects. I have a tremendous admiration for the work of this young writer. An important novel." *New York Times* critic William Goyen wrote that O'Connor's first novel featured a "Tennessee-Georgia dialect expertly wrought into a clipped, elliptic and blunt style, [which] introduces its author as a writer of power." *Time* magazine was less flattering: "[A]ll too often it reads as if Kafka had been set to writing the continuity for L'il Abner." *Commonweal*, however, called it "a remarkably accomplished, remarkably precocious beginning."

Summer arrived. Gordon returned to Princeton. O'Connor traveled to Connecticut to stay with Sally Fitzgerald and her children for five weeks; Robert Fitzgerald was teaching at the Indiana School of Letters. With trepidation, Sally told Flannery what Regina O'Connor had felt unable to reveal to her daughter: Flannery had lupus, the autoimmune illness that killed her father.

That June, O'Connor and Gordon met in person for the first time in New York. With characteristic helpfulness, Gordon suggested that O'Connor send a copy of *Wise Blood* to her friend, influential British poet and literary critic Herbert Read. Gordon's support carried weight: her novel *The Strange Children* had been nominated for the 1952 National Book Award alongside J. D. Salinger's *The Catcher in the Rye*, Truman Capote's *The Grass Harp*, Herman Wouk's *The Caine Mutiny*, and James Jones's *From Here to Eternity*, which would win.

O'Connor remained in Connecticut until illness forced her home to Georgia. There, for six weeks, she was confined to bed, though she minimized her "come and go ailment" in letters to Gordon.

Flannery O'Connor to Caroline Gordon

11 September 1952

Last night I happened on this picture of your connection here.* Since I had sent him two bucks in memory of Mark Twain (before I asked you about him), I figure I must have at least paid for the license. He's mighty well preserved.

I am up again now and looking forward to a recessive period of my come-and-go ailment. It's very good working again. I am just writing a story to see if I can get away from the freaks for a while.

This summer while I was at the Fitzgeralds, I read *The Strange Children*. I thought it was a beautiful book, part one probably in the development of Grace in these people. Of the characters I noticed that the Catholic, Mr. Reardon, was the least filled in. Was that because he would have taken the book over if he had been? It was not his story of course but it takes some doing to put a Catholic in a novel.

I have just read *Victory*. Everything I read of Conrad's I like better than the last thing. I've also just read *The Turn of the Screw* again and to me it fairly shouts that it's about expiation.

Have you seen the Fitzgeralds? Sally seems to be having a bad time still. I had to leave in a hurry on account of my fever a few days before she lost the baby. Benedict has had the chickenpox but they say it has only given him more zest—which he didn't particularly need. The day before I left, he climbed in the car, drove it twelve feet over a chair and into a pile of rocks, climbed out the window, looking exactly like Charles Lindbergh, and received a whipping from me (Sally was in bed sick) as if it were a great honor.

I suspect you are getting ready for Minnesota.

Caroline Gordon to Flannery O'Connor

20 September 1952
1908 Selby Street
St. Paul, Minnesota

I was indeed glad to hear from you and so awfully glad to know that you are up and at work again. We were disappointed not to have a visit from

---

* A cousin of Gordon's who was associated with the International Mark Twain Society. See *HB*, 48–49.

you at Princeton. I found myself wishing that I had kidnapped you and taking you on there that day we had lunch together.

I was fortunate that Cousin Lee—dreadful old blatherskites and lecher—was off on his wedding trip when I visited my brother in St. Louis the other day. I therefore didn't have to see him. His house-keeper is much relieved that he and his "secretary" are wed after a good many years together. "It may cut down the talk," says she. My brother says it must have been something to do with income tax. Cheaper to wed than not.

Allen is still reeling all over Europe—Rome one week, Venice the next, but he will have to come home by September twenty ninth as the U. of Minnesota, an institution that is doubtless far from his thoughts these days, opens on that date. He has had such a good time that he is positively dazed. At some time or other he was due to have a talk with the Holy Father [Pope Pius XII]. He had things he much wanted to discuss with His Holiness. I am curious to see whether awe in the pontiff's presence will keep him from saying all he thinks about his fellow Scribner-author, Francis Cardinal Spellman.

I got to St. Paul about a week ago and have been busy settling into our new (rented) house. It is just heavenly to be able to unpack and hang your clothes up in your own (rented) closet. This has been a hellish summer. I have not got a chance to put in as much as one hour's work on my novel and in the last few weeks I have been getting pretty peevish about it.

About *The Strange Children*. I think you are right about Reardon. He isn't quite right. I think now that he is mis-cast. He had to be a "little" man, one whom they could all rather look down on, but he could have had another variety of littleness. I see a different character in his role now—a man who has little intellect and who would reveal himself more than Reardon does, trying ponderously to account for his conversion and never being able to, yet holding on to whatever it was stubbornly, nonetheless. Ah well—one reason for writing another novel is the chance to avoid the mistakes you made in the first! While we're on the subject, I'll point out another flaw in that novel.

Must take another paragraph for that. The story, as I see it, is the journey which every human being must make, from the natural to the supernatural. Lucy's mother lives more easily in the natural world than her father—she looks at the waterfall with her mother but she looks at the stars with her father. In the middle of the book there is a shift of emphasis from mother to father. It is her father who picks her up when she falls off the pony, her father who comforts her when she is afraid of Dr. Reardon and in the end she stands behind her beside her father, with his arm about her. But that old nigger preacher I'm always telling my students about: the one who said "First I tells 'em I'm going to tell them, then I tells 'em I done told 'em"—Seems you have to do it every time. Steven Lewis' part should have been underlined at a certain point. I should have told them that I am going to tell them. Instead, I just told them and none of them got it. That's one thing you can count on: their not getting it if there's any way humanly possible not to get it. You think as old a bird as I wouldn't have made that particular mistake!

I took advantage of Allen's absence to go up to Dorothy Day's "Maryfarm" at Newburgh to what she calls "the basic retreat." It lasted five days. I had to come back in the middle to see Allen off, so got in only three days in all—rushed right back the minute he took off. It was an extraordinary experience. Dorothy says that for several years after she entered the Church she got little help, little more than platitudes from parish priests. Then she went to a retreat given by Fr. La Couture in Canada. He is dead now but she keeps the retreat alive, training first one and then another priest to give it. It is tough sledding—this particular retreat is frowned on in many quarters.

They call their joint a "Hospitality House"—any bum is free to wander in off the road, and many do. The audience was therefore pretty motley, but you ought to have heard those bums sing the Latin. Prime before Mass and two conferences in the morning, then dinner and a short rest and an afternoon conference and supper and another conference. I don't think I could have stood up under five days of it, but when I got back from Princeton towards the end of the retreat they were all as fresh as daisies.

The approach was frankly mystical and I was reminded often of what Jacques Maritain says, that every real novelist is a mystic, "for nobody else knows what is in the human heart." Jacques was invoked often. So were Aristotle and other worthies. And the whole series of talks was based on a figure of St. Augustine's: *"pondus animae"*—spiritual gravity, as it were. The father also threw in the mediaeval schoolmen's demonstration of the existence of God and a good many other things that have hardly been heard of in the academic circles in which I move. It really was something!

I had such a good time that I didn't even envy Allen his trip to Italy. I guess we are going there in 1954, though. Allen has got himself a Fulbright professorship at the University of Rome for that year—I reckon Minnesota will let him off.

I do hope you get good news from Sally. I haven't heard from her since her illness. I do so hope things are going better there. I was dreadfully disappointed not to get over to Ridgefield but Sue Jenkins whom I was visiting at Sherman was ill and I couldn't get transportation over at the time I'd planned.

Let me hear from you when you feel like writing. If I don't answer you'll know it's because I'm wrestling with my novel. Getting back to work after a four or five month interruption is a grim business, isn't it? Luck to you, always.

↪ That fall and winter, O'Connor completed two short stories, "The River" and "The Life You Save May Be Your Own"—without advice from Gordon—and began work on her second novel, *The Violent Bear It Away*. In October, she purchased her first set of peahens. O'Connor learned in December that she would receive the $2,000 Kenyon Fellowship sponsored by the Rockefeller Foundation.

Meanwhile, Gordon tossed the first year's drafts of *The Malefactors*, then worked in "fits and starts." A providential visit from her friend Dorothy Day in November offered Gordon a new model for her novel's character, Catherine Pollard. But Gordon's writing, more and more, was interrupted by her commitments to lectures and book reviews—all necessary to relieve financial burdens. Mentoring young writers (like Walker Percy and Flannery O'Connor) also took an inordinate amount of time away from her writing.

In one missing letter from this time, Caroline Gordon shared with Flannery O'Connor a draft of a lecture that she delivered at the College of St. Thomas in St. Paul.* Gordon's proposition, with credit to Jacques Maritain's *Art and Scholasticism*, was that the craftsmanship of artists like Joyce and Flaubert made them "more Christian writers." Christian art, according to Maritain, was an

---

* The only existing draft of Gordon's lecture from the College of St. Thomas discusses (among other works) O'Connor's *Wise Blood* and is missing a page, as O'Connor notes in the next letter (CG to FO, 29 January 1953). The lecture was ultimately published as "Some Readings and Misreadings," *Sewanee Review* 61.3 (Summer 1953): 384–407.

encounter with "redeemed humanity": "everything belongs to it, the sacred as well as the profane." Gordon also shared Allen Tate's belief, outlined in an essay he wrote for the *New Republic* (and referred to in the next letter), that "Vague and ignorant piety (piety ignorant of literary standards) is the greatest enemy of a Catholic literature."

Flannery O'Connor to Caroline Gordon

29 January 1953

Thanks so much for looking for the missing page [from Gordon's lecture]. It was the one before the one you sent but I will look for it in *The Sewanee Review* and send that to such of my kin as will be impressed with the sight of this much stately printed matter mentioning a niece. The size of it will fairly stun my 83 yr. old cousin. Nothing stuns her but sheer bulk. Mr. Monroe Spears [*Sewanee Review* editor] wrote me and asked if I had a story. My stories are adequate, there's nothing in particular wrong with them but they sicken me when I read them in print; however, there's that money.

I liked the piece in the *New Republic** very much but where it ought to be is expanded is *Thought*. Though who reads *Thought* that don't go to Fordham? Maybe it ought to be in *Our Sunday Visitor*. Could His Eminence keep it out of *Our Sunday Visitor*? My attitude toward him [Cardinal Spellman] and his works (literary) is more lenient than yours and more crafty. It is—If we must have trash, this is the kind of trash we ought to have. This states your case and at the same time flatters the Cardinal. Somebody has to write for my cousin and she might as well have a prince of the church, and with him so well-suited to the task etc. etc. I suppose it's a problem that there's nothing for but the Holy Ghost. I dreamed one night about a Pope named April the 15 and woke up thinking this must be Francis. Then I realized Francis would be the 1st and this would be one of his far descendants. It was a mighty comforting dream.

I read *Middlemarch* a few years ago and thought it was wonderful all but the end. I suppose that was a connection to the century or something.

* Allen Tate, "Orthodoxy and the Standard of Literature," *New Republic* 128 (January 1953): 24–25.

I got me the Modern Library edition called the *Best Known Novels of Geo. E* then and thought I would have a great time with them but I didn't. I started on the *Mill on the Floss* but that thing must be a child's book or I don't have any perseverance or those big books are just too heavy to hold up. I started on one about some Methodists and didn't finish that either. I remember something from *Middlemarch* about "the roar on the other side of silence." That's what you have to pick up in a novel—I mean *put down* in one, I suppose. I want to read *Middlemarch* again and see if she wrote about freaks.

Do you know a man named Brainard Cheney? I found a review of my book by him in a quarterly called the *Shenandoah* that I hadn't known but that comes from Washington and Lee. It was a very good review, one of the only ones. This quarterly had a review of *The Old Man and the Sea* by Faulkner. He said Hemingway had discovered the Creator in this. It was just a paragraph. I think where he discovered the Creator in it was that sentence about the fish's eye—where [it] looks like a saint in a procession. I thought when I read it that he's seeing something he hasn't seen before; but I haven't really read many of his books.

I guess you are right about Cal [Robert Lowell]. I remember about the preacher who bought the sailor's parrot but finally had to give him up because whenever he cried "How shall we get God into our hearts?" the parrot hollered, "Pull him in with the rope! Pull him in with the rope!"

Caroline Gordon to Flannery O'Connor

Undated [February 1953]

Damn it: It was *not* the one before the one I sent. I have sent you all there is of that version of that lecture. You aren't reading it right. But alas, what I sent you was only a lecture and had to be revised drastically as well as cut before it could be published as an essay. And my advisor, Mr. T [Tate] (who gets pretty irascible, anyway, when confronted with my prose style— "Your sentences have no snap," "That's nonsense," etc.), he made me cut *Wise Blood* out, allowing as how it was all right to bring it in the way I did in a lecture but that in an essay it would introduce a whole new notion that I didn't have time to deal with and that ought not to be in there anyhow. I had bit off as many writers as I could chew by that time. Sorry.

My essay ventures are usually productive of great suffering, one way or another. But I doubt whether your cousin would have been much impressed. At her age I guess there is little that you, or even I at my advanced age, can do to impress her.

Allen isn't allowed to publish anything in *Thought* on account of his sassing Cardinal Spellman. It is a great grief to the editor, Fr. Lynch, who wishes that both Allen and Cardinal Spellman were a little different from the way they are.

In the same mail that your letter came was one from Brainard Cheney, saying that he was going to send me his review of *Wise Blood*. He is an old and dear friend of ours. I have been aiming for some months to become his god-mother but haven't made it yet. However, I think I will. Both he and his wife are taking instruction now. "Lon," as we call him, comes from that Wood family in Georgia. It has produced Julia Peterkin and Lon and many generations of is it Methodist or Presbyterian divines? Anyhow, Lon, who is as full of what I call "Protestant clichés" as any egg of meat, wrestles mightily with the Spirit. As Allen said once of him and another old friend who is all snarled up in Protestant theology, "Tommy wants to roll on the floor and froth at the mouth and Lon wants to speak in tongues." He does deal with the Spirit in a mighty high-handed way but he is one of the finest fellows that ever lived.

Must get to work. I do hope things are going well for you.

[postscript]

Robert [Fitzgerald] wrote Allen a letter of reprimand about that piece in the NR [*New Republic*].

Allen says tell you he disagrees with you completely in what you say about trash and Cardinal Spellman. He doesn't believe that we ought to have trash, in the first place, and if we do he thinks that the last person who ought to write it is Cardinal Spellman. I think I'd line up with him. I don't believe that anybody ought to write for your Cousin. Let her tell her beads. I believe that one thing that is the matter with the world today is that practically everybody is writing with one eye slanted at your cousin. That is one reason *Wise Blood* didn't sell any better than it did. There is far too much printed matter.

My great-grandfather Gordon debated all over the South with McGuffey, the author of the famous readers, McGuffey was for having everybody taught to read—so he could sell more readers—my great-grandfather maintained that reading was a strain on the mind and that not all minds were fitted to bear it. He used to cite as evidence a dear and illiterate old friend of his, "Uncle" Sam Bunch, from "the Ragged Mountains" who used to come visit him every time he drove his team of fast-stepping oxen down from the mountains into Charlottesville. Uncle Sam was of the same opinion as my grandfather and would often say: "Now look at me. Don't know a letter in the book and my mind is as strong as it ever was, while you are getting weaker every day, Billy Gordon."

My gt. grandfather had to defend Uncle Sam once in a law suit over a "breachy" sow of a neighbour's whom had dropped in her tracks, nine inches from the door to the dung-hill. My gt. grandfather, when he put Uncle Sam on the stand asked him what the letter "G" stood for in his name, Samuel G. Bunch. Uncle Sam exclaimed that here was an example not only of a man's mind being weakened by reading but his character being impaired. My gt. grandfather was lying, he said, when he pretended that he didn't know what "G" stood for in his name. "Billy Gordon," he said, "we was play-boys together. You know my mother was a Hancock!"

If you aren't convinced by all this I have many more antiquarian reminiscences that finally will convince you—give us both enough time. MUST, MUST get to work!

If you liked Lon Cheney's review of your book I wish you would write and tell him so. He has written two novels himself but has had to give up writing for the last year or so while helping to elect the new governor of Tennessee—Lon is a newspaper man [on] the side. His address is 2412 Kensington Place, Nashville, for the winter. In summer they live at Smyrna, Tennessee, thirty miles outside of Nashville where they have a lovely old house that they call "Cold Chimneys."

⁓ Fannie and Lon Cheney were certainly old and dear friends of Gordon. Caroline helped Lon revise his first novel in 1937; Fannie served as Allen Tate's secretary at the Library of Congress (1943–44); Lon lived briefly with the Tates while Fannie taught in Japan (1951–52); and, finally, Caroline and Allen were Lon and Fannie's godparents when they entered the Catholic Church, in the summer of 1953. Gordon's introduction would lead to a lifelong friendship between Flannery O'Connor and the Cheneys.

Flannery O'Connor to Caroline Gordon

22 February 1953

I am much obliged for Mr. Cheney's address. I wrote him that I liked
the review though I had to admit that I hadn't thought of the patrolman as
the tempter on the mt. top or H. Motes as embodying the Christ "myth."
I leave the word *myth* to Mrs. Roosevelt anyway. The Fitzgeralds have a
friend in the UN who took his eleven-year-old daughter to one of the sessions one day. He told her to act intelligent and to show that she knew who
the people were he introduced her to and to say something to show that
she knew. She did very well, he said. He introduced her finally to Mrs. R
and she said, "Oh hello, Mrs. Roosevelt, I always listen to your radio program while I'm waiting for the Lone Ranger." Which is how I know *myth*.
Maybe it's the myth business that [is] keeping him out of the Church.

I do think with you all that the Cardinal is the last person who ought to
be giving the world fiction and verse and what I mean by its being the kind
of trash we ought to have is that it's several cuts above Mickey Spillane.
I suppose Prudence is all you have to worry about in the order of trash
and the Cardinal is very prudent though I think he sins against it in ways
he don't know it exist. Anyway, you tell Allen it's just as well he doesn't
acquaint himself with the great masters of the novel in the 19th century.
That would be exactly your point of: too much reading. He would go on
fattening the foundlings with even more horrible prose. Somebody was so
good as to give me [Cardinal Spellman's] *The Foundling* when I was sick in
the hospital. I was taking big doses of ACTH which prevents concentra-
tion, but this wasn't necessary for that. It was the purest pablum and if I
had been fifteen years old I would have liked it fine.

My trouble I suppose is the usual Catholic sin of not paying much attention to the Church's temporal hardtimes, knowing the gates of hell
won't prevail. I certainly enjoy watching them prevail here and now, or
anyway, when they're prevailing in the Protestant body. Chief Thum and
the Sunshine Evangelistic Party are nothing to laugh at but I would mighty
well like to hear the musical paint buckets and see the fourth singing heart
in the world. When it gets around to Catholic vulgarity, that is too Pious-
Business Business-Pious and being too close to home, hurts too much;
hurts too much to write about. I've often wondered how J.F. Powers stands

to write about it. It certainly must be a torture and he [is] a strong man. The whole subject sharpens my sympathy for him. The other day I got a "check" for One Hundred Hail Marys on "The Bank of Heaven," from a nun in a convent in Canada where I had sent a dollar for some mission or other. All made out with a picture of the Christ Child on it in the corner—"President," and signed by the sister who said the prayers. Now this is worse than the Cardinal's works. This is bringing it too close to the altar; his is a good distance away. I know the Hail Marys were said in all charity and may save my soul.

Have you read that history of the Church by a Dominican, Phillip Hughes? He says something to the effect that the Church is like a river and the times like a river bed and when the bed is low, the river is low but still pure.

I have just finished reading a piece in the *Commonweal* by a man named Lukacs* who says there's no more literary correspondence and that good writers don't pay any attention to young ones because there's no more charity among them. This has not been my experience. I think of your detailed letters to me about my book and wonder what makes him so sure of what he says.

* John A. Lukacs, "On Literary Correspondence," *Commonweal* 57.20 (20 February 1953): 500–504.

Part 2

A Good Man Is Hard to Find
(March 1953–March 1955)

The D. P. [the Displaced Person, Mr. Matysiak] and Shot nearly choked
each other in the wagon the other day and now my mother is almost afraid to
send them to the field together for fear one won't come back. She gave him
a long lecture that night through Alfred, the 12 yr. old boy. She kept saying,
"You tell your father that he's a gentleman, that I KNOW he's a gentleman
and that gentlemen don't fight with poor negroes like Shot that don't have
any sense." I think he then told his father in Polish that she said Shot didn't
have any sense. Father agreed. Too much agreement. She knew it hadn't gone
through and started again. "You tell your father that he is, etc." Finally Alfred
admitted he didn't know what a gentleman was, even in English. She was very
successful in communicating with Shot, however. "Now Shot," she said, "you
are very intelligent. You are much too intelligent to fight with a man that we
can't understand very well, now you know you are above this, etc. etc."
He agreed with every word, but said Mr. Matysiak had hit him first.
—Flannery O'Connor to Caroline Gordon, 8 February 1954

I particularly miss landscape after the Misfit comes on the scene.
One wonders how the grandmother is able to keep her mind on her
conversation with him when Bailey goes off in the woods with the two boys.
—Caroline Gordon to Flannery O'Connor, undated [May 1953]

≈ In the spring of 1953, Caroline Gordon accepted a ten-week teaching position in Seattle as the University of Washington's Walker-Ames Lecturer, while Allen Tate remained in Minneapolis. She earned $2,000, what she called "movie pay." She sold paperback rights for her 1941 novel *Green Centuries*, and relieved some weighty debts. Gordon left her longtime publisher, Scribner's; Harcourt, Brace offered to publish *The Malefactors*. (Gordon's editor at Harcourt, Denver Lindley, would later become O'Connor's editor.) Finally, Gordon negotiated a contract with Viking for a nonfiction book, *How to Read a Novel*.

Three days after Gordon arrived in Seattle, she set aside her book projects to write "Emmanuele! Emmanuele!" In a writing career that would last thirty more years, this would be Caroline Gordon's last published short story. (She would, however, publish excerpts of novels.)

Back in Milledgeville—and despite her illness—Flannery O'Connor's world was expanding daily. The lifelong fears and physical challenges that would accompany O'Connor's lupus diagnosis make the next stage of her life all the more remarkable. Health stabilizing, O'Connor wrote to Robert Lowell, "I have enough energy to write with and as that is all I have any business doing anyhow, I can with one eye squinted take it all as a blessing." She wrote each morning, a practice she would maintain throughout periods of good health. Over the next two years, O'Connor produced some of her finest work: "A Good Man Is Hard to Find," "You Can't be Any Poorer Than Dead," "A Circle in the Fire," "A Temple of the Holy Ghost," "The Displaced Person," "A Late Encounter with the Enemy," "A Stroke of Good Fortune," and "Good Country People."

Gordon's critiques during this period are insightful and unselfish. O'Connor's revisions are a testament to her strengthening resilience and expansive artistic humility. What Gordon taught, O'Connor was willing to learn.

In May 1953, O'Connor sent "A Good Man Is Hard to Find" to Gordon.

Caroline Gordon to Flannery O'Connor

Undated [May 1953]
"The Moated Grange"
4337 Fifteenth Avenue, N.E.
Seattle, Washington

Your story has just come. This is the first day I have been free of a dreadful old man of the Sea who leaped on my back two days after I got here—to wit, Uncle André Gide—and there are 52 letters that I ought to answer before writing you. However, I like your story so much that I will write you before tackling the rest. Also while my impressions of the story are fresh in my mind. You probably know by this time that there are some things you do better than anybody else. The dialogue is marvelous. What an ear you have! But the effects are achieved unobtrusively, subtly, always—never thrown at you, the way some people throw 'em.

I am reminded, though, of something General Forrest wrote to a young lieutenant: "I told you tweist. God damn it, KNOW!"

I am presuming that since you sent me the story you will not be averse to receiving my criticism. I told you some months ago that I thought your stories suffered from too narrow a focus. I also told you that the omniscient narrator does not speak colloquially—but here you are, at it again.

" . . . the son she lived with's . . ." That is something that a person could say. The omn. narrator cannot talk like that. Yet you have him talking like that in the second sentence. As a result your story doesn't have the proper dimension, will not seem to the reader as important a story as it might otherwise seem. You seem to choose to look at the universe through a peep hole, as the result of this technical fault. The reader will unconsciously be tempted to say: "All right. She's only a girl looking through a knot hole in the fence. If she could really see what's going on her report would be different." This failure to master this technical secret seems to me a major fault of your work.

It comes, partly, I think, from the terrific, unremitting, almost unbearable effort to achieve intensity. You all but screw up your eyes in the effort. When you first tried to learn to write letters you made similar contortions. Now you write effortlessly. Once you have learned how to do a thing you must do it without thinking about it and go on to learn something else.

The omniscient narrator speaks of the "rag" tied about the children's mother's head. "Rag" is a word that is not in his vocabulary. Your authority—if the story is to have its proper dimension—ought to be more Olympian. You impeach your own authority when you use words like "rag" in the context in which you are using it here.

The story, on the whole, does not have enough "composition of scene" to borrow a phrase from St. Ignatius of Loyola. It is not well enough located in time and place. Remember that the Lord made the world before He made Adam and Eve. Events take place in time and space. The apricots help, but they aren't enough.

Look how Yeats in "The Second Coming" locates his "shape with the lion body and head of a man" and "gaze blank and pitiless as the sun" [...] "somewhere in sands of the desert" [...] "while all about reel shadows of the indignant desert birds." The poem wouldn't work without those desert birds.

I particularly miss landscape after The Misfit comes on the scene. One wonders how the grandmother is able to keep her mind on her conversation with him when Bailey goes off in the woods with the two boys. I think she ought to register Bailey's going and bringing herself back to The Misfit in an effort. Incidentally, I think that goes too fast. Even if Bailey doesn't resist I think we ought to know the attitude his body assumed as he went off.

And right here you come up on a difficulty handed you by your method. You are using the omniscient narrator yet you go into the grandmother's mind when it suits your convenience. If I were doing it—and that, after all, is all I'm saying amounts to—I think I'd use the device Flaubert uses in the seduction scene in *Bovary*—he renders Emma's emotions by her reactions to the landscape—I'd show the grandmother's reactions to what is happening, or what she barely suspects may happen by the way the world—these trees, this road—looks to her. Then have her resolutely concentrate on her talk with the man. You take it too fast. I'd work this device three times, I think: when Bailey first goes off, then when the shot comes, then when the second shot comes. The way you handle it there isn't quite enough tension, it seems to me. You get over the ground so fast we aren't made to realize what is happening.

On page 13 the paragraph beginning "I was a gospel singer onct . . ." is magnificent.

I think that the grandmother is perhaps a little too much of a disembodied voice throughout. We want to know how she looks when she says this and that. You hardly ever show us.

I keep coming back to my point on page 13 just before the paragraph beginning "I was a gospel singer onct . . ." That is, just after the two pistol shots we need to know how the road, the woods looked after the shots were fired.

In Chekhov's "On the Road," we know most of the time what the characters were doing—what attitudes their bodies assumed—and how the room looked, even though What's His Name delivers a long—but highly dramatic—dialogue. If you will try to remember that story you can see the people all the time—even the pot boy. That is because Chekhov has given you enough specification to enable you to see them. I don't see your grandmother the way I see Chekhov's folks—you haven't given me enough specification to enable me to keep visualizing. Your task is to keep the reader visualizing all the time. If he ever stops visualizing there's a hole in your canvas, waste motion in your story. You are more on the bean than any young writer I know, and as talented, Lord knows, but you suffer from the modern complaint: Abstraction. The business of art is incarnation, according to Jacques Maritain.

I am at the University of Washington as a "visiting professor," at what seems to me movie pay. However, it's only 10 weeks, so I won't get rich at it.

I am mad about Seattle. The city is almost wholly encircled by the Sound and two huge lakes, which, in turn, are encircled by two mountain ranges, the Olympic and the Cascade. The two highest peaks are "Baker" and "Rainier." The natives refer to them as "they." "They are out" is a synonym for fine weather. They are very seldom out but when you [sic] are they look like Fujiyama. There is a roof garden on top of this hotel. When the sun shines I take my typewriter up there and work and sun-bathe all day. If I ever look up from my work I am likely to have my breath taken, the view in any direction is so spectacular.

I go to a Dominican church here: the Blessed Sacrament. The Newman chaplain, Fr. Dooley, tells me that this is the most pagan campus in the U.S. Maybe it is. Anyhow, I gather that Bob Heilman, head of the English department, picks his visiting profs with an eye to stemming the rising tide of Logical Positivism—as if worms like I can do anything about that! What they need out here is the Old McCoy—Jacques Maritain, I say.

I go to Mass by way of the alleys which are simply wonderful. Every little house is set in a mass of flowers. I have never seen anything like the flowers in this city. And the flowering fruit trees! It rains most of the time, so everything grows and blooms like mad.

Allen is going to be Fulbright professor at the U. of Rome next year. He also has to teach six weeks at Oxford, so we will probably go abroad around the first of July. I have a writer's conference among the Mormons [University of Utah] between me and the east, though—and so much work on hand I can barely remember that we are going abroad. Allen says he dreads asking me to Rome. "You will be delirious the whole time," says he.

I was awfully pleased when Lon and Fannie Cheney "came through." I hope you will keep on writing to Lon and advising him if he ever asks your advice. He is a perfectly splendid fellow and he has something, too. But he could not write a decent sentence if he were to be hanged for it. Still, neither could [Theodore] Dreiser!

Tongue cannot tell my sufferings with Uncle André G. I just sent the ms [manuscript] of my story EMMANUELE! EMMANUELE! (I hope the title sounds like a cry of anguish!) off to Allen yesterday. Come near killing me. I had thought I was to be let off writing any more short stories in this life. But the *données* were too much for me. I think you would find them interesting—God knows about the story. My son-in-law, Percy Wood, had a terrible old trout of a grandmother and a perfectly darling, saintly grandfather. When the old trout finally died at eighty-something, the funeral was quite a confused affair on account of so many of the members of the family not speaking to each other. Grandpa, according to Mrs. Percy Wood, Jr., went through all the muddle as if oblivious, riding the ninety miles to Indian Mound, with his head tilted back and his hat over his eyes. As the body was lowered into the grave he clapped his battered grey hat against his breast and leaning far over said in an audible voice: "Goodbye, my heart!"

We now switch the scene far afield. A highly respectable prof. of English, poet, too, was describing to me with admiration André Gide's amorous pursuit of the little Arab boys. He was also regretting that Gide had declined an invitation to come and lecture at his university! It occurred to me that I would have felt that I ought to pay money to keep him from lecturing to my students. Anyhow, all these *données* lay fallow till Walker Percy told me I ought to read the correspondence between Gide and [Paul] Claudel.

I did. Claudel said finally that he thought Gide "had no real talent," a conclusion I share. When I got here, Jackson Mathews, on the floor below, who is learned in contemporary literature, gave me *Madeleine*, the memoir Gide wrote of his wife after she died. He never mentioned her name in his journal except casually but the letters he wrote her were supposed to supply that omission after his death. I think he hoped to cut a figure posthumously as a great, sort of Dantesque lover—he took the theologically unsound view that his love for her was so spiritual that it inhibited all carnal desire, leaving him free to sport with Arab boys or even to have illegitimate children by other women. Anyway, one day when he called for the key to the secretary in which the letters were kept he found that they no longer existed—she had burned them. He says he cried steadily for a week and never afterwards felt as if he were alive—felt instead that he had a hole in the place of a heart, which brings us around, full circle, I hope, to Grandpa Russell.

I have got to get to those letters! I envy you those guineas [O'Connor's birds]. Baby guineas are something out of this world! Georgia must be wonderful now. All the flowers that bloom here and sunshine, too.
[postscript]

I hope you don't mind being harangued about your story! It's the evil effects of teaching.

Flannery O'Connor to Caroline Gordon

20 May 1953

I thank you the Lord knows for haranging me twice on the same counts and at the expense of boring yourself stiff. This is Charity and as the good sisters say Gawd will reward you for your generosity. I hope quick. But you are wrong one place—I do not suffer from the modern complaint of Abstraction; I suffer from the 7th Deadly Sin: Sloth. The slothful are always in a big hurry, I know all about it and how it catches up with you before the end. My contrary disease is called lupus but it's only the Aggressive Sloth made Manifest. I'd like to persuade myself that I hear time's winged chariot and so on and so on but then I think you take such good care of yourself you'll have the embarrassment of being around like your cousin when you're 85, in spite of the ailment and the agony and the outrage. The effort to achieve some intensity is terrible but it isn't as terrible as it must have to be or there'd be more intensity coming out somewhere.

Anyway I will work on the story longer. I keep asking myself: how would the damn woods look after two pistol shots? The Omniscient Narrator is running me nuts. I thought he could ease into a brain and rifle it and ease out again and look like he had never been there in the first place. Mine is just a bungler. Also I think I will start talking like Dr. Johnson as a matter of course—if this is possible. My mother says I talk like a nigger and I am going to be out sometime and say something and everybody is going to wonder what kind of people I come from etc. etc. Her predictions turn out on the double and worse than true and here it has affected the Om. Nar.

There was a man at Yaddo who used to say Gide was the "great Protestant spirit." I was glad they put him on the Index* as it meant I wouldn't have to read him. Otherwise I would have thought I had to. If I had charge of the Index, I'd really load it up and ease my burden.

Somebody brought a man out here, a textbook salesman for Harcourt Brace [Erik Langkjaer]. He was a Dane and had studied at Fordham with Fr. Lynch and was interested in Dorothy Day. He wasn't a Catholic and said what he couldn't understand was why she fed endless lines of endless bums who crawled back to the gutter after every dish of soup. No results. No hope. No nothing, he said. The few Scandinavians that I have seen have impressed me as being very antiseptic about everything. I said it was Charity and there was nothing you could do about it. He seemed to be fascinated and disgusted both. What I can't understand about them is the pessimism. If Charity were in the form of a stick I can imagine beating a lot of people over the head with it.

I would hate to [cope] with [a lot] of young Logical positivists.† I will pray for you.

The Cheneys wrote that they would try to stop by before St. Simons and I hope very much that they'll do this.

---

* A list of books and authors the Catholic Church found heretical; this practice was abolished in 1966.
† In this letter, the archival documents are partially illegible. Bracketed insertions contain editorial inference.

Caroline Gordon to Flannery O'Connor

21 May 1953

I was tight the other night and held forth at some length my friends tell me on the sin of "Gloth" with which I kept assuring them I was grievously afflicted . . . I wonder if you're right about that sloth. It's bad but Abstraction is even more insidious. Be that as it may, view-point is something anybody in your business to needs to know something about. I don't understand it very well, myself, but what little I know about it, is, of course, at your service.

The Om. Nar. eases up to people's brains, as I understand it, but never manages to get really inside, though he'd like to. It's a matter of distance. If I go up on the roof of this hotel I see Mt. Rainer and other things I can't see from the ground. But I can't see the blade of grass on the ground outside my window. Any narrative is a mixture of panoramic and scenic views. Your stuff is mostly scenic, wherein lies your excellence as a writer. You are nearly always down to brass tacks. [William] Thackeray was too often like a lordly uncle lolling in a window seat and calling to a nephew who is almost too short to see over the sill: "Come here and let uncle show you." Half the time Nephew doesn't bother to look. It takes the scenic to convince.

In a book called *The House of Fiction*, by two wights hight Tate and Gordon (Scribner's) there is in the appendix a discussion of four points of view, which, the authors say, may be used.

One is the om. nar. but you can hardly write a book from that view point. You need something more immediate for your effects. There is the first person view point. It has obvious merits. One gets an immediacy which is hardly to be secured in any other way. But, as [Percy] Lubbock pointed out before T. and G. in his *The Craft of Fiction* and if you haven't read that book you ought to read it at once, this method has also disadvantages. Your first person narrator may be, as is the case with so many of E. Hemingway's heroes, a perfect dope. If you stick to the first person viewpoint how are you going to let the reader know that your hero is not as smart as he is?

Gustave Flaubert solves this problem in *Bovary* by using what T. and G. call The Effaced Narrator viewpoint. His narrator is at all times exactly as close to his characters—all of them—as he needs to be. He does not confine himself exclusively to any one, but stands right beside them, or at a distance from them or slides inside them as his need requires. He stays closer to Emma than any of the other characters but doesn't hesitate to go inside the consciousness of the others when he wants to. A brilliant example of a sudden and dramatic shift in the view point is when little Justin, the apothecary's assistant, looks out of the window and sees Emma coming with "the air whirling in her hollow head" and "she had never appeared to him at once so wan and so majestic."

At times Flaubert gets far enough away from Emma to allow a superior, ironic intelligence—his own—to play on the scene: "She longed at once to live in Paris and to roam the high seas etc." At other times he absolutely slips inside her as when she and Rodolphe are riding in the forest and the succession of brown trunks makes Emma giddy. He is walking close beside her at the beginning of one sentence—when she starts up the attic stairs with Rodolphe's letter in her hand and midway of the sentence is inside her, looking with her eyes at "this horrible piece of paper she is holding in her hand:" the letter. There is only one person in the world to whom it is horrible: Emma. Rodolphe thought it was a pretty nifty piece of work and the plough-boy who brought it wonders why anybody should turn pale on receiving a note from a neighbour. The rest of that scene he is inside Emma, too, when she leans out the window and the hollow square below combines with Binet's lathe to call: "Come!"

I think that the Effaced Narrator Technique is what you need. Why don't you study *Bovary* from that standpoint? I had a student one term, as illiterate a youth as e'er I met who did exactly what I advised: took scene after scene in *Bovary* to pieces to see how Flaubert got his effects. In fourteen weeks it turned him into a professional writer. His first novel was called *So Many Doors*.* (Also turned him into a teacher of Creative Writing at the U. of Iowa.) In a couple of years he became a best-seller. His novel this year *The Corpus of Joe Bailey* has been much talked about and has sold mighty well. If Flaubert could do that to him think what he would do to YOU!

While I am on the subject of view point I will just fire the remaining barrel. There is a fourth method which Henry James called "The Central

---

* Oakley Hall, *So Many Doors* (New York: Random House, 1950).

Intelligence." This does not mean that events are seen through the eyes of a central intelligence. It means something a damn sight more difficult. I do not know of but two people now living and operating who know what James meant by this. One is Your Humble Servant, who does not understand it very well, but who, as far as she knows, is the only novelist except James who has ever used the method. The other initiate, the one who initiated me, is Percy Lubbock. I grieve to state that I do not think my collaborator, A. Tate, quite gets it. He wrote the Appendix in *The House of Fiction* and called this method, most mistakenly, he now admits, "The Roving Narrator." I have a devil of a time when I am teaching to conceal my disapproval of what he says about this method.

I'm sorry to say that from what I see of your work I fancy that you will be using this method before you are done. That is why I recommend that you read Lubbock. But you had better master the Effaced Narrator Viewpoint before you tackle the Central Intelligence.

In a preface to *The Portrait of a Lady*, James says that "The house of fiction has not one window but a million." These windows, he goes on to say, are of every size and shape. The window is the temperament, the capacity to perceive, the artistic form the author gives his stuff. But, says Uncle Henry, at every window stands a figure, either with a pair of eyes or a pair of glasses. What goes on outside, on the broad, spreading plain outside the window—in, that is, the human scene—is reflected in this spectator's eyes. Lubbock, attempting to make it plain, says that in *The Ambassadors*, Lambert Strether's sensations and emotions and reactions are the actors.

I think of it this way: The reader is, as it were, a prisoner, seated on a stool so low that he cannot see out of the window. Therefore he sees of the human scene only what he sees reflected in the eyes of the figure at the window. At first glance this would seem to restrict what he sees: he will see only what is reflected in a pair of eyes. But when you stop to think of it that is all anybody can see ordinarily: what he sees through his own eyes. If he sees through his own eyes what is reflected in another pair of eyes he will see twice as much as the next man, who is looking only through his own eyes sees. Here is a great mystery of the craft. I can't explain it. I merely try to tell you how it seems to me.

There is one little trick, though, that I think you need which you could get from Lubbock. I think perhaps the best way to put it before you is to tell you something of the origins of my novel, *The Strange Children*. I use

James' method of the Central Intelligence there. My heroine is nine years old, James' hero is fifty-four, but they are handled by the same method. (We won't go into the reasons why the results are so different.) Every event in the action is reflected by nine-year-old Lucy and morally evaluated by her. James himself said that to use this method you had to have a character who was capable of morally evaluating what happened to him. There were times when it seemed difficult to refer everything to Lucy. For instance, I wondered at first how I was going to reveal the fact that Mrs. Reardon and Uncle Tubby were lovers. In the end, I used exactly the same method James used when Strether sees Madame de Vionnet and Chad Newsome on the river. His innocence—up to that time he has not realized that Mme. De V. is a woman capable of having an illicit love affair—and Lucy's innocence make each scene more dramatic than it otherwise would have been, I think. I could not have written my book, however, without a hint from Lubbock. He says that sometimes the recording intelligence records more dramatically when it does not know what it is recording. I think the *donnée* of my book was a remark I heard Nancy make when she was four years old. I used to let her stay out in the country with her great-grandmother as much as I dared. One day I heard her say: "I got to die some time . . . I got to die some time." It was said rather merrily but through the childish voice I heard my grandmother's saying grimly something she'd never said to anybody else. If you will notice in *The Strange Children* we don't get Lucy's thoughts. It's her sensations and emotions that are the actors.

I think that this very little trick: the consciousness recording something it doesn't understand—children often do that—would be very helpful to you. I feel that your grandmother [in "A Good Man Is Hard to Find"] ought to record the fact that something is happening or is going to happen without understanding it. She is just the kind of character who is made for this device. Without Strether's innocence James couldn't have turned a wheel.

I guess that this is about enough lecture for one day. I still haven't got back to my novel after that round with André Gide [the story "Emmanuele! Emmanuele!"]. We went on a long boat trip yesterday, with two admirals. One French, the other a home product. Dined on the boat, served by Filipino sailors. There are houses along the shore all the way. The gardens slope down to the water. I never saw such masses of flowers. Even the trees were in bloom—at least the madrona, dogwood and hawthorn. Dogwood

blooms twice a year here. I don't know that I could stand that. Like Peter
Taylor who came up from Louisiana one year, stayed in Tennessee a stretch,
another in Maryland and got to New England in time for his fourth spring.
He said the emotional strain was almost more than he could take.

I am amused at your profession of gratitude for my lectures on the craft.
I suppose you ought to be grateful to me for haranguing you, for I really do
want to be helpful. But mighty few people take it that way.*

Flannery O'Connor to Caroline Gordon

2 June 1953

All this is very helpful to me and I intend to take the slow tour of
Madame Bovary. I read *The Craft of Fiction* periodically but I am still at the
stage where I have to worry about if anything is going to BE than HOW. I
notice Mr. Lubbock says Flaubert never had to hold down his subject with
one hand while he wrote it with the other. Me neither. I have to go in search
of it. I don't know whether I get blood out of the turnip or the turnips out
of my blood. The novel I am writing now [*The Violent Bear It Away*] is very
exciting to me but I keep writing the wrong thing, proceeding like the mole.
It has three boys for heroes—all very guilty and sharp. They burn a cross
on one of them's papa's lawn and the cross is something different to each of
them and the papa etc. etc. It is going to be kind of impossible to do but I
think it must be the impossibility that makes the tension.

My method is more likely to be affected by my mother's dairyman's
wife than Mr. Henry James. She hangs around all the time and all her sentences begin: "I know one time my husband seen . . ." It works like you
say. He sees everything and she sees twice as much as he sees but she has
never looked at anything but him. They both read my book and said: it just
shown you how some people would do.

Don't be amused by my profession of gratitude. It's drastic and the fact.
I have had a few people apply to me for advice about their manuscripts
but they are always hopeless, and have a mission, or are just plain crazy.
One of them, a lady, said, "You use the block style, don't you?" Another is
a disciple of Henry Miller. The other is a bank clerk and when he brings a
paper, he sits on the arm of the chair smoking heavily while I read it and

---

* Letter incomplete. Final phrase reads: "They seem"; the page that follows is missing.

every now and then his finger descends on a word and he says, "See? That's where I use muh iron-ny." It scares me to death when I think how good the Lord is to give you a talent and let you be able to use it. I re-resolve to become responsible, and to *Madame Bovary* I go.

I do pray for you but it strikes me I ought to pray for the logical positivists. A distasteful business.

⟿ In 1953, Flannery O'Connor's summer began with an optimistic doctor's visit: "He says I am doing better than anybody else that has what I got and he's very pleased with his work." O'Connor published "A Good Man Is Hard to Find" in *The Avon Book of Modern Writing* and "The River" in the *Sewanee Review*; Signet released the paperback edition of *Wise Blood*. On June 6, Lon and Fannie Cheney—recent Catholic converts—visited O'Connor for the first time while driving to St. Simons Island. O'Connor reciprocated with an August visit to their home in Smyrna, Tennessee. At the end of the summer, O'Connor travelled to Connecticut to see the Fitzgeralds.

Caroline Gordon's summer was equally busy. Gordon left Seattle and taught at a writer's conference in Utah before returning east. Bantam published the paperback edition of her novel *Green Centuries* and Gordon sold "Emmanuelle! Emmanuele!" to the *Sewanee Review*. In late July, she sailed to England to meet Allen Tate at Oxford. Gordon and Tate stopped in London and Paris before settling in Rome, where Tate's year-long Fulbright would house them at the American Academy. Free of household chores, Gordon immersed herself in writing.

Back in Milledgeville that September, O'Connor began to prepare stories for her collection *A Good Man Is Hard to Find*. The Fitzgeralds were moving to Italy and O'Connor wrote to them, "I had a letter from Caroline in Paris & from Ashley [Brown] in Dublin & I feel like the world is moving off and leaving me in the United States alone."

Caroline Gordon to Flannery O'Connor

1 September 1953
Hotel des Saints Peres
Rue des Saints Peres, Paris 6

Yesterday I read your story "The River," sitting in the little inside court of our hotel on the rue Saints Peres. I am convinced that Lambert Strether once sat on the very chair I was sitting on to read that communication from his formidable fiancée, while Waymarsh watched him through the glass. Jack Mathews thinks it was another court, but let us leave that aside for a moment. The point is what a beautiful story you have written: I had a feeling that it was going to be good from the moment Mrs. Conin took that little boy by the hand, and you sure didn't let me down. Just as I finished the story, John Prince, a young friend of ours who practically knows every word of Eudora Welty's "Petrified Man" by heart, came along. "Here you are," says I and he, too, was charmed. As was Ward Dorrance, another friend of ours and a very gifted fiction writer, who is staying at this same hotel. There are so many of these people about that I called him the "*sainte peres.*" I seem to be the only *sainte mere.* But to get back to your story, or rather, to your work in general. I see even more clearly with this story what you are about. It is original. Nobody else has done anything just like it. And it is something that much needs to be done. I'd sort of like to write something about your work—I'm beginning to feel that I might be able to point out some things about it that other people may not have noticed— and I'd like to review your novel when it comes out. Will you let me know as far ahead of time as you can so I can ask either [the] *Times* or the *Herald-Tribune* to let me have it? I suppose Francis Brown [editor, *New York Times Book Review*] would let me have it. But I gather that he got a lot of indignant letters about my Willa Cather review.*

Allen flew over to England July sixth for some sort of conference at Oxford. I followed by boat, with our impedimenta. We had a fine time at Oxford—I spent most of my time on the river, with the swans. There are five cygnets this year, all still the colour of lead. Somebody was incautious enough to lend us a house in London and we stayed there a week and then started for Rome but couldn't resist stopping over in Paris. It is twenty years since I've been in Paris! It's heavenly being back, in spite of all the changes—the house we lived in on Vaugirard has been torn down. The wall opposite this little hotel is still cracked and defaced by German machine gun fire, and every now and then one comes on over near the Place de la Concorde a plaque informing you that a certain *gardien de paix* fell here to liberate France.

---

* Caroline Gordon, "A Virginian in Prairie Country: Two New Studies Explore the Life and Work of Novelist Willa Cather," *New York Times Book Review*, 8 March 1953, 1.

Speaking of mortuary plaques the only errand I had in Paris was to buy two *couronnes funebres* with which a friend of mine wants to ornament the grave of her departed Cairn terrier. I finally settled for two perfectly darling little "monuments" of vrai marble. One had a metallic wreath with a dove in the middle of it and bore the legend: "Nous ne l'oublierons pas." The other, designed for Uncle Bud's son, "Cubby," who isn't dead yet, but is mortal, in spite of all his charms, said simply, "Souvenir" and was a little smaller. It never took me more than three days to find *ces articles mortuaires*.

We leave here Thursday for Rome. Allen has prevailed on me to fly. I always have hated it, but flying across the channel was such fun that I'm willing to try the Alps. We left England, flying above a bank of clouds that were so dense that they looked like another world. The channel itself was the most heavenly cerulean I've ever seen, except at the shore where it was blue green.

We have spent more money than we should have and are going to try to re-coup by staying at the American Academy for a while. However, the best address for us is rather a formidable one: American Commission for Cultural Exchange with Italy, Via Ludovisi 16, Roma, Italia.

Allen has a Fulbright professorship, so we'll be in Rome all winter. However, I expect to make a few pilgrimages: to Assisi, of course, and Orvieto, and Siena and to a little town near Arezzo named San Sepulchro where Pieta della Francesca's great "Resurrection" is. I suppose the whole town constitutes a sepulcher for it, in a sense!

I expect to work every morning but I also expect to go out and look about a bit every afternoon. When I lived abroad before I was so busy writing my first novel that I never saw anything at all.

To go back a moment to your own work. I know that it's nearly always dangerous to say anything about anybody else's work, and, in a way, dangerous to become too conscious yourself of what you are doing. But I do feel that one reason your work is so original and powerful is that—for the first time that I know of—the Catholic viewpoint is brought to bear (however unobtrusively!) on sectarian country people in America. It is a rich field and you are certainly the one to work it. I do congratulate you most heartily.

Write and let us know how things go with you. I am wondering whether you made the visit to the Fitzgeralds. We are looking forward to seeing them in October.

[postscript]

The way I happened to see Haze Motes [from *Wise Blood*] was when I went to Hyde Park to hear Maisie Ward lecture from the same soap-box she's been mounting these thirty years. She followed a ranting Franciscan who cracked vulgar jokes with the crowd. We thought that she was terrific—but the people who lecture for the Catholic Evidence Society are really trained for that sort of speaking.

We are dining tomorrow with Princess Caetani—edits *Botteghe Oscure*. You might send her a story if you have one. I'm sure Cal [Lowell] has told her about your work, but we will tell her about it all over again, to make sure.

Flannery O'Connor to Caroline Gordon

Undated [September 1953]

I am highly pleased you liked that story "The River." I had been thinking about a woman baptizing a child that didn't know what it was about for a long time and finally I thought myself up to the point of writing it. The Church's ceremony of Baptism is so elaborate! I keep trying to think of some way in fiction that I could convey the richness against the threadbareness of the other but my thought is none too productive. The Church takes care of everything and I am always struck fresh with it on St. Blaise's Day when you have your throat blessed. The One True Holy Catholic & Apostolic Church taking time out to bless my throat! And these people around here have to scratch their religion out of the ground.

Which brings me around to what I wish you would do in Rome—see those Texas Baptists that are there to convert the Italians. I think that is the story of the century and if I knew anything about Rome I would be at it myself but I'll probably never get there. I saw the picture of one of them in *Time*—he looked like a clipped lion with a raging headache, a little like a stupid Cal. You could wring that subject dry!

Guess what I did this summer. I spent a weekend in Nashville with the Cheneys. They had me and Ashley Brown* and we had a lovely time, mostly listening to Lon whom Fanny says is a non-stop talker. They had some people in one night and let me read "The River." I like to read once

---

* Samuel Ashley Brown, literary scholar and founder of the journal *Shenandoah*, was a mutual friend of Gordon and O'Connor. He also corresponded with poet Elizabeth Bishop.

I get started and quit thinking about it. They had a picture of yours of a peacock and some other birds and wild animals that I was much taken with. It was the only peacock I'd ever seen with the face of a mandrill. My peafowl seem to just die for meanness. I have a cock and two hens left. She hatched one peachicken this summer and raised it big enough for a weasel to eat before he went to bed. Next year as soon as they hatch I am bringing them in the house and going to raise them in the bureau drawer. The Cheneys have been in Ripton, Ver. and were going by to see the Fitzgeralds on their way back home. I got to the Fitzgeralds too. You are the Oracle around there. Everytime those children do something awful which is none too infrequent they say Aunt Caroline let me do that etc etc. Benedict is very superior, having visited you. Things finally got evened up when they let Hugh visit the Maxwells. Now when Benedict says Aunt Caroline had a ferry boat, Hugh says the Maxwells had a bear-skin rug that was a real bear. When I left they hadn't been able to rent the house yet and their trip to Europe was hanging fire but I am hoping they have got it rented by now.

You will see quick enough that I am enclosing two things. The one called "Whom the Plague Beckons"* is the first chapter of my novel and that is all there ain't no more and I do not know where the next word is coming from. By the time I get it finished we may both be dead and gone to our reward. My intention is to take Tarwater on to his uncle's, the ass in town, pursued all the time by the cross he didn't set up—which he finally sets up on his uncle's lawn with the appropriate consequences. It's full of stuff but I am nowhere near it yet. The other is a long story ["A Circle in the Fire"] (long for me) that I don't know whether it comes off or not but would appreciate your word on the subject. I have sent both of these to Mr. Ransom [Kenyon Review] and have asked him to send me back the one he doesn't want. Nothing like presumption. I would like to send something to Botteghe Oscure but I would also like to paint the side of the house so I will be sending it to Madam McIntosh† instead to have it buried in some fashion magazine for a price. I had one ["A Late Encounter with the Enemy"] in the Sept. Harper's Bazaar, wedged in between all the skeletons in pill box hats. It made me sick to look at it.

* Published as "You Can't Be Any Poorer Than Dead."
† Mavis McIntosh, O'Connor's literary agent.

Since I aim to be so long about the novel I have inveigled Giroux into saying they will publish a book of my short stories in the fall of '54—to be called *A Good Man is Hard to Find*. They take a dim view of it of course and I take a dim view of it myself though it's my idea. The fact is I am uncertain of the stories. Three early ones would have to be included and I can't even bring myself to read them over. If you say so, I would like to send them to you and get you to say if you think they ought to be included. Did you see that one of mine in the Spring [1953] *Kenyon* called "The Life You Save May Be Your Own"?

One of these stories, the first I ever published ["The Geranium"], was written after I had read one [of Gordon's stories] called "Old Red" which you are doubtless familiar with. "Old Red" was the making of me as a short story writer. I think I learned from it what you can do with a symbol once you get a hold of it. Beforehand I hadn't even known such a thing existed.

I was mighty glad to hear from you. I live in a Bird Sanctuary but the birds are not enough.

Caroline Gordon to Flannery O'Connor

22 September 1953
American Academy in Rome
Via Angelo Masina, 5, Rome

We have finally landed at the above address, a top the Janiculum hill, with all Rome to look down on. (Just strolled out a minute ago and take a look at the Coliseum. Hadn't realized it was there till somebody pointed it out the other day.) The Academy has three apartments clinging to the skirts of the director's stately Villa Aurelia and they like to exhibit an "artist in residence" in each one. In return for letting himself be labeled "Writer in residence," a label he's well used to, Allen gets this apartment, high ceilings, marble floor, divine terrace etc. for forty-five dollars a month. We are surrounded by the Aurelian wall which used to encircle the whole city. The Porta di San Pancrazio, which was the starting point for one of the most famous pilgrim routes, is just outside the gates of our villa. We even have a fine little catacomb within five minutes' walk. Saint Pancras—he was a little Roman boy who was stoned to death while carrying the Eucharist to prisoners. San Pancras' catacomb doesn't have any art work in it, except a

dove or a fish or the monogram XI Ro here and there on a wall but it has
as many skulls as any catacomb I've seen yet. Still piled up thick there. I
suppose it was such an insignificant catacomb that Pope Damasus didn't
bother with it.

I have just finished reading the first chapter ["Whom the Plague
Beckons"] of the novel—haven't got to the story yet—and I think it is
simply terrific. Simply terrific. The first sentence is a gem, such a gem that
I hesitate to pick a flaw in it, but nevertheless am impelled to do so because
it is such a gem. You are evidently a city girl and haven't realized that dogs
don't root things up. They dig them up. " . . . Keep the wolf far thence that's
friend to man, or with his nails he'll dig them up again."* It is hogs that root
things up, with their snouts. "Dig" is not as good as "root." You need the o's
for the end of that sentence. If it was me I'd make it hogs instead of dogs.
However, it's your story and you may well be proud of it.

I'm glad to hear that the short stories are coming out in a volume. I will
write Giroux and tell him that I want to write something about your work
and ask him to send me a copy of the book as soon he can. Will also ask
Francis Brown to let me have it for review, or maybe I'll try to get one of
the literary magazines to let me do a piece. Send me the early stories you
have doubts about including if you want to, for whatever my opinion is
worth.

I will now tell you what your work reminds me of. It will be quite a
compliment if I can get it said so it can be understood. It reminds me of
the little chapels one sees in the catacombs, all Roman arches, but Roman
arches that never get far off the ground. We were out with Peggy Erskine, a
young art historian, the other day and she took us into San Ivo's, murmur-
ing that she didn't know whether we'd got so we liked the baroque "yet." I
felt like saying, "Honey, I was born Baroque and have been trying to work
my way back ever since."

We were also in Santa Agnese that Sunday. It is in the form of a cross,
and each chapel abounds in more than life-sized statues and incredibly
bouffant draperies. The ceiling is seventeenth century. Nymphs, well, I
guess they're really saints, but they act like Renascence nymphs, all very

---

* In *The Waste Land*, T. S. Eliot quotes from act 5, scene 4, of John Webster's revenge-tragedy
The White Devil.

bosomy, floating about on cushiony clouds in a very posh heaven. I got a terrible crick in my neck staring at them. What fascinated me was the contrast between what we were seeing then and what we had seen the day before in the catacombs of Saint Priscilla on the Via Saleria.

Saint Priscilla was the mother of Pudens, the Roman senator, converted by St. Peter. Pudens turned part of his house into a private oratory, so it is the oldest church in Rome, Santa Pudenziana, called after his daughter, Pudentiana, who, with her sister, Prassede gathered up the bodies of three thousand martyrs and dug a catacomb under the house to bury them in. A bone from the arm with which Prassede gathered up the bodies is still exhibited, in a handsome bronze container shaped like an arm, the fist rather small and feminine but clenched martially, a hole in the bronze arm so that you can see the thin little bone. Santa Pudenziana has what I believe is the oldest Christian mosaic in its apse, but the church itself is rather ugly. What makes it so moving is that it has the look of something that was made for one purpose and converted to some other use. The columns of the nave are made from stone which was just picked up off the street, having been judged to be not fit for municipal buildings. They have cut a section of the floor out so that you can see the foundations of the original house and a base on which a column used to rest and they have made another small excavation at the foot of the altar at which St. Peter must have said Mass so that the faithful can set hand or foot on the sacred soil.

But let's get back to the cemetery. You walk forever down winding corridors lined with graves, tier on tier, and come finally on a tiny chapel deep in the earth. Mass is evidently still said there on occasion, for there is an altar with the cruets or whatever you call them that they put the water and wine in all ready. Over the altar there is a fresco: the most beautiful Lord's Supper I have ever seen. The background is that saffron colour that almost everything in Rome is, the fresco is faded greens and yellows, with touches of Pompeian red. Six figures, three men and three women seated at a table, with Our Lord in the middle. Our Lord has just taken a fish up from a dish that sits before him and holds it in his hand. At the end of the table, one of the men, evidently a priest, holds a loaf of bread out eagerly. At each end of the table baskets holding bread are ranged, evidently a reference to the loaves and fishes. The other walls have frescoes showing the three children in the fiery furnace, dancing among the very lively flames, Noah riding the Flood in the ark, Abraham sacrificing Isaac, Susanna and the Elders. Farther on there is another small chapel which has on its ceiling a fresco showing Christ, the Good Shepherd. A goat perches comfortably on his shoulder. Two sheep stand beside him, looking up at him trustfully. In the outer circle of the fresco are peacocks and doves with olive branches in their mouths and the vine curling around everything. All very gentle, very faded and modest, the finest embodiment of the Christian virtue of *humilitas* that I have ever seen in architecture, or in art, for that matter. If I had my way every artist who paints an altar-piece would spend some time with that Last Supper.

In another part of this catacomb is the earliest known painting of the Virgin. Tiny and sort of tucked into the corner of a bas-relief of the Good Shepherd, with two sheep, whose flanks have peeled off but whose hoofs still stand sturdily. Our guide—every now and then one gets one who not only knows his stuff but is actually devout—was pleased to recount that the present Pope once stood exactly where *il professore* was standing at the moment and saying a Te Deum to that Virgin. Wasn't that nice?

Being in these tiny chapels in the catacombs and then coming out into the light of day and going into Santa Agnese or St. John Lateran, where Bernini's more than life-size Apostles stride down the nave as if on their way to a four alarm fire, reminds me of the South. There is the same contrast between these chapels and the artwork in them and the big churches that one sometimes finds in the South between the big house and the nigger cabin. I think particularly of the house Andrew Jackson built at Nashville as soon as he came into the money—called ironically "The Hermitage." It is handsome but bad architecturally, with false what you call 'ems sticking out on each side of its portico. Back of the house is the cabin where his butler, Uncle Alfred lived. It is a little gem. I suppose having to hide and being persecuted did something for the art of the early Christians. These little chapels have got something you don't find in the big jobs.

That peacock picture of mine at the Cheneys' was the first version of that particular subject. It's too light. I did another one that has more depth. It's at Benbrackets. Nancy says that whenever Fr. Jean de Menasce, the famous Dominican monk ("When Israel Turns to God")—he comes of a family that has had walled gardens in Alexandria for three hundred years and is part Egyptian, part Spanish, part Jewish—whenever this worthy comes to BenB. he stands in front of my Transfiguration and nearly splits his habit, laughing. I wonder if the Cheneys explained the symbolism? The peacock, of course, is a symbol of the Transfiguration, a fact which obsessed me long before I set foot in the catacombs. The couchant beasts are the Glory that Was Greece and The Grandeur That Was Rome. The goose in the corner, sitting on infertile eggs, is the Anglican Church, the pensive pea-hen is the Roman Church, the broad-bottomed, gabbling gander is all your friends taken at the moment you enter the Church, the duck scuttling across the pool is a little convert duck who is saying, "Here am I, Lord, send me!"

I'm awfully glad you visited the Cheneys and glad Lon got to work. He loves to talk but it's hard for him to get wound up. Sometimes he turns purple from suppressed conversation—when in the presence of some re-lentless talker. I suppose Lon is re-working his novel. I shudder to think of the struggle he must be having with it. He cannot write a decent sentence but he's got something to say. I hope he'll get it said one day. Otherwise, he may just burst. I know how he feels. One would think that seeing all this art in Rome would make me feel like giving up painting. Unfortunately, it stimulates me to further effort. I am going to do something with a Good Shepherd, holding a goat on his shoulders, with sheep at his feet, and pea-cocks and dogs disporting themselves in the outer circles and the Vine wreathing the whole works. Bosio copied that ceiling from the Priscillan catacomb. Why can't I?

Later: I have just finished reading "A Circle In The Fire." I like it very much. It seems structurally sound to me. The passages like "Sometimes the last line of tree . . . The child thought the sky looked as if it were push-ing against the fortress wall . . ." and the concluding sentence do a lot for the structure, do, I think, just what you intended them to do. The dialogue is wonderful. You have a marvelously true ear. (Wish I'd thought of "bid-nis" first!) We have been reading or trying to read, for I defy any human being to get through the whole of it, Red Warren's long poem [Robert Penn Warren's *Brother to Dragons*]. It is a shocking performance. One of the most shocking things is the way his ear has failed him for the speech of his own people—or maybe he never really had a good ear. We just thought he had. He forces everything and in order to get the violence he delights in has forced his dialogue to the point where it becomes ludicrous. His heroes, or villains, the Isham boys, nephews of Thomas Jefferson (my own cousins, incidentally), talk like niggers or poor whites. "I wasn't Isham what had killed his brother" [and] ". . . Killed my bubber what I loved so good" are two of the most appalling lines. Your dialog does its job dramatically and at the same time delights by its verisimilitude. This is the way certain kinds of people talk in our country. . . I'm not sure that I like your title. Or rather I wonder if you couldn't phrase the idea so that the sound would be mouth-filling. I guess it is the "i's" in "Circle" and "Fire" with which I am dissatisfied. The effect is somehow too light. Flames might be better. "The Circle in The Flames"? Not too good. But "Flames" is a word you can bite down on. "The Fiery Furnace?"

I must get to work. For Heaven's sake tell me how I can contact the Texas Holy Rollers. If you'll get the dope I'll gladly contact them and pass the dope on to you. Years ago we had a friend, came into our lives on Red's coat-tails, who was the son of the Methodist Bishop of Rome. The Bishop kept up a good deal of state while trying to convert the Romans and had many servants for his palazzo. His son was converted to homosexuality while the Bishop was trying to combat Romish heresies. The last we heard of him he was in the pen for raping two C.C.C. boys . . . These missionaries you speak of, are they Holy Rollers, or emissaries of Billy Graham or what? I do hope so.

Love. I hope the work continues to go as well as it's evidently going. I shouldn't think you could ask for more. Your first chapter of the novel strikes me as very sound and full-bodied. When Tarwater plants the fiery cross on somebody's lawn the reader will unconsciously say "I told you so." By the way there is no such thing as "bob-wire," at least, within the ken of that Old Debbil Omniscient Narrator. It's barbed-wire. "Bob" is the way people like you and me pronounce it. But the Omn. Nar. doesn't speak with a Southern accent, alas.

Flannery O'Connor to Caroline Gordon

2 October 1953

You will think I never appear but what I am loaded. I don't know if I'm writing these stories to keep from writing that novel or not but I suspect myself. Tarwater is a mighty sullen companion. Anyway it cheers me that you find him worthy. I'm distressed that dogs don't root things up but we don't know anything about dogs here. My mother won't allow one on the place because she has the grande dame cows, all neurotic. There's no such thing as a contented cow. If one of hers sees a particularly fierce horse fly, the milk production falls off. Also she won't have a hog on the place. She just don't like to look at them. I guess I will change it to hogs and then I'll have to insert a couple of hogs somewhere in the scenery. I am a city girl. One time Mr. Ransom had to point out to me that you don't hunt quail with a rifle.

I've been scouting around in the book of Daniel for a better title for the story ["A Circle in the Fire"] but all the stuff there is too heady. What the angel really did was to "make a wind in the heart of the furnace, like the wind that brings the dew." I need something that won't wag the dog but perhaps I'll think of the right thing before the book comes out.

I'll send you the old stories by a slower freight. I have just finished this one ["A Temple of the Holy Ghost"] and as is my habit I am very pleased with it. I always am for about twenty-four hours. You are mighty good to look at these things and it means a great deal to me.

The Fitzgeralds have found themselves a tenant and say they set off Oct. 12 for Milan. This will be an experience for the Italian Airlines.

All I know about these people from Texas is they're Baptists. I haven't seen anything about them lately but last year they were raising cane about how they were being persecuted in Rome. Maybe by now some Swiss guard has walled them up in an unused catacomb or they have moved on to see what they can do about Spain. I think I could handle their end of it; what I have no idea about is Rome. You must feel you are living on several levels of reality, or maybe I mean I see you are, right clearly—coming up from the catacombs to catch a streetcar or whatever. The Fitzgeralds sent me a clipping about The New Jerusalem—to be built by Eddie Dowling at Pinellas, Florida. A 4.5 million dollar project, an exact replica, the smell of camels, real olives from Gethsemane, etc. etc. Dowling said, "Once the site is determined, you can have the custodian come over from the Garden of Gethsemane. Right from that day, you're in business with an attraction." All this is in the vicinity of Palm Beach. Non-sectarian. Big name stars for the major roles (Jesus—Gregory Peck; Mary Magdalen—Rita Hayworth!!!). Tourists from all over the world. I see Haze and Enoch prowling around here, sniffing the camels.

The enclosed [feather] from Peacock. His regards, my love.

Caroline Gordon to Flannery O'Connor

Undated [October 1953]

Allen and I, and several other people who have read the stories you have been sending us—Harry Duncan and Edwy Lee, for instance, think that they are perfectly terrific. I'm hard-put to know which one I like the best. By the way, I wouldn't worry about that title, "The Circle in the Fire." I think that I was probably wrong. The more I think about it the more I like it. And as you say, anything else from Ezekiel [Daniel] would probably be too heady.

You sent me these stories and I presume you'd like some criticism of them. The fact is that when I am reading them I find my powers of judgment suspended more continuously than I am in the habit of finding them suspended. There is so much in your stories that I admire, so much that seems to me done about as well as it can be done. But I have been trying to think about your work in general, the way I sometimes try to think about my own, and I am going to set down at random some thoughts that occur to me. Perhaps I can illustrate what I am going to say by using an example from my own work.

I got the Bantam edition of *Green Centuries* [1941] the other day and read it almost as if it had been written by somebody else, couldn't remember what was going to happen next. But the book seemed to me to have a major flaw. I don't know [how] to put it except by quoting that old negro preacher we used to lean on so heavily in GS 39 at Columbia, the one who had the formula for the perfect sermon: "First I tell 'em I'm going to tell 'em, then I tells 'em, then I tells 'em I done told 'em."

Green Centuries ends on a rather exalted note, with symbolism, elevated tonal effects, even classical allusions, but it starts in a much lower key. I just dive into the action, as it were, with Rion Outlaw seeing a stranger coming down the Trading Path. This man is, I suppose, a symbolic figure—never having attended Paul Engle's School of Writing,* I can use that word without quivering—The man is a symbol of what is going to happen, but the reader can't take that fact in till he's finished the book, so the symbol, at a given moment—when the book opens—isn't working. The reader psychology is the instrument we have to play our tune on and it's

---

* University of Iowa's Writers' Workshop.

a pretty ram-shackle affair. Coleridge's idea was to make the reader listen like a three-year [old] child. I'd say he's never over thirteen—when he's reading fiction for pleasure.

Anyhow, I feel that in the beginning of GC I don't do something that needs to be done. I don't tell them what I'm going to tell them. Homer does. Virgil does—both of them in the first lines of their poems. The chorus of a Greek play fulfills the same function. Sets the tone, prepares the reader's imagination for what is going to happen to it, plants the seed of the happening, as it were, so that it will be working underground all through the book and when it swells up at the end the reader will say, "I thought so all along" and feel smarter than he is. I do this in a story of mine called "The Last Day in the Field." The story begins: "That was the year the leaves stayed green so long," and is a story about a man saying goodbye to youth. (Of course I didn't discover I'd done this till fifteen years after I wrote the story!)

Doing this sort of thing, giving a story a frame of reference, as it were, gives it more stature, more dimension. You dive into your actions so promptly—and God knows that that is a virtue—that the reader hasn't time to realize whether he's going on a long trip or a short one. I would hate to relinquish an atom of the remarkable objectivity which you achieve—real three dimensional effects—but I think that if you occasionally stretched a hand out to help the reader over some relatively unimportant stile he'd have more breath left for the long stretch. An example of what I'm trying to say is the hats of Mrs. Pritchard and Mrs. Cope. They are rendered marvellously, one of the best things in the story. But the reader is asked to give them an attention that is perhaps out of proportion to their importance. A sentence indicating that Mrs. Cope had to wear Mrs. Pritchard's old hats would be that helping hand over the stile and would not take away from the dramatic effect—I think. I may be dead wrong about all this. However, what I've just said is the only criticism I can muster of your work. I am just crazy about it.

This note is written very hurriedly. We are about to set out for Ostia, having just got a hold of our new Austin. The Fitzgeralds have arrived in Milan, we see by the Rome *Daily American*, but we don't know how to get in touch with them yet. However, they will surely remember us before many more days. We are dying to see them.

Don't worry about *Botteghe Oscure* if you don't have a story handy for them. Allen likes the Principessa but doesn't think much of her magazine. I have never minded appearing in the fashion magazines. On the whole they print as good stories as any of them.

Flannery O'Connor to Caroline Gordon

23 October 1953

This is absolutely the last one of these things I am going to let myself write until I have my foot well on Tarwater's neck again. I would like to know if it ["The Displaced Person"] works or not. I'm afraid the end is too abrupt. After about 18 pages I always get the to-hell-with-it feeling and sign off. I think the reason I don't help the reader over the stile is because I am too busy getting myself over it. I don't always know what's happened even after it has.

Let me know where the Fitzgeralds are when you find out and give them my blessings. My mother wants to know where to send their fruitcake. She has her fruit cake seizure about this time of year and there's nothing to be done about it but get out of the way.

Robie [Macauley] writes me that the Lowells have bought a big old house in Duxbury, Mass. Mansion about 300 years old, from which they aim to commute to Iowa. Cal also has a big old Packard named "The Green Hornet." I hope Elizabeth does the driving. The Fitzgeralds thought Cal was going to be at Cincinnati this year but apparently he is still at Iowa.

Lon wrote that he was back at fiction after doing the Governor's paper work for his conference with the President about TVA [Tennessee Valley Authority]. It was very successful he says. This Governor Clement is a big friend of Billy Graham. I saw old Billy on the tellyvision this summer at my aunt's in Boston. They had a real repulsive announcer—the good-looking dreamy variety—and then a real repulsive singer—same kind—and then Billy. Billy was very vigorous and less repulsive than the other two but I suspect they were chosen so that this would be the case. He looks like Onnie Jay Holy [from *Wise Blood*] only he's better dressed.

I think Mr. Ransom has forgotten I sent him the story and the chapter ["A Circle in the Fire" and "You Can't Be Any Poorer than Dead"].

Incidentally Cal has a long review of Warren's poem in the last *Kenyon*; he read it three times, he said. I read the part that came out last year but haven't read the whole thing; I have no perception about poetry though. I can tell Edgar Guest from Shakespeare but that is about all.

Caroline Gordon to Flannery O'Connor

Undated [31 October 1953]

I finished the first section of my novel [*The Malefactors*] the other day—it took only seven chapters to carry the hero from breakfast to the time when he sank around four o'clock in the morning into a troubled sleep. I hardly know which is the more sullen companion—he or Tarwater. You wouldn't think it to look at—or listen to him—but he's busy with his Fiery Crosses, too. Seems they all are, one way or another. Anyhow, I made the mistake of turning my back on him long enough to do a bit of sightseeing and here it's three weeks I been letting him lay—and without the kind of excuse you have for turning your back on Tarwater.

I wrote "Old Red" in somewhat the same frame of mind in which you seem to be turning out your stories—stopped in the middle of writing a novel and felt guilty about stopping, but couldn't shake Old Red off. But I wrote only one story that time. You are having such a creative bust as is seldom seen. I'd sure try to make the most of it. (Intended to write "burst" there but "bust" seems to do as well.) Such seizures don't come often.

"The Displaced Person" has some of the most brilliant passages you've written, notably Mrs. Shortley's conversations with the two Negroes. I like them so much I've read them aloud to various people, all of whom have gone into the proper stitches over them. Allen likes them, too. In fact, our reactions to the story seemed to be about the same. I'm going to give them to you as best I can, but for Heaven's sake remember that I may very well not know what I'm talking about. I'm really just thinking aloud—mulling over what seems to me to be the problem. We both feel that the story doesn't quite come off at the end, though superb up till then. Neither of us is quite sure what the trouble is. I'll hazard some guesses.

Mrs. Shortley's vision, though fine in itself, doesn't seem to be integral to the story. The connection between the vision and the denouement isn't established, really, seems to me. If the vision is in there it ought to "work," ought to have some particular job to do.

I am wondering whether the trouble, after all, isn't in the handling of the viewpoint at the end? I don't like the touch of levity ("I have been made regular etc.") in this context. It cuts the ground out from under Mrs. Shortley's feet, makes her pathetic rather than tragic. But you have been building her up for a tragic role—a mountain of a woman, or at any rate, a woman of larger size than most of her companions, a woman who thinks as deeply as she can, and, certainly, ponders even if she isn't capable of ratiocination.

It seems to me that the denouement ought to take place on a larger stage. Mrs. Shortley ought to see herself in somewhat the same position as those heaps of bodies of dead, naked people that she saw in the movie. Damn it! She ought to see or feel herself and Mr. Shortley being dismembered!

As I see it, the structure of the story rests on three supporting scenes, the way your roof might rest on three columns: the sight of all those naked, dead bodies in the movies, the vision and the command to prophesy and, lastly, her realization of what it is she is prophesying: hers and her husband's destruction.

Mr. and Mrs. Shortley are Displaced Persons, Dismembered Persons, more displaced, more painfully dismembered than the Gobblehooks if they only knew it, and your story is Mrs. Shortley's realization of what is happening to them. It's all there—and magnificently—it seems to me. All you have to do is bring out a little more what is already implicit in your action.

This being the Vigil of All Saints we are hieing ourselves today to a holy, if pagan spot: The Lake of Nemi, the Mirror of Diana. It was from a study of the rites that went on in the sacred grove there that Frazer got the idea for his thirteen volumes of *The Golden Bough*. The priest was called Rex Nemorensis and every year, I think, was challenged to a fight to the death by an aspirant to the priesthood who was usually an escaped slave and who also had to pluck a branch from the mistletoe bough before he could slay the priest, after which he reigned in his stead, till somebody came along and killed him. He was called Virbius, too, and there is a legend that he was Hippolytus, brought there by Diana after she had had Aesculapius restore him to life by his arts.

It was the fact that he found these religious rites different in some ways from any he had ever come across that started Frazer off. It certainly is one of those places. You feel as soon as you step in there that it's holy ground. Allen, whose first inklings of religion (he was brought up an "advanced" Presbyterian, poor boy), gets mighty excited when he gets into that sacred grove.

All these places, religious as well as historical, are kept rough. If there's any good grazing around them the sheep, cows, chickens are turned in. You go through a gate mended with barbed wire, as if by a Southern tenant, and go through shallow terraces planted with violets, carnations, orange trees and cacchi (persimmon) trees until you come to what is left of the temple: Fifty or sixty arches made of stone, cut and cemented in that pattern that's supposed to make the Roman arch so strong, set against the side of the hill, or sort of fitted into a natural cavern. A statue used to stand in each arch, they say. But the statues, of course, are all in the museums now.

Nemi, itself, is a valuable valley situated in an extinct crater, a perfect bowl, with "the mirror of Diana" at the bottom. The slopes of the valley are terraced and cultivated to the very top. It is the most fertile looking place I ever saw, all set for the worship of a vegetation goddess. You feel as if the worship were still going on—only, I hasten to add, in a quite Christian way.

On the other side of the valley, opposite Diana's shrine, the spring into which Juno turned Numa Pompilius' girl-friend, Egeria, when she got annoyed with her, still plashes down the hillside. I must have heard Egeria's voice as we first drove into Nemi, for I suddenly thought of her for the first time in many a year—and asked some savant if Egeria hadn't operated out here. He said No, that she was in Rome. When we got up into the town we took our stand on a spur that gave us the best *bella vista* and I forgot all about Egeria but kept hearing this plashing. At first, I couldn't see any waterfall anywhere but finally located her slipping down the hill, almost covered up with canes and ferns and things, but still Egeria.

We have just got back from a three day trip to Naples and Paestum. It rained every day but we had a marvellous time, nevertheless, at least I did, until we got to Pompeii where I succumbed to an attack of "Roman stomach" that I had been fighting off, so violent that they had to stow me away in a Pompeian hotel while the rest of them did the scavi and the museum. I was so sick that I never got to see anything but the "Villa di Mysteri" but now that it's over and I can face food—even pasta—again, I'm rather glad it happened that way. If I had to choose one thing to see there it would be the Villa di Mysteri.

It's time for the picnic to get started. I am keeping the copies of the stories. But you can have them back any time you want them. Hastily, with love. [postscript]

By the way, it's "carcase," not "carcus." Also, I don't at all like "squinch" on page 21. Here is an example of the thing I was talking about in my last letter. There is no such word as "squinch." It is not in the vocabulary of the omniscient narrator, who is above colloquialisms and that sort of thing. The word therefore can come only from Mrs. Shortley's vocabulary. The use of Mrs. Shortley's vocabulary, which is to say, her view-point here, abruptly contracts the field of vision and also lowers the tone of the action—at the moment when you need a wider vision and an exalted tone.

You have here, in a nut-shell, it seems to me, the chief weakness in your work: the tendency to use too restricted a viewpoint at crucial moments, thereby cutting down the scope of your action. You are superbly agile in slipping in and out of your characters, borrowing their eyes and ears and mouths in the interest of verisimilitude. In fact, it is through this very agility that you achieve some of your finest effects but I would like to see you learn to do something else—to soar above the conflict, to view it as if through the eyes of an eagle, at certain crucial moments. And this passage is one of those moments. After all, you have a more exalted subject matter than any of the other young writers. Your language ought to match it—but without relinquishing anything of what you have already got, not even one double negative. Of course this will be hard to do but you have got what it takes to do it. I feel very certain of that.

I think that this group of stories you've just done are among the finest that have been written by any American.

Flannery O'Connor to Caroline Gordon

8 November 1953

I enclose my new ending [for "The Displaced Person"] which you can plainly see is a heap better than the other one. That last one was just one more thing attributable to the 7th Deadly Sin—too lazy to do what ought to be done. The view point at the end may not be that of an eagle exactly but at least it's a buzzard on a very high limb. I have also done away with the word—the not-word—"squinch." This is very difficult as I have a natural fondness for it.

Will you please tell Allen that Mr. Ransom decided he wanted to use "A Circle in the Fire," so it can't be sent to *Encounter?* I was quite surprised as I thought he would want the chapter. Anyhow, he thought I ought to work on the story more, said it wasn't as economical as it ought to be— Mrs. Pritchard talked too much and some other things, so I have written it over and sent it back to him. The speed with which I did this is probably unequaled but I told him he could send it back as many times as he could suffer to. I can't stand to have them hanging around, ever. He thought the chapter was a little complicated, that the reader had to work too hard, but he said he would print it too if I liked. I am afraid to fool with that right now. I rather think it's all right as it is, and I have to get on with Tarwater even though it kills me.

My mother has a D.P. family along with her regular dairyman and his family. They are becoming Americanized fast. The little boy asked my mother the other day if gold came from Mexico, where did silver come from? My mother didn't know. He said from under the Lone Ranger.

It's getting cold here and my peafowl have ruffled necks all the time and step very high. I heard a great commotion out there the other day and went to find that the cock had taken on the entire flock of turkeys—about ninety five. When they would charge him, he would fly straight up and land on the shed room and look at them a while, then he would descend straight down and scatter them. This would have gone on all afternoon if I hadn't put a stop to it.

I'm much obliged for the Fitzgeralds' address. I reckon they decided Siena was too cold.

Caroline Gordon to Flannery O'Connor

Undated [November 1953]

You may have a fondness for the word "Squinch" but it doesn't like you—as the ladies who can't eat cucumbers put it. I wish you would pluck it out of your vocabulary. I've never seen you use it right yet and I've seen you muff some of your best effects by using it. Your best effects are got not by that particular kind of violence, but more subtly. Here on the Janiculum certain people who have read your stories will tell you that "It is a shop on the Largo Tritone where you can get shoes made by hand for fourteen

thousand lire." I myself prefer the sentence: "I knew a man that his wife
was poisoned by a baby that she adopted out of pure meanness." That's real
colloquial style! "Squinch," nine times out of ten is childish. So is "Zlurp."

Yes, I think the new ending is much better than the other one. The vision really comes off for me now. Part of that is the excellent timing. You
give it time to take hold of the reader. But the vision itself is really brought
off. So is the scene at the end where Mrs. Shortley's realization of herself as a displaced person is made dramatic by being made visible. I have
one criticism of it, though. In the very last paragraph you do the thing
that I seem to be always begging you not to do. You lower the tone of the
paragraph and thereby diminish the range of your whole story—give it a
smaller stature than it would otherwise have—by abruptly and it seems to
me inadvisedly narrowing the view-point to that of one of the girls. You
borrow her eyes, look through them and say her mama is acting "kittenish"
and that her papa is imitating a dead man. But at this point you do not
need either the eyes or the idiom of that illiterate, insensitive young girl.
You want somebody who can see a lot farther than she can and expresses
herself a lot better, in a higher style. *Oedipus Tyrannus* ends with the chorus observing that it is better not to call any man—that takes in the whole
human race—happy until he is dead. But if it had ended with some kid re-
marking—in idiomatic Greek, of course—that it looked like the old man
had the blind staggers, why, I don't think that Aristotle would have called
it the perfect plot.

Mrs. Shortley may be a poor white woman but she is in the act of dying
and therefore is bound for one of three states of awful dignity: she will
either be received as one of the Brides of Christ in a few seconds or she
will go to Purgatory or she will be cast into outer darkness. Anyway, this is
no time to call her "Mama." And no time to call the old man "Papa." "Their
mother" and "their father" is the least you can give them at this moment.
All the same, I think you have made a brilliant revision of these last pages.
I think that it is a superb story.

I like "A Late Encounter With the Enemy" very much, too—all but one
passage. That is where the old man is dying and you say "he saw the faces
of his children and of his wife and of his mother." This doesn't seem dramatic to me. This is a time when you ought to borrow his eyes and show
us through them how his wife looked to him. You wouldn't need to show

us all the faces that appeared to him. Two, at the least, three at the most, would do it. But saying that somebody saw something doesn't make the reader see anything. James' *The Beast in the Jungle* has, I think, too long a foreground and too much palaver in it, but it ends with John Marcher's seeing and feeling the hot breath of the beast that is springing to devour him. This, I think, is the chief flaw in your story and it is still one of the best stories I have ever read, and I don't think that there is anybody else operating today who could have written it. The use of the black-robed figures, the Boy Scout, the Hollywood premiere are all wonderful—a real creative imagination is at work here.

My *creche*, or as I am learning to call it, *mio presepio*, is progressing marvelously. A lonesome little girl named Caroline, who can't speak anything but French, comes in sometimes and helps me paint or model the figures. I have a wonderful grotto now, with ledges of rock outcropping for the strategic placing of beasts and birds who have come to the Nativity. The peacock already sits on the roof, all blue and gold. The Christ Child has been modelled once and being very fragile broke into bits and will have to be done again, but the Virgin and St. Joseph and a wise man who is a student of Confucius and wears long black moustaches and a yellow robe are holding up nicely. The ox is white and has long, branching, twisted horns, like the cattle you see here in the fields. The donkey looks, I flatter myself, much like the donkeys you see around here, like, in short, a perfect angel. (Every time I see one of these darling, patient little creatures I am glad to remember that every hair in their tails are numbered, for they sure have plenty of burdens to bear here.) This donkey is suckling a colt no bigger than a rabbit. I have two more Wise Men to do, but have reduced the shepherds to one, the god Apollo, who has come to the Nativity in the guise of a shepherd, bearing a goat on his shoulders—after the Good Shepherd in the Calistan [Callisto] Catacombs. The inside of the grotto has The True Vine wreathed all over it and the walls are illuminated—very simple to achieve, with a little gold paint.

My novel [*The Malefactors*] is not going so well. I came to the end of a section and stopped to take that trip to Naples and Pompeii and have never succeeded in getting started again, though I go through the motions of one who is about to write something every day. I have confronting me what seems an almost insuperable technical problem: three dead people in my book whose lives unfold chronologically but in a movement counter clockwise, shall we say, to the main action. They are important parts of the main action and I haven't been able to think of any other way to handle them, but they are sure hard to handle. Flaubert had some such idea once in a novel that was to be called *La Spiralle*, a hero who dreamed by night of marrying a prince and living high on the hog, but by day sank rapidly towards the gutter but Flaubert had sense enough to confine himself to thinking about his plot, not writing it.

Allen was mobbed the other day in the Largo Tritone. I mention the fact apathetically as it has been so much talked over that we are all, including Allen, rather bored by the fact. He and his car got in the path of a student demonstration over Trieste and a yelling mob of four or five hundred students surrounded the Austin, yelling "Inglese" and doing the car all the damage they could by kicks. They also broke the headlights, ripped off the license plates and leaped on top of the car and stamped on the roof. Fortunately the windows were locked, so they couldn't get Allen out of the car. When one resourceful youth ran for a pick to break the windows in an old gentleman walked through the mob and took his stand with his back against the car. Other middle-aged people followed suit, together with several "deserters" from the mob, and they succeeded in diverting the mob and then escorted Allen to a side street while the mob swept by.

Our maid, Assunta, says that when her fourteen year old son, Lelo, stays at school all day, it is safe for us *forestieri* to go out on the streets. But that morning Lelo's school had been dismissed—presumably so he could take part in the demonstration. Our car will be in the garage—two hundred dollars to hammer the body out and re-paint it—for another week. But we would not have dared to drive it for at least a week after the Trieste business. We sometimes get a bit weary of the gauntlet one has to run when one goes in or out of the Villa Aurelia: three or four gate-men, each of whom has to be buona giornoed or buona seraed or buona notted—till sometimes we just mutter "Buoni tutti" as we go through—but the night of Allen's "mobbing" it was quite a relief to know that we had the ancient Aurelian wall running practically all the way around the garden, and high iron gates, manned by Giuseppe, Mario, et al.

I simply must get to work. Many thanks for sending me "The Late Encounter." I'm keeping the pages because there are people here who

much enjoyed reading your stories—you may hear from one of them a
writer named Ward Dorrance. But I'll preserve the page[s] and return
them in case you need them. When you are getting up a volume of stories
it is the very devil to find copies.

Love, and keep up the good work. It is such good work!

[postscript]

And let us hear from you whenever you have time for letters. What luck
for you that your mother has got those D.P.'s. There is something inher-
ently dramatic in a Displaced Person, as poor Allen discovered the other
day, as did Henry James before him.

One more thought. I don't like that phrase "an entire cat" in the end
of your story. It sounds flippant, almost "magazine style"—and woman's
magazine, at that. I repeat: This is a solemn moment. You've spent a lot of
time and energy building up to it. Don't belittle it!

Flannery O'Connor to Caroline Gordon

15 December 1953

I have just got back from spending a weekend with the Cheneys. I like
them both very much. Lon seems to be in the middle of one novel but
wanting to write a different one. I suppose you always want to be writing a
different one. They had the Spears up Saturday night and I read them "The
Displaced Person," having doctored on the end of it according to your di-
rections. I took off the mama and the papa business and added a sentence
to the effect that they (the girls) had never known that she had been displaced or that now her displacement was at an end. You were right; it gives
it another dimension.

The D.P. is currently telling Shot, the colored man, that he can get him
a wife from Germany but that he'll have to pay five hundred dollars for
her. My mother says "Oh get out, Mr. Matysiak, you know all those folks
over there are white." She has had a lot of trouble anyway with Shot's mat-
rimonial complications. He is estranged from his first wife who used to
have him put in jail every month because he wouldn't support his child.
My mother finally after paying his bond several times had it arranged so
that she sends the check for the child every month—twelve dollars. She
was talking to his mother the other day and told her that she was mighty

tired of having to be Shot's bookkeeper (she also pays his policy man, his board, & his incidental debts). His mother said well she wished he'd go back to his wife and then he wouldn't have to send out that twelve dollars every month. My mother says why you know that woman doesn't want him back. "Oh yesm she do," his mother said, "she wants him worsen a hog wants slop." I happened to be present and nearly fell off my chair but my mother didn't bat an eye until the old woman had gone, then she said, "I hope you are not going to use that in one of those stories." Of course I am as soon as I can find me a place to.

You would probably be interested in Mrs. Steven's children's Sunday school organization. It is called the Meriwether Mites. Meriwether is their community. Very Very Very Methodist. The Mites are mostly interested in the social opportunities in religion; the decent ones that is. They have "no drinking, no smoking, and no setting around in cars."

The story I enclose ["A Stroke of Good Fortune"] is one of those old ones that I am undecided about including in the collection. It is very funny when read aloud but I'm afraid there's not much to be said for it otherwise. Anyway I'd like to know what you think.

I hope your mobbing experiences are over. The people I saw in Nashville were powerful interested in it. Merry Christmas.

Caroline Gordon to Flannery O'Connor

26 December 1953

We were delighted to know that you spent part of "the Christmas" with the Cheneys, and I'm sure they were, too. Assunta, our maid, says that Natale makes her *molta nervosa*. It always has me, too. It seems even more hectic over here than in the United States. Complicated for us by a couple of the Academicians getting married on the twenty-fourth. Party every night for a week. We are all nearly dead.

The Midnight Mass was a big disappointment to me or, rather I was to it. I wanted to go to Matins and Mass at San Anselmo and had a book of the office guaranteed fool-proof by Fr. Anselms, a friend of ours, but we got involved with this Church-shopping that people go in for here and missed Matins and were a bit late for the Mass. After dinner everybody rushed wildly from church to church. A young coloured sculptor from the

Academy told us probably when we met him at Santa Maria Maggiore that he already had five churches under his belt. Santa Maria Maggiore was lit up without and within—I never saw any object as brilliantly illuminated. It was the only chance I've ever had to see the mosaics—it's so dim in there you can't ordinarily see them—and I would have liked to stop and peer around more, but our friend had heard that they had bagpipers at Aracoeli—it was on the steps leading up to that church that [Edward] Gibbon had his big idea—so we had to rush over there . . . Well, enough of these complaints. All I can say is that if I don't succeed in getting back to work soon I'll go nuts.

That's pretty good about wanting him back like a hog wants slop. My grandmother once made exactly the same remark to me that you[r] mother did to you, only she didn't say "those" stories. Seems she may have thought more kindly of my stories then your mother does of yours. She once told me that my stories reminded her of "Miss Austen," which please[d] me no end. A very lonely old woman who lived by herself in an old house out in the country till the age of ninety seven. Right now her way of life strikes me as perfectly delightful, but at times it did seem a bit grim.

I don't think "A Stroke of Good Fortune" is one of your best stories, but I think it might be good enough for the collection if you would do a little more work on it. It's the old story in my opinion: the thing I seem to be always talking about when I write to you: a mis-handling of view-point.

You see the whole action through Ruby's eyes, tell the story in her own words. This automatically takes away from the stature of the action. Ruby is not very bright. If you confine yourself to her view-point you will not see all that is going on: she is too dumb to know what is happening to her.

I am offended by the word "toting" in the first paragraph. The use of that word gives the story an amateurish air. The first sentence, "Ruby came in the front door etc." sounds as if the omniscient narrator were speaking. But the omniscient narrator could not utter the next sentence. The word "tote" is not in his vocabulary. But you haven't established the fact of Ruby's existence yet and therefore are not entitled to use her view-point or vocabulary. So "toting" just won't do, any way you take it.

This paragraph is to me an example of the chief weakness of your work. You don't seem to understand the handling of view-point yet. I wish I could say all this better. I don't seem to be able to make it plain.

Have you read Lubbock's *Craft of Fiction* lately? He's awfully good on this particular thing. *Harry Richmond* [by George Meredith] is his example of the narrowing of a story's scope by sticking exclusively to the hero's view-point. Of course Lubbock is tough going. Allen says he read him once when he was considerably younger than he is now and didn't have much idea of what he was getting at. But he certainly repays rereading and re-reading.

I find this eye-plastered-against-a hole-in-the-wall view-point particularly unfortunate in your stories because of the scope of your action. You have a much, much wider range than any of your contemporaries and much more serious subject-matter. You've got to see all around your subject.

Think, for instance, of what *Madame Bovary* would be if Flaubert hadn't constantly shifted his view-point with almost miraculous agility? In one paragraph he is walking beside Emma, in the next he has jumped on the horse she is riding and then jumps inside her and sees through her eyes. (The succession of tree trunks going by made her giddy.) But even more startling, he can shift the view-point in the midst of a sentence. He and Faulkner are the only novelists I know who can do that. When Emma mounts the attic stairs to read Rodolphe's letter Flaubert is moving beside her until the middle of the sentence when he uses the word—I forget the French, dreadful, horrible, something like that. Anyhow, the view-point shifts with the use of this word, for this letter is not horrible to anybody in the world except Emma. I think that if you would study that paragraph it might clear up some of your difficulties for you.

Also, consider what the story would be like if told exclusively from Emma's viewpoint. Her love affairs, her debts etc. might seem perfectly proper then. Charles Bovary might appear so loathsome that one would have no sympathy for him. All our sympathy would be for this lovely young woman who is being smothered to death. We might not even realize how foolish Emma is—if she told her story plausibly enough.

I have my nerve, giving anybody advice about anything, with my head feeling the way it does—like a stewed simlin! So don't take what I say too seriously.

It's too bad you and the Cheneys and all my friends couldn't see *mio presepio* this year. I must say that I felt that it received almost as much praise as it was entitled to at our Christmas party the other night. Rufus

Morey, the iconographer, was particularly struck by my god Apollo, clad in a simple fig-leaf, and attending the Nativity as a Good Shepherd (Effect of the Catacombs.) I am going to do one next year which will be out of this world.

Here are some fine Protestant remarks we've heard lately. Dom Anselms says a friend who was thanking him for getting him a ticket to some audience of the Pope lately said: "Thank you so much. The Pope was the one thing I wanted to see most in Rome." Jackson Matthews, who is doing the definitive edition of Valery's works, asked me the other day if I "believed in the Catacombs." I said, "Yes, and I believe in the Empire State Building, too." We were driving along the Appian Way with Harold Strauss, editor in chief at Knopf's not so not long ago and passed the Catacombs of San Sebastian. "I don't suppose there's any anything of any real interest in there," said he comfortably.

I must go and soak my head in hot water in lieu of holding it under a pump. This letter is very incoherent, I know, but so am I. Better tomorrow, we hope, we hope. Tell the peacock his feathers make a wonderful sort of halo for a carved wooden *putto* I bought in Venice and was going to work off on Allen as a Christmas present and then lost my nerve. Allen, by the way, gave me a lovely St. Michael trampling on the Devil—in alabaster.

Love and our best wishes for a fine New Year. If it's as productive as the last year you'll be doing well.

Flannery O'Connor to Caroline Gordon

10 January 1954

You are certainly right about that story ["A Stroke of Good Fortune"] but at least I console myself with the fact that it was written five years ago and I've improved some. Right now I am back on the subject of Displaced Persons. Anything to get away from Tarwater; also I decided that I had not exhausted the possibilities in that particular situation so now I am busy displacing Mrs. McIntyre. I am going after it very slowly and hope to send it to you in a few weeks. I have a peacock in this one. I aim to render the highest possible justice to the peacock. Have you ever read anything about the peacock as a symbol for the Transfiguration? I don't know if it appeared as that in medieval paintings or tapestries or what. If you know of anywhere I could read about it or see it I would be obliged to hear.

Mr. Ransom has renewed my Kenyon Fellowship [$2,000], which is a great help. How many minutes a day do you suppose I ought to pray for the repose of Mr. Rockerfeller's soul? I suppose I ought at least to learn how to spell his name—that don't look right. I sold that story called "A Temple of the Holy Ghost" to *Harper's Bazaar*. I object to having them in there because nobody sees them.

I had a note from Cal [Lowell] who said he was fed up with teaching and wished he lived in a world of illiterates. I thought Brother you may and don't know it.

I'm afraid my mother doesn't think highly of my fiction. Anyway she likes the fact that I do it and her tone is greatly softened by the situation of my being her child. If I was anybody else's I would hate to hear what she'd say about it. Robie says that after his mother read his book, she said, "Is it funny? Chuck said it was funny." When my mother read mine she took it to bed with her every afternoon for about a week. She would start reading and in about ten minutes, she would be snoring. She always says, "That was very interesting," when she hands anything back to me.

Two weeks off I have to give a talk on the novel to the local college—600 girls who don't know a novel from a hole in the head. I asked the head of the English department how she wanted me to approach the subject. She says, "I don't care how you approach it. They don't know anything and they aren't interested in anything but personality." I am going to tell them that Henry James said that the young woman of the future wouldn't know anything about mystery or manners. Then I am going to tell them that the novel is a celebration of mystery. It's going to take me a half hour. Afterwards I am promised a Coca Cola in the Student Union. Pray for everybody.

Caroline Gordon to Flannery O'Connor

Undated [1954]

Sorry to be so slow about reporting on the story but la vita here in Rome is terribila, as Assunta complains every morning. She has a refrain that runs through her day: "Molta trista la vita d'Assunta!" Her vita, naturalmente, is the saddest of all. Mine is just hectic.

First, as usual, I want to give my reactions which may be absolutely screwy, for all I know. I think this ["The Displaced Person"] is one of your best, or will be when you have done a tiny bit more work on the first two or three pages. The first two pages are not dramatic enough. You don't make enough of a scene between Mrs. McIntyre and the priest. You tell us about them instead of presenting them in action. Let Mrs. McIntyre do something, if only to arrange her bangs before you tell us she has them. Until we have seen her we don't care whether she has bangs or not. You ought also to let us have a peep at the priest before you begin telling us about him. The informatory passages, the "long views" will then become dramatic. What Mrs. M. thinks of the priest, what he is trying to do to her will be part of the action then.

I think the peacock as a symbol of the Transfiguration is handled splendidly and planted in just the right place to prepare for the denouement but you hurry your effects too much. Crowd too many ideas in any one speech of the priest's. Your timing is off. If you followed the example of your hero, Mr. Mozeley T. Sheppard, who follows Yeats' advice and always sets off the "tense line" by a "numb line" you'd do better here. Or if this passage were more like old Astor's report on what Mr. Guizac said when he was dying. You take plenty of time there and succeed brilliantly. These are all the criticisms I have to make. I think it is a wonderful story.

I feel a little ill-at-ease, though. Princess Caetani wants one of your stories and asked me to let her see the copies I had here. She, of course, wanted the one that was already sold. She has been asking me to let her see this one. I have put her off, telling her that it was sent to me for criticism and that you may not have thought of its being submitted to an editor. But she keeps asking to see it, so I have written a note, explaining the circumstances clearly and saying that I feel that we are both rather taking things into our own hands but that I think you'll probably overlook it—it does take so long to get letters across the water. Do write her, anyhow.

Bill Faulkner has been here this week, making a movie, of Pyramids and something I forget what [Land of the Pharaohs]. We were all a little worried over how he might behave at the con gins and dinner parties that were given for him. He seemed a bit plasterato once or twice but his conduct was impeccable. We all had a late, tipsy dinner together the other night after a big party. Bill and Allen kept toasting the Old South and then Bill after intervals would say "Where is Mr. Maury?" I thought he was referring to

Rufus Morey, the iconographer and would reply, "He spends his days in the Vatican, cataloguing the Pope's collection of gold-glass medallions." "I certainly wish I could meet that man," Bill would say and I would say, "I'm sure he'd be delighted to meet you," wondering meanwhile whether Rufus Morey would care to meet Bill or anybody else so contemporary. Finally I tumbled to the fact that Bill had been talking all along about Mr. Maury.*

The peacock is generally regarded as a symbol of the Transfiguration, or was in early days. There is a book on the saints by Lucy T. Menzies, which gives the various symbols. I like it better than any I know, but there must be dozens. Consult the Master Librarian, Fannie Cheney, about this. She will fix you up in no time. It's just the kind of thing she's good at. She'll send you a book from one of the joint libraries.

It is almost impossible to get any work done in the Eternal City, but I am trying. This morning I woke with a neat little bit from the underground work-shop. I have a homosexual named Max Shull in my book, sometimes called "The Black Widow" as he lived with the poet maudit, Horne Watts, before that worthy committed suicide. Anyhow, my hero, a great man for reflection, is reflecting how odd fairies are and wondering why Max has never availed himself [of] the professional services of a psychiatrist friend who is also present. Then he remembers that his wife once tried to lead Max to this same psychiatrist but Max demurred, paraphrasing the Marquis de Montespan's famous remark when Louis XIV wanted to make him a duke—in return, the Marquis felt, for cuckolding him—"Sire, I was born a marquis and I prefer to die a marquis," so Max says, he was born a "Queen" and prefers to die a "queen." It's not much. But it's comforting to know that that little stranger is working away below stairs. And now I have to dress and go to a party for Wallace Fowlie.

Love, and thanks for sending the story. I really hated to see Mr. Guizac go. I have got attached to him.

Flannery O'Connor to Caroline Gordon

8 February 1954

I am fixing up the front of that story ["A Stroke of Good Fortune"]. It does read very flat. Miss Caetani [editor of *Botteghe Oscure*] wrote me a

---

* Gordon's fictional character from her novel *Aleck Maury, Sportsman*.

note asking for the one Mr. Ransom had and I wrote her a politeness to the effect that he had it and told her I had sent you another but I didn't think I was finished with it; as I am not. If she likes it, I suppose she can have it when I am through with it but my concern right now is to get them published before Fall so I can have out this collection. I think she only has two issues a year or something; maybe she won't want it which will suit me just as well. Incidentally, I called her Miss. What am I supposed to call her? The Mozely T. Shepperd in me objects to calling her anything else. I refuse to be any urbaner then I have to be. Anyway, if she likes it well enough to want the corrected version, would you ask her to let me know and I'll send it to her.

It has been on my conscience to send Poor Ritt* something. Do you know Poor Ritt? I don't know why I should call him Poor but he has written me about how much money he has lost on A.D., and of other of his trials. A.D. was something they started at Fordham, or something somebody started at Fordham, anyway it was no good, just terrible in fact, and he has taken it over and is trying to make something of it. Poor Ritt and I remember each other in our prayers but I have never met him. He has a nine-year-old child that he hasn't seen in nine years—wife departed and "remarried." M. Maritain is now a contributing editor, I think, and other people.

I was thinking about going to see the Fitzgeralds in the spring but my doctor squashed that one. Too much risk, said he. He says I have enough blood to be a Southern girl. I better not be anything else.

The D. P. and Shot nearly choked each other in the wagon the other day and now my mother is almost afraid to send them to the field together for fear one won't come back. She gave him a long lecture that night through Alfred, the 12 yr. old boy. She kept saying, "You tell your father that he's a gentleman, that I KNOW he's a gentleman and that gentlemen don't fight with poor negroes like Shot that don't have any sense." I think he then told his father in Polish that she said Shot didn't have any sense. Father agreed. Too much agreement. She knew it hadn't gone through and started again. "You tell your father that he is, etc." Finally Alfred admitted he didn't know what a gentleman was, even in English. She was very successful in communicating with Shot, however. "Now Shot," she said, "you

* Thomas F. Ritt, editor of the literary journal A.D.

are very intelligent. You are much too intelligent to fight with a man that we can't understand very well, now you know you are above this, etc. etc." He agreed with every word, but said Mr. Matysiak had hit him first.

I had a note from Paul Engle today after I had written to congratulate him on his O. Henry collection. He said the *Saturday Review* had just attacked it and the [Iowa Writers'] Workshop. He seemed sad about it but I think it's obviously an honor. Love and thank you for seeing that story. I am going after it.

≈ That winter, O'Connor prepared her story collection, acknowledging to Robert Lowell how much she relied upon Gordon's feedback on her stories: "I send them all to Caroline and she writes me wherein they do not meet the mark." Gordon's work on her novel *The Malefactors* came to a halt when, in Rome, she discovered Jungian analysis with a practitioner who guided her through dream analysis—new, intuitive, and emotional terrain for Gordon—alongside a familiar, intellectual discussion of archetypes. Later, Gordon would tell O'Connor, "There is too great a gap between the Freudian practice and the poet's daily life but Jung is dealing with the same material the poet has to deal with every day." Then, in April 1954, she received an emergency cable about her daughter Nancy, whose mental health had become precarious. Gordon flew to Princeton the next day. She spent the spring and summer back in New Jersey before returning to Minnesota.

More than six months passed before her correspondence with O'Connor resumed. With a new story finished and a collection in development, O'Connor once again hoped for Gordon's consultation.

Flannery O'Connor to Caroline Gordon

27 October 1954

I met Bob Giroux in Atlanta yesterday and he told me your daughter had been ill and that you had been back some time. I will pray for her—he said she was better. I have not heard from anybody for great lengths of time but I suppose all of my acquaintances are as glad to get shut of the summer as I am. Grace after the season. He told me about Cal.*

---

* Robert Lowell spent three weeks in 1954 at the Payne Whitney Psychiatric Clinic.

We've been besieged lately by rabid foxes—to the extent that we've lost three cows, one a good one, of hydrophobia—so the government has come in and set traps. Every morning the traps have to be investigated. I never knew so many skunks, possums & coons had been created. Every night the negroes take home a possum or so and yesterday they went home with two possums, a coon, & a fox-squirril. I asked the colored woman how she cooked the coon and she said, "First I boils him and then I bakes him." I was going to ask her to send me a piece but now I'm not so sure I want him.

Where are the Fitzgeralds? The last I heard they are in some kind of moated castle belonging to one of Mr. Pound's connections and this was teeming with theirs and other people's children.

I have a new story called "The Artificial Nigger," that I want to send you if you are not too busy & if you are really in Minnesota. Apparently Harcourt is going to put out my collection of stories in August [*A Good Man Is Hard to Find*]. I have ten & have gone over them and removed all such words like "squinch," "scrunch," "scrawnch," etc.

I managed to raise two peachickens this summer. They are fearfully tame and both are vicious. I can't tell what sex they are yet though a man we had working out here told me that the way to tell is you hold the chicken upsidedown by its two front toes and if it tries to turn rightsideup again, it's a hen and if it just hangs down, it's a rooster. He swore this was a sure way and that he had used it many times to separate three-day-old chickens. One of mine turned up and the other hung down but they still look exactly alike.

Remember me to Allen.

Caroline Gordon to Flannery O'Connor

Undated [6 November 1954]
1409 East River Rd.
Minneapolis, MN

Do send me "The Artificial Nigger." What a marvelous title! "The Displaced Person" looks just as good in the SR [*Sewanee Review*] as it did in manuscript.

I have been wanting to write you and to have news of you for ages but I dropped behind the procession five or six months ago and I'm just catching up now we are back in Minneapolis.

Nancy had what old fashioned people would call a nervous break-down. She is married to a psycho-therapist, who, naturally, has other terms for it. The "episode"—we took on the vocabulary while we were staying with them—is doubtless only an incident in the savage and unremitting sexual warfare that goes on between that handsome, healthy, charming and, for the most part, well-disposed young couple. I really think that they are definitely on the up-grade now. But it was sure tough while it lasted—tougher than I could have imagined. In fact, I look back on myself of six months ago as just a slip of a girl of fifty-eight, lingering with the reluctant feet where the Tiber and Trastevere meet. I knew it would be tough but I was naïve enough to think that if I kept my mouth shut and worked awfully hard that I might be of some help. Vain delusion! Nancy's doctor, whom I met at a dinner party, explained to me about that. "My patients," says he, "all do the work of four or five women, including the work of a professional chauffeur and a trained kindergarten teacher—and then feel guilty if they don't look like glamour girls." Nancy, in addition to all that has to—or is fool enough to think she has to—administer therapy to three (child) patients. Matter, I suppose, of being too "identic." (Pardon the language. It grows on one.) Her husband treats one patient at a time in a seclusion calculated to spare the nerves of both patient and doctor, but she has to take on three while doing six and eight hours [of] house-work a day.

Working six or eight hours a day, myself, I wasn't able to help her much—though I did paint part or most of the inside of three houses— but I found a woman who could: a nice old coloured woman who ran away to get married at thirteen and thus was as well equipped to help one who lunged from the frying pan into the fire at the age of eighteen. It cost a good many thousand dollars to find the old soul. Wish now I'd spent some of the money in detective work up and down Witherspoon Street. Anyhow, she's still with them—and I, thank God, am back at my novel. There were five months when I couldn't even answer a letter.

Our little house, which was ideal for a middle aged couple, proved to be a torture chamber for the mother of three, so we sold it and bought a run-down Victorian mansion at the other end of town. It is late Victorian, gone perverse, but it has six bedrooms and three or four bathrooms and an orafectory—we thought we were the only people in the world who had a combined oratory and dining room but Jacques Maritain says he has a friend in Paris who had one. Anyhow, we all—of every age and size—adore the house and we had just got it fixed up in our fashion when Percy, who has just ended nine months training, got an offer from a near-by sanatorium at a salary so fabulous that he couldn't turn it down. But he has to live in a house that the hospital furnished, nine miles away from Dulce Dorum (Chillon, Wildfell or Locksley Hall, as it is indifferently called). So they had to move just before we left. We were fortunate enough to rent the house to another young couple. All most confusing. But the house is still there and Allen and I expect to spend next summer in it. I do hope you can come and visit us. You can have the choice of several suites as we'll be rattling around in it by ourselves. Do plan on coming.

We are moving into a house on the Mississippi River Boulevard here next week but have been staying with some friends on the, as they unblushingly call it, The Lake of the Isles, while waiting to get into the other house. The weather has been mild. Heavenly, in fact. I walk around the lake almost every day. On the next lake—there is a chain of them through the city—all sorts of exciting wild-fowl came down yesterday. Snow geese, whistling cranes, God knows what other fowl, all on their way south and whooping and hissing as they went. But they lit for one night on Lake Calhoun.

Imagine being able to raise two peacocks! I hardly dare mention the little devils' names for fear they'll hear me and take to pining away just by way of self-assertion. Marvelous, maddening birds . . . Allen and I are reading Jung's book on Religion and Alchemy. He certainly does a lot with peacocks—and unicorns—in that. It's amusing to watch him slowly making his way to the Church through the alchemical symbols in the dreams of his patients. I wish I could wrap up every poet I know and mail him the Jung or one of his disciples. I wish so much that poor Cal could be in the hands of a good Jungian. There is too great a gap between the Freudian practice and the poets' daily life but Jung is dealing with the same material the poet has to deal with every day. I tried to make Elizabeth see it but with no success. We lunched with them shortly before they left. Cal was in the depressed stage. He summoned me to come to see him while he was in the hospital and explained the secret of the universe to me. It is the Counterpoint: the Father, Son and Holy Ghost strain ceaselessly against one another.

The Fitzgeralds have been staying in a castle in the Tyrol [Schloss Brunnenburg Castle, Italy] with Mary Pound, Ezra Pound's daughter, and her husband, Prince Boris de Rachewiltz and their several children. Mary is an awfully nice girl, a sort of bigoted Catholic—except on the subject of Ezra. She considers him an ideal father. The old rascal has managed to hood-wink three women: Mary, her mother, Olga Rudge, and Dorothy Pound. Poor Boris has dedicated himself to getting Ezra out of St. Elizabeth's [Hospital]. They go around trying to get people to help them. I think Robert finally sent for some of the records and tried to make Mary see that her father had been guilty, technically, at least, of treason and that she was going about things the wrong way. Both she and Boris seem to take everything Ezra says as gospel.

The Fitzgeralds are having a new baby, so decided to take a trip to Greece while they were mobile. Indomitable souls.

I must get back to work. Have to make up for lost time. Do send the story and also some news of you—and be planning to come and see us next year. Love.

[postscript]

Get Bob Giroux to send me the proof of the book as soon as he can. I asked the *Times* to let me review it months ago.

Please pray for Nancy and Percy. They need it sorely. Percy is going to be a wonderful Christian some day. Right now he can't see anything much but psycho-therapy—all the world's his patient! He is, nonetheless, a mystic at heart. He really dotes on me but feels it is his duty to sell Nancy the idea that anything wrong with her is the result of some untoward word or gesture of her old mother's!

Flannery O'Connor to Caroline Gordon

14 November 1954

I am being very piggish with your time sending you "The Displaced Person" again but I have made a novella out of it or maybe I only think I have. Anyway, the business of the peacock and the priest etc. etc. was not done to my satisfaction before and I think this is better. I am not sure it works though, and if it doesn't I don't want to use it for the collection. Mr. Ransom took "The Artificial Nigger" for the *Kenyon* but I think without enthusiasm. He complained it was very flat and had no beautiful sentences in it. I rewrote it but there still aren't any beautiful sentences. It may be too long.

The first freeze came and carried off my frizzly chicken (she was molt-
ing and didn't have but ten feathers and they turned the wrong way) and
my youngest peachicken.

I suppose you have heard from the Fitzgeralds that Sally and Barnaby
are coming back at the end of this month to see her father who apparently is dying in Houston. She plans to stop here and I hope she will stay
a couple days and rest. My mother is afraid she won't be able to walk up
the steps, being pregnant, but I tell my mother it is a state Mrs. Fitzgerald
takes lightly.

It must be very fine to look at your family and see it becoming Catholic.
We look at ours and I am afraid I see the Catholicity washing away. The
grandchildren get married outside the Church, etc. etc. Part is from poor
instruction and part from that awful jell the Irish manage to set their religion in. They pass it on from generation to generation. We all prefer comfort to joy.

I am doing very well these days except for a limp which I am informed is
rheumatism. Colored people call it "the misery." Anyway I walk like I have
one foot in the gutter but it's not an inconvenience and I get out of doing
a great many things I don't want to.

You are mighty nice to ask me to come see you next summer when you
get in your house and I entertain the idea with great pleasure. And you are
mighty nice to read this stuff. I don't know who else would.

Caroline Gordon to Flannery O'Connor

Undated [November 1954]

Business before pleasure—as our vagabond cook, Willie, said when
Allen wanted her to sweep the front porch and she felt called to the post
office, to get a real special delivery letter. You asked for it and here it is:

As usual, I think you have improved your story ["The Artificial
Nigger"] by revision. (One reason that makes me reluctant to advise
you is the danger that in re-working a story you will lose some of the
good stuff. People nearly always do. But I don't think you do). I shall now
treat this revised version as if it were coming out of my own work-shop.
I would read it over now, for God knows the how manyeth time, for tone
and dramatic effect.

I think you can improve your first paragraph. The tone is not yet elevated enough, authoritative enough for the story you have to tell. Its subject matter is even more important than the subject matter in Joyce's "Araby," and look at the high and mighty tone he takes throughout that story of something that has happened to every one of us in our time—to be promised a treat as a child and then disappointed. Joyce takes that universal experience and makes it an analogue of man's situation in the universe, a small, lonely figure under a vast, dark dome, a figure whose eyes "burn with the anguish and anger" as the child-man realizes his plight. Your story is about an old man who realizes that all along he has been no better than a child. Your subject matter entitles you to take an even higher tone. So does your Christianity, which Joyce forsook and which you didn't.

Have you ever studied any of the paragraphs in Joyce's short stories or in *The Portrait*? It is very rewarding. Each paragraph has in it at least three kinds of sentences and each sentence does its appointed task with something that approaches perfection. You should learn to write the long, complicated—in the sense that it carries a lot of stuff—kind of sentence with which Joyce ends "The Dead." You ought to have a sentence like that to end this story with. The sentence you end on isn't quite strong enough, not weighty enough.

But let's go back to the first paragraph. Mr. H [Head] awakened to discover that the room was full of moonlight. You state that the room was full of moonlight but you do not substantiate it. It takes at least two sensuous details to make anything "come alive" in fiction (except in the case where exhaustive preparation enables us to do the job with one). Your moonlight isn't in the room, though you say it is. Put it in the room. Show us how some one object *looked*. You go at it too fast, try to leap straight up in the air by metaphors: The reckless air of the trousers, the straight chair.

A metaphor (why can't I lay my hand on a piece I wrote called "The Use of Metaphor in Prose Fiction"? Because I am so damn disorderly, for one thing, and also because I live in a different house every year.) Anyhow, a metaphor is, acc. to Aristotle, a transference of names or qualities by means of similarities. It is a vehicle of transference from one plane to another. Shelley says "Make me thy lyre even as the forest is," but even [Percy Bysshe] Shelley doesn't expect to be made into a stringed instrument—serve him right if he had been! A metaphor is like an airplane. An airplane does not take off vertically into the air. If it does it will crash on its nose. A metaphor, like an airplane, has to taxi along the ground, has to glide off into the empyrean, usually through sensuous details. You don't prepare enough for your metaphors.

Have you ever studied any of the great metaphors in James' novels? For instance, the image of Charlotte Stant as a beast, sometimes confined in a cage, sometimes loosed and ranging, runs all through *The Golden Bowl*. It is prepared for the first time she comes on the stage when the Prince thinks that there is something of the huntress in her appearance. She comes on the stage as the huntress but she goes off as a beast, controlled by the silken cord which her husband has tied around her neck and which he twitches or will twitch the moment she is not obedient. Metaphors take time.

You go at your first scene too fast. So fast that we cannot accept the comparison of Mr. Head with Virgil or the archangel Raphael. If you have really got the moonlight into that room, though, we could, I think.

Here is something I wish you'd think about, too. A sentence is a miniature story, just as a paragraph is a story in miniature. A story must have a climax. A sentence must have its small climax. A sentence is more telling if it ends on the word that is most important. I'd rewrite "like the servant of some great man who had just flown the garment on him" as "like the garment that some great man had just flung to his servant." "On him" trails, makes what in poetry we call the feminine ending: "later," say. "Late" is a masculine ending. If you expect a sentence to have a real effect you had better give it a masculine ending. There are very few times when a feminine ending like "on him" won't weaken a sentence.

"Any time he wanted to be awake at a certain time he was awake at a certain time" sounds very much to me as if it were Mr. Head, himself, talking. We don't want him or his vocabulary or even his thoughts here. We want to see him, at the beginning of the story, as God sees him. The least flavour of colloquial speech lets the tone down. You ought to learn to write a whole paragraph that is as free from colloquial flavour as one of Dr. Johnson's. You need such paragraphs for the elevated effects you aspire to.

Madame Bovary rests, as solidly as a building on its supporting columns, on three views of Emma: Emma, as she appears the first time Charles is alone with her, standing on tip-toe, trying with her tongue to lick the last drops of sweet from the liquor glass, Emma, running on tip-toe to pursue her pleasures in illicit love, and Emma, on her deathbed, in the same attitude we first saw her in, only she lies prone now, neck on the stretch, mouth pressing on the crucifix "the fullest kiss of love she has ever given."

Your story has the same form, the same three great supports: first Mr. Head in the moonlight, second, Mr. Head and Nelson waiting for the train. I don't think you give this scene enough attention. It corresponds to Dante's "mid-way in the forest of our life." You ought to set this scene more carefully—that is by using more sensuous detail—ought to make it more mysterious, for it is the "forest" out of which your action will emerge. You go at it too fast and don't choose your words carefully enough; "stuck" is not good there. Set the scene. Were there any trees there? If so, how did they look then? Did the tracks run through a flat place or did the train emerge from a small defile? Were the tracks straight or was there a bend? You do put the trees in but too late to have the right effect.

Again, on page 21, you scant an important effect. Mr. Head stares forward like a sleepwalker. Only one detail here, at this, perhaps the most important moment of the story, the moment when, in denying the boy, he denies his best self. "Forward" is vague. "Straight ahead," which you perhaps avoided for fear of being trite, would be better here. You need something else to make us see him at that moment. Our picture of him is blurred for lack of the data that would enable us to visualize. The reader cannot visualize unless you furnish the necessary data.

There's a trick that Flaubert works at important moments that will always work. In the seduction scene in Bovary he registers the way Emma feels by showing us the way the world looked and sounded and, if I remember right, even smelled at that moment. This seduction meant a lot to Emma. Rodolphe, on the other hand, is whistling immediately after it, as he mends with his pen-knife one of the horses' broken bridles. That bit does marvellously to render Rodolphe's attitude toward the affair. It wouldn't have worked for Emma. This moment, so important to Mr. Head, ought to be enlarged. This might be a good time to use that device. Show what he saw when he stared ahead like a sleep-walker.

On page 25, I think you go too fast again, substituting a sentiment of your own: "The two of them stood looking for almost a minute etc." when what we want is to see them. Perhaps they might even exchange looks at that point. At any rate, you have scanted the action again in a very important moment. If you made us see them at that moment your paragraph of commentary and statement would follow, all right.

I'd make "The boy nodded, with a strange shivering about his mouth" the start of a new paragraph. Anything important ought to have a paragraph to itself. When you run the boy's reactions on to his grandfather's you mar the effect of both.

I think you can do better at the end. It needs a little more detail. How did the place they took off from look when they got back? And how did it look to God—or Dr. Johnson? None of this "like it never had before" stuff. When I was younger than I am now I learned from Ford Madox Ford a way of handling dialect and colloquial speech that I still follow. His theory was that dialect and colloquialism is to a writer, like white to a painter, precious and therefore it must be properly displayed, enhanced by surrounding speeches. One word of dialect will flavour a whole sentence. He never used "'s". They bristled too much, he thought. And indeed, people are inclined to lay off stories that have a lot of "ain't s," "war's" and the like.

It's dangerous for me to say this to a young writer who is such a master of colloquial dialogue as you are, but I dare say it just because you are such a master. Your dialogue delights me. I wouldn't like to see less of it in your stories. I ask only to see it more set off, better displayed. That can be done, I think, by elevating the tone of the rest of the story—more beautiful, high-toned sentences. More paragraphs without a colloquial word or phrase in them. In that way you would get a contrast that would make your dialogue sparkle even more than it does.

Faulkner can do it—when he's in the groove, but he, poor fellow, is bogged down, I judge from his last book, in what Allen calls "Mississippi theology." You have an advantage over him there. For God's sake make the most of it!

Allen and I have been reading a lot of Jung lately. It's amusing and exciting to watch him making his way to the church by way of alchemical symbols in the dreams of his patients. We are also reading a book by a Fr. Victor White called *God and the Unconscious*, a discussion of Jung and Freud, which Allen is going to send poor Cal for Christmas. (How I wish I could wrap that boy up and mail him to a good Jungian practitioner.)

I think you'd find this book very interesting, also a book of Jung's called *Religion and Alchemy* (Pantheon Press). It is fascinating and ought to be very helpful to any fiction writer. It is to me, at least.

By the way, you ought to be able to get any book you need through your local library. They ought to purchase any book you need for your work if they follow the almost universal custom of extending special courtesies to writers. If they do not you can get them to order books from the Library of Congress' Inter-Library loan service.

I've got to get work on the ill-wrought paragraphs of a promising old writer named Gordon. Love and congratulations on your revision. I don't think you've lost a thing and you've gained an awful lot by the revision.

Caroline Gordon to Flannery O'Connor

Undated [November 1954]

Yes, I think this version is much better. I think that those two land-scapes—the one in the bedroom in the beginning and the moonlit rail-road tracks are very important in the story's architecture. There are times when the reader has to know what the landscape looked like before he will believe the action took place. James, Chekhov and Flaubert—each in his own and slightly different way—are masters of this principle. In James' critical scenes the landscape always plays a part.

I don't like the way you use the word "paused" about the moon. It's an adjective as you use it. "Paused" makes a damn awkward adjective.

And there is no such thing as an orange moon, an orange cat, an orange dress. If you mean that the moon or cat or dress is the same colour as an orange say "orange-coloured," for God's sake.

I certainly hope I'm not wrong in the advice I give you! And I hope you have a merry Christmas. *Mio presepio* this year is *terrifico*—more like a real sculpture than ever before. Allen and I are thankful we don't have to journey anywhere to see anybody. The news from Princeton is encourag-ing. Nancy had a block about writing letters for a while, so we didn't even know how they were getting on. But we had a letter the other day in which she sounded like her old self.

MUST get to work. Have thirty-five thousand more words to write. Think they will kill me. Why does anybody choose to write fiction when there are so many delightful occupations—like sculpting or even sewing!

Love—and best wishes ever. Ask Giroux to send me a copy of the book as soon as he can, so I can be thinking what to say.

[postscript]

Ran across this piece on metaphor the other day and am sending it along on the chance that you may be interested.

We are reading a book called *The History and Origins of Consciousness*, by a Jungian named Erich Neumann (Bollingen—I mean Pantheon) which I wish I could put into the hands of every fiction writer I know. Poets, too. Poor Old Cal, for instance! Neumann's book is a sort of study of mythology, mythology as the drama enacted in every consciousness.

~ O'Connor submitted the manuscript of *A Good Man Is Hard to Find* in November, in which she included the revised, expanded version of "The Displaced Person," as well as all the major revisions that incorporated Gordon's critiques. In December, her story "Circle in the Fire" won second prize, $200, in *Prize Stories 1955: The O. Henry Awards*.

O'Connor's story collection was considered complete—until she sent Gordon a new work-in-progress.

Caroline Gordon to Flannery O'Connor

19 February 1955

GOOD COUNTRY PEOPLE is a master-piece. Allen and I are in complete accord on that. Can't you get it into the volume of short stories? I do wish you could. It somehow sets the tone for the whole works. And what a tone! It's a terrific story—terrific in more than one sense. In one way, the most shocking story I ever read. But the shock is implicit in its reality and one realizes one has got to take it. Mrs. Freeman is marvelous. So is Mrs. Hopewell. So is the Bible Salesman. He is a super-Haze Moats, Haze Motes in the act of realizing his evil genius. Gosh, what a story! It's beautifully written, too. . . . Well, I don't know anybody else who could have pulled it off. It makes most of your contemporaries look like children busy with their all-day suckers. It's as good as Maupassant in execution but it's got what he lacked—moral seriousness. A dimension that his stories haven't got.

I have, of course, being me, a few strictures, minor ones to which you may well pay attention, having got the job done in such a masterly fashion.

The child: Allen and I both wonder about calling her the child. And that brings up that old debbil, View-point. I think I see why you call her the child. When you do that you are referring to her immortal soul. St. Isaac of Nineveh or is it Evagrius the Monk? —anyhow one of the worthies of the *Philokalia*, says that the soul has three ages, which correspond to infancy, youth and age and that when St. John the Evangelist says "I am addressing babes, young men and fathers," he is recognizing that fact. Anyhow, I gather that something like that is meant when you call her the child—but from whose viewpoint do you call her the child? St. John is using the Lord's viewpoint, in so far as he is able to. If it is from her mother's view-point, then it might be well to make that fact clear.

I was inclined to say that she ought to be capitalized, The Child, then I realized that you had doubtless considered that notion and decided against it. Anyhow, on page 3, I think you have a muzzy spot.

Here I must get didactic for a minute: Ideally, when you write a story, you reproduce the conditions of real life. You present a room, say. You cannot possibly portray every object in it, but you must give the reader the impression that you are doing just that. Faulkner does it in "A Rose for Emily" with three pieces of furniture, arranged so that the imagination fills in the (so to speak) dotted lines that connect them and makes a rectangle. On page 3 you direct our attention to the child but when we follow your bidding and look at her we can't see her. Should we see a real child "whose constant outrage etc."? If we do, we get mixed up. You have failed to furnish the data necessary for visualization and the reader escapes from you and has to be re-captured, which you do quickly and featly enough—but still there is a weak spot right there. What Uncle H.J. [Henry James] would call "weak specification." One page 5 you let us see the child as she really is. This is too late. You can not introduce a person, say, for instance, "This is Mr. Simpson" and have the other person acknowledge the introduction without taking some kind of look at Mr. Simpson, but that is what you asked us to do on page 3.

I should think that it might be effective to use Mrs. Hopewell's viewpoint for making her "the child." I see no reason against it, whereas holding off from any viewpoint worries the reader.

On page 18 you say "He gave her a kind of dying look as if he felt his insides dropping." Dropping where? Dropping is a transitive verb and requires an object of some kind or a prepositional phrase. Also, there is the question of view-point again. Your subject is one of high seriousness. It is the Omniscient Narrator who observes the way he looks there—not Hulga—and the Om. Nar. does NOT USE EXPRESSIONS LIKE "kind of." Particularly at crucial moments.

On page 24 you say "She realized that for the first time in her life" . . . . Is this strictly true? Is he really innocent? If he is, "realized" is the right word there. If he isn't, wouldn't something like "thought" be more exact?

Here is something that occurred to both of us. I mean we both had the same reaction to Hulga's academic career. Allen doesn't think it is well enough established. That passage that her mother read in one of her books is fine, but if you want to get anything important across you seem to have to do it three times—some relation to the Trinity, no doubt. Anyhow, it is a fact that I discovered many years before I realized that the Trinity existed. Another stroke might be well on that. Allen thinks that it would open a sort of vista which would give the story another dimension, and that that would strengthen its already massive impact.

I am just letting my imagination roam over the possibilities here. Hulga is a miraculously suitable name. I don't know where or how you got it, but if somehow her choice of a name could be connected with her learning, her other life . . . ? That is, her choice of another name, her adoption of it might be a symbol of her whole life, that is, her life lived in relation to her mother and Mrs. Freeman. You might invoke mythology here. Venus, the goddess of love, "took a bandy-legged smith for mate", [a] fact which is of enormous mythological significance. What I'm trying to say is that in the act of choosing her symbolic name she might display a little of the learning the reader is now asked to take on hearsay. It's just one corner of the canvas whose colours aren't yet quite bright enough to "carry."

But enough of this. I am satisfied with the story as it stands. It's a masterpiece. A very important story, I think.

If I am more incoherent than usual it is because I [am] on the home stretch of my novel [*The Malefactors*]—I hope, I hope! I have just finished the next to last chapter and hope to start the last chapter in the next day or two. I started the thing in 1951 and can hardly believe that I am about to get out from under it—I have carried it around in so many places. By the way, I hope you won't let them bully you into writing a novel if you don't feel like it. Publishers seem to have no sense about that and never seem to learn from experience. When they get hold of a fine short story writer, then demand a novel and often dry up the flow of short stories and get no novel, either. Katherine Anne [Porter] is an example of that. Eudora Welty has tried to write a novel but succeeds only in writing long stories. Jim Powers is up the Mississippi river eighty five miles from here, sweating away, trying to write a novel, when he ought to be writing short stories.

By the way, it's quite possible to sweat here. In fact, I have suffered more from heat here than I have suffered from cold. The houses are kept infernally hot and then the sun shines dazzlingly almost every day during the winter. I went out to Mass the other morning at seven o'clock, stepped on a sheet of black ice and nearly cracked my noggin. As I righted myself I felt, along with a sense of outrage that this should be, a wave of nostalgia. When had I last been doing that kind of thing? "In New York, in Princeton, in Nashville, in practically every other place you ever lived except Rome" came the answer. We had had a rain during the night—the only rain we have had this winter, or probably will ever have, and "every twig on the elm tree was ridged inch deep in pearl"* as a result, but as a rule, the ground is just neatly covered with several feet of fine, white, dry snow. The sun shines so bright you some times have the illusion that it is full summer. I have a nut-hatch [that] comes to my bird feeding table every morning and a jay-bird who comes every few days. The squirrels are so tame they come and rap on the glass door if you fail to put their peanuts out and will even come in to the kitchen after them.

I have got myself *Early Fathers from the Philokalia* (Faber and Faber) translated by E. Kadloubovsky and it is about to make a Schismatic out of me. Those Eastern fathers just naturally seem to have more soul than the western fathers!

I must get to work, or, at least assume the position of one who might work in case I can get started on that chapter. As for you, I should think

---

* "Every twig on the elm": From James Russell Lowell's poem "The First Snow-Fall": "the poorest twig on the elm-tree / Was ridged inch deep with pearl."

you could recline on your laurels with right good grace. And many thanks for sending us the magnificent story.

Flannery O'Connor to Caroline Gordon and Allen Tate

1 March 1955

I do appreciate both your letters and I am glad to have my opinion on that story ["Good Country People"] confirmed.* I really thought all the time it was the best thing I had done. Hit was a seizure. Anyway, Mrs. Freeman's remarks are not much credit to me. She lives on this place and all I have to do is sit at the source and reduce it a little so it'll be believable. As for the other lady I have known several of her since birth and as for Hulga I just by the grace of God escape being her; the Bible salesman also came without effort. I am mighty afraid he is my hidden character.

I have corrected the business about the child and now only use it from the mother's point of view. This is a great improvement. Then I have added two touches to support the intellectual life of Hulga; one, like you said about the name, and the name's working like Vulcan in the furnace, etc. Hulga thinks that one of her greatest triumphs is that her mother has not been "able to turn her dust into Joy, but the greater one was that she had been able to turn it herself in Hulga." That helps some. Then while Mrs. Hopewell is thinking about Hulga and how she is getting more bloated, rude and squint-eyed every day, I stick in this (from Mrs. Hopewell's viewpoint):

> And she said such strange things! To her own mother she had said—without warning, without excuse, standing up in the middle of a meal with her purple and her mouth half-full—"Woman! Do you ever look inside and see what you are *not*? God!" she had cried sinking down again and staring at her plate, "Malbranche was right: we are not our own light! We are not our own light!" Mrs. Hopewell had no idea, to this day, what brought that on. She had only made the remark (hoping Joy would take it in) that a smile never hurt anyone.

Anyhow, with these changes, I sent it airmail to Giroux and he wired me he would try to get it in the collection if it didn't cost too much to throw away the old type and do the resetting. Seems there can't be but so many

---

* Allen Tate also wrote O'Connor a letter expressing his admiration for the story.

pages or they will go broke. I was to get the proofs this week so I suppose he could wring my neck.

I know you are glad to get out from under that novel, or anyway where you can see out. If I could just get where I could see a little daylight in mine I would be happy. It hasn't moved an inch in 18 months and when I stop it and write a story I feel like I am letting myself down from the penitentiary by a rope. I mean a thread.

The story of Powers in the [1955] O. Henry collection ["The Presence of Grace"] is better than any of the others in the book. If you ever see him I wish you would tell him he has one solid admirer in Georgia.

More thanks.

Caroline Gordon to Flannery O'Connor

Undated [March 1955]

Allen sent Giroux a telegram yesterday to the effect that hit war his considered opinion that "GOOD COUNTRY PEOPLE" is the best study of maimed souls that's come along in his life-time. Giroux wired back that he'd like to use the remark as a blurb for the jacket and said that the story would get into the collection. I wish you were calling the volume "Good Country People." Anyhow, I am glad this story got in.

We both think that your revision—the passage you quote in your letter—is masterly and will quite do the trick. The use of view-point is masterly there, whether you know it or not. Putting it in the mother's view point does a lot towards putting it over—making it convincing. And the juxtaposition of quotations from mother and daughter is extremely effective. "A smile never hurt anyone" is inspired.

But I had better stop praising you a while and return to my own *moutons*—lest they take a chill in this winter weather. I have found that if I sit up after dinner—instead of slumping in bed and reading the *Philokalia*—and listen to the radio straight through Edward Murrow, the Chesterfield Caroleers, Amos and Andy—whom I hadn't heard for twenty years till the other day—Bing Crosby, Ernie the Pea-Packer on to Cedric Adams, that I go to bed so bored that I sleep like a log and can get up and face that last chapter easier the next morning. But it is a fearful price to pay. And you hear an awful lot about the weather, in and out of

the "Twin Cities." Forty-nine below it went one night in a town with a
name beginning with W.

Thank God, though, people do come to dinner—and you have to stop
and get it for them. The other night I was so hard pressed in my prepara-
tions that I taught Allen how to make crepes Suzettes. He has never showed
much talent along those lines and it was a little like teaching a horse to
count—and his performance was received with the same kind of astonishment. When he entered the dining room, bearing his flaming burden, the
guests with one accord, rose to their feet and sang the Marseillaise!

Love and again congratulations. Let us hear from you some time when
you are not in the midst of giving birth to a story. I hope you don't suffer
too much over the novel. Feeling guilty over not writing on it may help
you get the stories written. But when you can write the kind of stories
you can write why should you worry over writing a novel? Our lives were
blighted for years by a publisher's conviction that Allen could write another novel and Allen's feeling that he ought to be writing one. It sure is
more comfortable now he realizes that he doesn't have to write a novel
if he doesn't want to, plus the realization that, having other fish to fry, he
doesn't want to.

⸺ As Gordon suggested, "Good Country People" would be the tenth and final
story included in *A Good Man Is Hard to Find*.

O'Connor travelled to New York on the last day of May 1955, to promote the
release of *A Good Man Is Hard to Find* in an appearance on *Galley Proof*, a new
television show hosted by Harvey Breit. Breit's interview of O'Connor accompanied a dramatization of "The Life You Save May Be Your Own"—all in all, an
experience O'Connor described as "mildly ghastly."

After the television appearance, O'Connor spent the weekend with Caroline
Gordon in Tory Valley, New York, where Gordon and Susan Jenkins Brown
hosted a party for O'Connor. "Dear old Van Wyke [Van Wyck Brooks] insisted
that I read a story," O'Connor told the Fitzgeralds, "at which horror-stricken
looks appeared on the faces of both Caroline and Sue. 'Read the shortest one!'
they both screamed. I read 'A Good Man Is Hard to Find' and Mr. Brooks later
remarked to Miss Jenkins that it was a shame someone with so much talent
should look upon life as a horror story. Malcolm [Cowley] was very polite and
asked me if I had a wooden leg."

Gordon described O'Connor's reading of "A Good Man Is Hard to Find" to Fannie Cheney: "It was interesting to see the guffaws of the company die away into a kind of frozen silence as they saw which way things were heading." To Walker Percy, Gordon wrote, "Flannery O'Connor spent the week end with us. Van Wyck Brooks insisted that she read one of her stories Saturday night. She read 'A Good Man is Hard to Find.' Van Wyck's white moustache quivered as he registered the dramatic impact of every stroke, but he didn't really get the point. He told my friend later that it was sad to see a young writer who was so talented having such a pessimistic view of life. In a way, though, he did get it. He took my friend during the course of the evening and interrogated her as to whether she had any religion or any belief in a future life."

That weekend, Gordon and O'Connor attended mass together; they also discussed the books they were reading: Romano Guardini's *Faith and the Modern Man* (Flannery) and Erich Neumann's *Origins and History of* Consciousness (Caroline).

It was a good summer for O'Connor. *Harper's Bazaar* published "Good Country People" and Harcourt, Brace offered O'Connor a contract for a new novel, to be delivered in five years. Late June also marked the British release of *Wise Blood*. The *Times Literary Supplement* proclaimed the work "intense, erratic, and strange." By summer's end, O'Connor enjoyed some relief in her treatment for lupus: a new medicine, Mericorten capsules, replaced her daily ACTH injections.

A Good Man Is Hard to Find received mixed reviews. *Time* described O'Connor's "ten witheringly sarcastic stories" as "arty fumbling" emerging "from another talented Southern lady whose work is highly unladylike," and instead of crediting O'Connor with a master's degree from University of Iowa, the anonymous reviewer dismissed her as "the product of a college writing class." In the *Kenyon Review*, Walter Elder called the collection "profane, blasphemous, and outrageous," but conceded that O'Connor had "an unerring sense of material monuments." Gordon published her own review of *A Good Man Is Hard to Find* in the *New York Times*. She described O'Connor's work as "characterized by precision, density and an almost alarming circumscription" and argued that O'Connor was "fiercely concerned with moral, even theological problems."

Earlier that spring, Gordon had been one chapter away from completing *The Malefactors*. But despite her assistance to others—or, more likely, because of it—Gordon did not meet her publisher's deadline.

Part 3

The Enduring Chill
(September 1955–December 1962)

≈

I'm busy with the Holy Ghost. He is going to be a waterstain—very obvious but
the only thing possible. I also have a fine visitor for Asbury to liven him up slightly.
—Flannery O'Connor to Caroline Gordon, 10 December 1957

Your chief weakness as a writer seems to be a failure to admit the august nature
of your inspiration. You speak almost always like FO'C. That is fine. You have the
best ear of anybody in the trade for the rhythms of colloquial speech. [. . .]
[Y]ou have this enormous advantage: what Yeats called the primitive ear.
He had it, too and got a lot out of it. But you have another kind of ear,
one that is attuned to—shall we say the music of the spheres? It is attuned
to that music or you would not choose the subjects you choose.
—Caroline Gordon to Flannery O'Connor, 26 January 1958

≈ After the publication of *A Good Man Is Hard to Find*, O'Connor and Gordon did not see one another for almost three years. O'Connor's move to Milledgeville, Georgia, was permanent; daily life at Andalusia farm with her mother, Regina, provided stability for her health and her writing. O'Connor continued to write to the Fitzgeralds and others, but it was O'Connor's deepening kinship with Lon and Fannie Cheney that would ensure a lifelong link between herself and Gordon. The Cheneys would act as friends and mediators as Gordon and Tate separated, reconciled, and divorced for a second time in 1959. Meanwhile, the Cheneys—Catholic converts with Gordon serving as godmother—enjoyed an easygoing relationship with both Flannery and Regina O'Connor. Lon's mother, like Regina, raised a family and successfully managed a Georgia farm after her husband had died. Lon was a novelist who shared Gordon and O'Connor's literary interests, as well as close friendships with other mutual friends, like Ashley Brown. Thus, where the Gordon–O'Connor correspondence stalls (or where physical letters do not survive), we can see the contrails of their relationship through their communication with others, particularly the Cheneys.*

In September 1955, Gordon finally completed her novel *The Malefactors*. She immediately returned to Rome, without Allen Tate.

---

* *The Correspondence of Flannery O'Connor and the Brainard Cheneys*, ed. C. Ralph Stephens (Jackson: University Press of Mississippi, 2008), contains 188 previously unpublished letters.

Caroline Gordon to Flannery O'Connor

St. Jude's Day, 1955 [October 28]
Presso Gargano,
Via Nicola Fabrizi 11A
Roma 28

I had a note from the Fitzgeralds last night. They plan to come to Rome around the tenth of next month. I sure hope they can make it. I am saving a few *giros* to make with them. Robert sent several sections of his *Odyssey* translation and said to pass them on to you after I've read them, which I will do eventually. But there are several people at the Academy who'd like awfully to read them and I think I'll let them have a look before I send the stuff on. I am up to my ears in Homer. I was halfway through Richmond Lattimore's *Iliad* when Robert's contribution came. I started my book hight *How to Read a Novel* the other day—at least I could make practically any point I need to make, using examples from the *Iliad*. Homer does all the things anybody else can do and more, it seems to me.

The Lord certainly moves in a mysterious way His wonders to perform. Here you are, in Milledgeville, Georgia, on crutches, damn it, and here across the hall from me in this *pensione* is a raw-boned Ford Fellow of Swedish descent who has been given five thousand bucks by the foundation for the purpose of enjoying herself and improving her mind. It turns out that she can do neither. Her brain-pan is as crammed with the brand of baloney purveyed at Columbia by that old rascal, John Dewey, and the fumes rising from that witch's broth are so powerful that she can't even see the Eternal City for her own smoke. I came very near recommending her one day to cut a hole in the top of her head and lean over some bridge till all her mental furnishings fell out into the Tiber. I choked that one back but the next minute heard myself saying, "Cut that sociological cackle, my dear. It's so boring." Relations have been quite the same since. But damn it, it is maddening to see the Eternal City withheld from you and wasted on her! I wish so often that you were here, for I see so many things I know you'd enjoy. Well, all I can do is pray for you in diverse places. Some of them very fine spots, too.

I had a wonderful little *giro* yesterday, all by myself. The house St. Benedict lived in when he was a student here in Rome is still standing. It is called "The House of Anicetus," he being supposedly descended from the Anicetan gens. I forget when it was made into a chapel but very long ago and it has somehow escaped any kind of restoration. The room St. B. stayed in is still there, but they take such little account of *tourisme* that you can't even get in to see it—have to view it through a grating, that is. I had a hard time finding it. It is right opposite that bridge Horatius kept, but back several streets from the Lungotevere, as they call the street that runs beside the Tiber. Nobody knew where it was or had even heard of it, till I finally ran and caught up with a very dirty Carmelite nun, who, it turned out, belongs in the convent attached to the church. The columns are rough stone, unadorned, the floor of the nave is Cosmatesque, but sunken in and much worn. The frescoes are quite dim and obliterated in some places. But it is a wonderful church, and you feel right off as you go in that it is one of those really holy places. An old abbot I met on the plane going from Paris to Rome gave me his list of the really holy places in or around Rome. Surprisingly few. Subiaco was one of them, and Paul Without the Walls and the Navicella chapel in St. Peter's where St. Catherine of Siena used to spend most of her time when she was in Rome. He didn't mention this chapel but it certainly is on my list, being the place where St. Benedict must first have started to "dwell with himself," as St. Gregory puts it.

I got passage the other day for December 11, so I expect to get back in time to have Christmas in Princeton with the children and grandchildren, and Allen who plans to fly in from Minnesota. He has just been in Princeton on some [Indiana] School of Letters meeting and was to arrive in Minneapolis yesterday. Percy has night duty sometimes at his hospital, which is twelve miles from Princeton. Nancy went over and spent the night at the hospital with him and Allen kept the children. He says that when he woke up the other morning Caroline was in bed with him. A pleasant surprise for anybody. She is three and a half now and a perfect darling. She accepts our comings and goings with equanimity. When I was there she would run over to my room every morning as soon as she woke up. I prophesied that she would find it quite natural for Grandma's head to be resting on the pillow one morning and Grandpa's the next.

I am living, like an aged student, *en pensione*, right around the corner from the Monastero, as they call it, of the Rosario Perpetuo. It's a cloistered order. The sisters sing the Rosary (very badly) night and day behind a grill. They also have the talent, common to American nuns, of defacing any landscape they come in contact with. But fortunately they are kept so busy with their choir work and also are cloistered and can't get at it, so haven't been able to do as badly by their visitor's garden as they might have done. They have only one "extern" Sister Colomba and one "familiar" (cross between a servant and a lay sister). Sr. Colomba is too busy waddling up and down the hill to market to do anything with the garden and they have turned it over to Sister Mary and me. Sr. Mary is a widow from Indiana—the kind of woman who is such a nuisance in the world, the kind that wants "to write." She was actually a newspaper woman of sorts, I believe. Anyhow, she and I are making the garden over together. Rodolpho, one of the gardeners at the Villa Aurelia, came down the hill the other day with a big wheelbarrow load of plants I'd begged from him. Every one we transplanted lived! He brought a lot of those darling little daisy-like things that look as if they had been executed by Fra Angelico, rose-coloured, white and blue, and I made a corona for the B.V.M. out of them. Alberto, the nuns' gardener (the cloistered garden is his chief interest), inclines to Papal colours, having worked twelve years in the Vatican gardens. "I would take the flowers up to His Holiness and he would talk to me just the way I am talking to you," said he to us from the heights of his condescension. Well, he slipped into our garden and stuck a row of calendulas right where I aimed to put my corona. We were appalled, but Sr. Mary, who has a powerful relic of Papa Pio Diecimo which tells her what to do in any circumstance, slept on it and the next morning ripped every calendula out. . . . I have begged about as much stuff as I can and next week am going out and [will] buy some roses for the Rosario. It really is lots of fun. I have always wanted to garden in Rome and here I have this garden dropped in my lap, as it were. I have a little suite at my disposal—the guest suite—and keep my garden clothes there and even take hot baths on the nuns when I work hard enough to get up a sweat. I am going over there in a little while and [will] try very hard to get up a sweat. It has turned cold much earlier than usual this year and I am freezing this minute. Also the *pension's* hot water heater is off again. Claudio, a high school boy who takes his meals here and learned English from Harry Duncan,* has the job of fixing a sign when the heater goes on the

---

* Founder of the Cummington Press, one publisher of Tate's poetry.

blink. Last time he affixed to it a paper which had on it a death's head and the words: "It is wrong. Do not touch." I was about to correct him and point out that the heater, being inanimate, was incapable of being right or wrong, when I suddenly realized that it is possessed by a devil which is certainly "wrong."

I left here in such a hurry last time that I didn't get any "loot." This year I prowl through the Flea Market every Sunday. Last Sunday I fulfilled a long cherished ambition and bought a picture at the Flea Market. It is a Tobias and the Angel. It takes a person who is both a papist and a Jungian and a Confederate to get its fine points. The actual painting verges on what Allen calls "Confederate Technique"—you know, those darksome oils that one finds in old Southern halls. Or rather, it looks as if it had been painted by me while apprenticed to Salvate or Rosa. The archangel is mighty upstanding. Tobias is a stocky boy but is pretty scared at the moment. He and the Angel stand under a tree whose leaves are a fine bronze colour, on the shore, with mountains in the distance and the city Tobias has come from at their feet. The little dog follows in the footsteps of Filippo Lippi's version, looking like a cross between a pug and a Pekingese. He is right down at the water's edge, holding at bay the monster fish. There is a strong family resemblance between Tobias and the fish—she's his mama, all right. I have it on the wall and wake up every morning laughing when my eye lights on it. I shall keep you in mind—I think our tastes in painting are pretty much the same—and if I come across any picture that I think is up your alley will get it for you, but they are hard to come by. This is the first one I ever found that I wanted.

I went to St. Bridget of Sweden's church the other day. The mother superiour there is a wonderful woman and graciously took me around. The rooms St. Bridget and her daughter, St. Catherine lived in, are now chapels. They still have the original, richly decorated ceilings and the original beams. Mother Richard says that St. Catherine of Siena gets credit for a lot of the work St. Bridget did. Certainly, St. C. carried it on, but I guess St. B was the first woman to start in making over popes. She came to Rome as a pilgrim and stayed on for years. Mother Richard observed pensively that she imagined that the walls of the room St. Bridget's daughter, Saint Catherine, stayed in had seen many tears fall. St. Catherine of Sweden was so fair—meaning so blonde—that her mother had to keep her shut up most of the time—the Italians, who love blondes so were falling over themselves to get at her, and she, being only a freshman saint, as it were, wanted to gad about a bit instead of being shut up in that room.

I am so cold that I have got to stop this and go over and warm up in the garden of the Perpetual Rosary. Love. Do write and let me know how things go. Not well, I fear. How *can* they when you have to go on crutches! It must be simply devilish.

[postscript]

If it's any comfort, may I say that I think that as a writer you have what the medieval scholars called "infused theology"—and I guess one doesn't get a gift like that without paying for it!

～ That December, Gordon's friend Susan Jenkins Brown contacted O'Connor confidentially, asking O'Connor for help promoting *The Malefactors* to the Catholic literary audiences who had appreciated *A Good Man Is Hard to Find*. When Gordon's editor, Denver Lindley, shared the page proofs of Gordon's novel, O'Connor expressed "all my usual admiration for everything she writes." O'Connor sent Lindley a list of suggested reviewers but demurred from writing one herself, explaining that "It would be impertinent for me to comment on the book, simply because I have too much to learn from it." (O'Connor would eventually review the book the following year.)

The Cheneys visited Caroline Gordon in Italy that December. Though O'Connor had been invited to accompany them, her health prevented it.

Flannery O'Connor to Caroline Gordon and Brainard and Frances Cheney

2 December 1955

I reckon you are all in Rome now, pilgriming and so forth and I do wish I was too. When you all were arriving in the Holy City, I was arriving in Atlanta, the state capital, to address a luncheon of the Ga. Writer's Association. I have now got to be famous enough to address this body. I set two down from Miss Lillian Smith* who asked me to visit her on her mountaintop. I allowed as how my infirmity prevented my going to the mountains right now. I sat next to a librarian named Miss Eunice Costa

* Author of *Strange Fruit* (1944).

(?) and whenever I find myself in the company of a librarian, I say in an impressive voice, "Do you know my friend, Mrs. Cheney?" At which they always say yes and accept me as a blood brother. After the talk, one lady shook my hand and said, "That was a wonderful dispensation you gave us, honey." Another lady said, "What's wrong with your leg, sugar?"

My mother has got another family on the place along with the D.P.s now. They are sort of half way between poor white trash and good country people—Mr. Buford May and his wife, Mayrene, and their two children with leaky noses and no shoes. My mother remarked to Mr. and Mrs. May that since they could smoke cigarets, she thought they could put shoes on the children, at which Mr. May told her with dignity, that smoking cigarets was a Habit. They have nothing but a red automobile and one suitcase. They make the Matysiaks look like John D. Rockerfellers.

I hope when you come back you'll be prepared to tell me what a catty-comb is like. I met a man at the thing in Atlanta who had a heavy French accent. He said, "You haf been on the left bank, haf you not?" and all I could think was: I stay on the left bank of the Oconee River, Brother.

≈ Few letters between Gordon and O'Connor from 1956 or 1957 survive. Biographers have provided some insight as to why this might be: Ann Waldron (*Close Connections: Caroline Gordon and the Southern Renaissance*) suggested that when Gordon did not write letters, it was "a sure sign that her life was in disarray." Nancylee Novell Jonza described—with both compassion and a clear eye—Gordon and Tate's escalating alcoholism during this period, Tate's infidelities and illnesses, Tate's financial negligence and the couple's ever-mounting debts, and their turbulent separations and attempts to reconcile. As always, Gordon accepted even the most inconvenient teaching, writing, and speaking engagements in an effort to secure financial stability, if not earn professional respect.

Gordon returned from Rome in January 1956, to teach for a semester at the University of Kansas. Of her three classes, one was a weekly lecture on the craft of fiction, open to the public and broadcast on a Lawrence radio station. O'Connor reported Gordon's news to Betty Hester: "[T]he two words not allowed to be used at the U. of K. are 'whiskey' and 'religion.'"* Nonetheless,

---

* Hazel Elizabeth "Betty" Hester, a fan of O'Connor's fiction, became a regular correspondent with O'Connor after the publication of *A Good Man Is Hard to Find*.

O'Connor continued, Gordon insisted that she would "make them see the difference in *Wise Blood* and the works of Truman Capote if she ha[d] to use the word 'religion.'"

O'Connor, meanwhile, returned to work on her novel, *The Violent Bear It Away*. She wouldn't request Gordon's feedback on the novel until 1959.

O'Connor's star rose. She learned that *A Good Man Is Hard to Find* was a finalist for the National Book Awards and that French publisher Gallimard would translate *Wise Blood*. O'Connor put her novel aside to write "Greenleaf" and "A View of the Woods." (No Gordon critiques of these stories survive, if they existed.) O'Connor now regularly received invitations to travel and lecture; she also started contributing book reviews to the Diocese of Atlanta's Catholic biweekly paper, the *Bulletin*.

Gordon's literary fortunes did not fare as well in this time. *The Malefactors* was published in the spring of 1956. Gordon had removed the book's dedication to Dorothy Day, who was not pleased by her representation in the character of Catherine Pollard. Among friends, O'Connor loyally defended the book against its critics: "I don't know anybody who has a greater respect for Dorothy Day," she said of Gordon. A March 1956 *Time* review called the novel "one of those Mary McCarthy–like exercises in intellectual cattiness in which one claws one's literary coterie in public." O'Connor responded, "They could not be expected to like such a book but what seems particularly low in the review is that it implies there is not even any honesty of intention in the writing." The *New Yorker* described Gordon's book as "tedious." O'Connor acknowledged the book's imperfections: "She is much concerned with the technical aspects of the novel, with the unities and the point of view and all that and *technically* the book is an achievement. I admire, purely and simply, how she has done it."

Some reviewers praised Gordon. The *New York Times'* Arthur Mizener wrote, "For twenty-five years Caroline Gordon has been producing good novels. [. . .] She is not simply a gifted novelist; she is also one with the intelligence to discipline and cultivate her powers so that her books have grown more skillful with time." In the *Sewanee Review*, Vivienne Koch called Gordon "the best woman novelist we have in the country at this time." Gordon was most gratified by a letter of support from Jacques Maritain, who praised "the sense of lovingkindness of Our Lord which permeates the entire book." Gordon thanked Maritain and told him that O'Connor had comforted her with the reminder of Maritain's godfather [Catholic author] Leon Bloy, who "went all over Paris, calling out loudly for 'a true Catholic Painter.'" O'Connor also reviewed the novel for the *Bulletin*, highlighting Gordon's achievement in bringing her "knowledge of the craft to bear upon a task that most novelists today would have neither the desire nor the courage to attempt." Her review follows below.

Flannery O'Connor, review of *The Malefactors* by Caroline Gordon (Harcourt, Brace, 1956)

In a critical essay called "Nature and Grace in Caroline Gordon," Louise Cowan has written that "though the surface of her novels ... moves toward destruction and despair, the current in their depths moves in a strongly different direction." In her latest novel, *The Malefactors*, this current comes openly to the surface and is seen as the sudden emergence of the underground rivers of the mind into the clear spring of grace. The novel's protagonist, a poet who is not producing, is provoked by a recurrent impulse to wonder where his years are bound. After an involvement with a lady intellectual poet, which takes him away from his wife, he comes to the conclusion that they are bound nowhere unless he can return to his wife who, in the meantime and after an attempt at suicide, has found her way to the Church. He comes to the knowledge that it is for him, as Adam, to "interpret the voices Eve hears."

A novel dealing with a conversion is the most difficult the fiction writer can assign himself. Miss Gordon brings a sure knowledge of the craft to bear upon a task that most novelists today would have neither the desire nor the courage to attempt. *The Malefactors* is profoundly Catholic in theme but it is doubtful if it will receive the attention it deserves from the Catholic reader, who is liable to be shocked by the kind of life portrayed in it, or from the reader whose interests are purely secular, for he will regard its outcome as unsound and incredible and look upon it merely as a *roman à clef*. The fact that the conversion is elaborately prepared for and underwritten by the force of Jungian psychology will be overlooked by those who are not willing to accept the reality of supernatural grace. Making grace believable to the contemporary reader is the almost insurmountable problem of the novelist who writes from the standpoint of Christian orthodoxy. *The Malefactors* is undoubtedly the most serious and successful fictional treatment of a conversion by an American writer to date.

⁓ That May, Gordon joined Tate in Nashville for the Fugitive Reunion. After finishing her semester in Kansas, she returned to Princeton for the summer. She planned to visit O'Connor and the Cheneys in Smyrna in that summer but was unable to get away.

Caroline Gordon to Flannery O'Connor and Brainard and Frances Cheney

Undated [June 1956]
54 Hodge Road
Princeton, NJ

I shall try to kill all three of you birds with one letter, things being pretty hectic here. It is the old people stirring up the waters this time. *Re* the matter of address, Flannery, 54 Hodge Road will reach me and I'll be glad to have the piece back any time you feel like forwarding it.

The reason you all didn't reach me by telephone is that the doctor [Gordon's son-in-law, Percy Wood] has his phones awfully muted so that he can't hear his patients' keening in the night time. He says he sometimes hears a faint moaning of the wires but always figures he dreamed it. The Woods have been in Memphis, visiting Percy's father, and I, who was cat-and-dog-sitting here alone for three weeks, got very few calls from my friends here in town on account of said muting. However it was just as well. And just as well you didn't reach me. I would have been so torn, longing to nip down to Smyrna—but I really had to stay here, with the animals. (As it was, one kitten (two months old, we figure) was arrested for attacking a Boxer and put right in the animal clink, whence I had to bail him out.)

I would not have been any help in the [Tennessee] theatre venture but I wish I could have been there and I sure hope something comes of it. Look at Paul Green.* All the gravy he gets. Of course he practically makes a career of it. All his work has gone clean to pot on account of it. Still, I'd be perfectly willing to take a chance on Lon's and Red's work going just a little to pot if they could just get their hands on the money.

Our thoughts are all of money these days and how in the devil to get one's hands on a few thousands. Anne Freemantle leased her little dump

* Pulitzer Prize–winning playwright from North Carolina.

on Mercer Street to us for seven years but omitted to report that she had previously leased it to the Inst. of Adv. Study whose lease has months to run yet. So we couldn't move in there June 15, as specified in our lease. We were furious at her. Allen was anxious to put her in jail—what she did was illegal—but she, characteristically, was on the high seas, and by the time she gets back to these shores we may be regarding her as a blessing in disguise. Anyhow, as a result of perfidy, we stumbled on the most divine little house, exactly suited to our age and condition. Part of it was built in 1780. Part in 1830. Three levels and none of them split. In an unfashionable part of town, down among the Italian gardeners. Near the shopping centre and sure to have a lot of horrible ranch houses built around it, but there is so much ground that you'd be protected. It's a sort of miniature Benfolly, only more practical. In perfect condition. We could move in right away and not even put on a coat of paint. We have re-mortgaged this house or whatever it is you do and are now scraping the barrel for three thousand bucks. If we rake them up we'll move in this week. All most hectic, with Allen at Harvard, conducting the foreign seminar and only coming down for week ends. However, we hope it'll be the last flurry—of that kind.

The Woods had a fine time in Memphis but all of them were glad to get back. Nancy said she got to feeling she might have to stay there and got panicky. They now regard Princeton as a summer resort. They say they don't see how people attain their full growth in Memphis. They say the heat is not only stifling but stunting. In short, they have turned into Yankees.

Percy's mother left provisions in her will for a swimming pool for her grandchildren and they did not delay in fulfilling her desires. I was in charge of it while they were away and it is no light matter as somebody has to come and do something to it every few minutes—mainly they don't come but send word that they will be there tomorrow.

Paul Williams* was killed in an automobile accident on Sts. Vitus, Modestia [Modestus] and Crescentia's day [June 15]. He had the most beautiful funeral I ever saw in my life. It was like a poem written by God. They had had a picnic and Harry [Duncan] says that he "drank my gin too fast" and was sleeping it off when Paul and a friend, Jack Leahy, set off for a near-by tavern. The village where they lived, Rowe, Massachusetts, is on a

---

* Artist and illustrator for the Cummington Press.

hill and the road is romantic but dangerous, with a beautiful river winding below it. The car failed to make a turn and the car was smashed but lodged in the trees in such a way that passers-by thought it was parked—till six o'clock when some fishermen discovered the wreck. The coroner thinks Jack died around two o'clock. Paul was breathing when they took him out but died soon afterwards.

He was lying in state at Smith's Funeral Service Home when I got there, while everybody in the village filed by to pay their respects. He had made a place for himself in the community by doing all sorts of menial jobs. Drove the school bus and was janitor for the school and last summer he and one of the town selectmen undertook to clear the brush and young trees off an ancient graveyard. Some of the graves go back to the seventeen hundreds and nobody had been buried in it for fifty years till the other day. The selectman told me that one day when they had worked all day in the broiling sun, they sat down in the cool of the evening to rest and the place was so beautiful that Paul said that he would like to be buried there.

His requiem mass was celebrated in the church by a young priest but the rector himself said the blessing at the grave. I had never before read the prayer for hallowing unconsecrated ground. It asks God to appoint a guardian angel for the spot who will loose from the bonds of sin everybody buried there, so Paul will have his hands full.

The road up the mountain is so overgrown they had to take the coffin out of the hearse and put it on a trailer which was hitched to a jeep. It was when they did that that I first really got an inkling of what was going on. The jeep and trailer looked as if they might have been driven by Paul himself and just as I thought that Harry turned to me and said it. But it was the rector—a pig-like Irishman, the kind that keeps people like Stark Young out of the church—who gave me the next clue. After he had blessed the grave he made a little speech about how Paul had endeared himself to the community and what an influence for good he had been and then he made the rounds and spoke a few words of comfort to all who might be thought of as being specially bereaved. Then he said he had to go and went off down the hill. Half way down he turned around, stared at us a few minutes—there was still a group around the grave—then came back and made the rounds again and spoke [to] a few more people this time. Then he went down the hill again, paused halfway and stood for a long time staring back at us and finally went his way. I think the man had a professional curiosity as to just where the Holy Ghost was lodged on that mountain. I, by that time, had no doubt as to where it was. The liturgy for the day was most explicit. "In the sight of the unwise they seemed to die and their departure was taken for misery and their going away from us for utter destruction, but they are in peace." Nancy always said he looked "just like a little sparrow." The Gradual is "Our soul hath been delivered as a sparrow out of the snare of the hunters. The snare is broken and we are set free: our help is in the name of the Lord who hath made heaven and earth." It was all simply marvelous. And his clearing the ground for his grave with his own hands was the final touch. He had told Harry a few weeks before that this was the first time he had even felt at home in a place in his life.

Nancy's baby is expected in September and I am going to stay over for her lying-in. (She has finally realized that I, myself, once had a baby!) The Woods are in such fine condition spiritually that it is a pleasure to be around them. I think that Bd. Meinwerk himself might approve of the children's conduct—at least more than he would have last year, say. Everything is different these days. If a grown person starts to say something he is encouraged to finish the sentence and if a child interrupts him he is told to shut up. If they start making horrible sounds they are checked. If you ask them to empty a garbage can they will actually do it. I do so hope no new theories come along. It is so divine this year!

Jacques Maritain's sister in law, Vera, has followed in his foot-steps with a coronary thrombosis and he is, he says, a prisoner. One can't even telephone him for fear of disturbing Vera. He summoned me by telegram last Saturday and I hot-footed it over. He was curious to know how my novel had been received and when I told him that with the exception of a few discerning critics, it had been dismissed as a *roman à clef*, his face lit up. "Ah," says he, "that is a good sign." He added that it was "a good experience for me."

Bill Elliott [at Harvard] is getting, or trying to get a lot more work out of Allen than Allen bargained for in his directorship of the foreign seminar. Allen comes down this weekend to try to put the buying of the house through. If all goes well we may move in Thursday.

Love for all of you.

Flannery, better address me at 54 Hodge till further notice.

Caroline Gordon to Flannery O'Connor

Undated [July 1956]
The Sabine Close—after another poet. He had a farm
but this place is as near a farm as folks like us can get.
145 Ewing Street
Princeton, NJ

We have got our house—if possession is nine tenths of the law. That
is to say, we are moved in and fairly straight. There are still papers to be
signed and some more money to be raked up—but we are IN!

It is the most divine little old fashioned house [that] ever was and exactly suited to our ages and conditions of servitude. We like every room in
it but we both like the garden best of all. The house is flush with the street,
which is good, as it leaves all the land in the back. There is a little terrace
at the back of [the] house, half-enclosed by ancient lilacs, syringas and the
like, which gives on a long sweep of greensward, on which one can still see
the marks of the furrow—as Pleasant Phlox, our part time gardener complains. At the end of the stretch of lawn there is a grove of young locusts
dominated by two huge willow trees. All around us ranch houses spring
up again. The "Shopping Centre," a village in itself, is two blocks away, but
when you sit on the terrace and watch the rabbits cropping the lawn you
can have the illusion that you are in the country—which is as much as
people like us can ask for in this day and time.

Poor Allen had to tear himself away day before yesterday and go to
Harvard where he is trying to turn an honest penny by conducting a foreign seminar. He hopes to get back here by August fifteenth.

I hope to get started on my book on *How to Read a Novel* before that
time—but the garden is mighty tempting. One thing about the garden, it
has held me up on painting, which was rapidly becoming a vice with me.
Have you yet had an idea wherewith to fill that canvas? My trouble is that
I have too many ideas for pictures.

My last venture is a Virgin and a Lion and Unicorn in a flowery mead.
The whole thing—I now see—is an illustration of a dream I had, in which
I came out of my rather gloomy house onto a path that was brightly illuminated. I told myself that I would just nip along the path till I got to
some dark place but it wound around back of the house and as I proceeded
along it I saw that it was more and more brightly illuminated all the time.

The path ascends a hill in a kind of spiral and the Virgin and Lion and Unicorn form a group halfway up. The woods below them are mighty dark and an owl—symbol of hersey (I don't mean John Hersey!) sits in the window of my house. . . . I sometimes think I'd get farther in my painting if I weren't so ambitious. I'll tackle anything!

By the way, please send me that essay—to 145 Ewing. I aim to incorporate part of it into this book. If you've already sent it to Dulce Domum it's all right. I'll be watching out for it—Mrs. Wood has a block about mail, and letters land in strange places there.

My only companion while Allen is away is a two months old kitten hight Toughie. He has already been mauled by two dogs and spent a night in the cat jail—arrested by the police for attacking a Boxer. But his third mishap was, in a way, the most frightening. I was roused around four o'clock by frightful howls and yowls and rushed down to the kitchen where I saw a huge yellow tom-cat plastered against the top of the screen door while Jennie, the Irish setter, leaped at him. He had evidently come in—through the cellar steps—with the intention of killing Toughie. I only hope he got a good lesson. I guess he would have finished Toughie if Jennie hadn't nobly protected her cats. She owed Toughie something as it was she who helped mauled him—the signal was a wicked glance between her and a neighbor dog, after which they both fell on Toughie and bit hell out of him. A large blue tom-cat now has fell designs on Toughie. He creeps out of the little wood that surrounds this close and comes right up to the screen door to menace him. Keeps me on the *qui vive* and is doubtless a good thing, or I might get too relaxed as I sit on the terrace and contemplate the rabbits on the far end of the lawn.

I have *got* to get to work on that book. Do write and let me know how things are going with you. Some time before Maurice Coindreau* gets back in the fall will you send me that review I wrote of your book in the *NY Times*. That is, if you still have it. I can't lay my hand on it. I want to expand it for that introduction. Revise it, too, of course. If you have any suggestions for said revision, I'd be glad to have them.

Do you ever see BOOKS ON TRIAL put out by the Thomas More Association? I sold them an article, written originally for Mlle [*Mademoiselle*], which Mlle did *not* like, called grandeloquently "How

---

* French translator of *Wise Blood*.

I Learned to Write Novels." (I should have called it "How *I* Learned to Write Novels.") Anyhow, their standards seem higher than R.C. literary standards are ordinarily.

One of the delights of this house is that we have Jacques Maritain for a neighbor. His sister-in-law has had a coronary thrombosis and as a result he is, as he says, a "prisoner." You can't even telephone him for fear of waking Vera who has come very near dying, in fact. Jacques summoned me by telegram the other day and I had a brief visit with them just before they left for Easthampton for the summer. Jacques looked better that he did a year ago, after his own coronary, but he complains that he has lost his *élan*, having been brought to a full stop on his book on moral philosophy when Vera fell ill. However, he said he thought that he would get it back "beside the sea."
[postscript]

One reason the typing is so awful is that Caroline ruined this typewriter. She says, "Grandma, you ought not to a let me got at it. You should a shut it up. Okay?" I said, "Nokay."

≈ That fall, Gordon worked on *How to Read a Novel*. O'Connor revised "A View of the Woods" and sent it to Gordon. When O'Connor realized her character (Mary Fortune) had quoted the same Bible verse as one of Gordon's characters from "Summer Dust," O'Connor wondered if she should change it: "Caroline has read the story and didn't mention it," O'Connor noticed.

Gordon was not merely distracted. As Nancylee Novell Jonza has explained, when Allen Tate traveled to India on a Fulbright lectureship that October, Gordon "found herself facing two years of accumulated bills Allen had forgotten to tell her about." At the same time, Tate neglected to deposit his paychecks in their shared bank account, "as promised." Gordon biographers Jonza and Ann Waldron have documented in detail how furious and frightened Gordon felt. Gordon put aside her book (and missed her December deadline), "took every job offered her," and borrowed money from friends.

By December, O'Connor heard that Gordon and Tate had separated. "I feel awfully sorry for Caroline, to have reached the age of 60 and have a husband who flits," O'Connor wrote to Betty Hester, "not that I don't doubt but what she is hard to live with and gives him cause to want to do that." While Lon Cheney blamed Allen's behavior, O'Connor saw alcohol as the problem for both Gordon and Tate: "Lord knows it creates a terrible waste, waste of time, waste of talent, waste of spiritual energy, waste of existence. It must come from some misunderstanding about the nearness of God. You get drunk when you aren't conscious that God is immediately present."

The new year arrived. O'Connor's "Greenleaf" won the 1957 O. Henry Prize. Her story "The Life You Save May Be Your Own" was adapted for a February 1957 episode of CBS's *Schlitz Playhouse of Stars* and featured Gene Kelly. In May, O'Connor received $1,000 from the National Institute of Arts and Letters.

That spring, Gordon taught four classes at three different schools. She finally completed her book in June 1957.

O'Connor asked the Cheneys that June, "Does anybody ever hear from Caroline?"

Gordon's *How to Read a Novel* was released that fall by Viking. O'Connor thought the title misrepresented the contents: it was a book more useful for writers than readers. Still, O'Connor recommended the book to others and credited Gordon's intellect: "Whenever I finish a story I send it to Caroline before I consider myself really through with it. She's taught me more than anybody."

Flannery O'Connor, unpublished book review of *How to Read a Novel* by Caroline Gordon

By now all are familiar with the famous ad found in a diocesan paper: "Let a Catholic do your termite work." In connection with literature, which is almost as dangerous as termites, this fraternal attitude abounds. Miss Gordon's book can therefore be recommended on the grounds that it is a Catholic who is writing. It would be painful to leave it at this.

As Miss Gordon points out, it requires a certain humility to read a novel; and perhaps also it requires a certain humility to read a book called *How to Read a Novel*, for everyone thinks novel-reading well within his competence. This book should satisfy any reader that it is not; and it can be particularly recommended for Catholics because Catholic groups are often vocal on the subject of "bad" literature, without knowing "good" literature when they see it. To pronounce judgement on a novel, one must first be able to read it. The suspicion with which the average Catholic approaches this particular art form is lessened only if the label Catholic can be applied to it in some way. Those moral principles which save us from counting ourselves among the admirers of such works as *Peyton Place* seldom operate in more subtle cases of corruption. We are liable to praise prose as poor, structure as weak, and psychology as dishonest if only the characters involved live, or at least die, according to the precepts of the Church. This is a cultural deficiency but it implies and it fosters a lack of moral insight.

No one will go through Miss Gordon's book and begin forthwith to read adequately, but he will begin to read more slowly and some of the fiction which satisfied him before will no longer do so. This book, along with Maritain's *Art and Scholasticism*, should be studied by any Catholic group making public pronouncements about literature.

~ At the end of the year, O'Connor told Gordon about a gift she had received from her cousin, Katie Semmes: a pilgrimage to Lourdes and Rome for the following spring. "I forsee a battalion of fortress-footed Catholic females herded from holy place to holy place by the Rev. McNamara to the point of holy exhaustion," O'Connor wrote to the Fitzgeralds.

She also sent Gordon a new story, "The Enduring Chill."

Flannery O'Connor to Caroline Gordon

10 December 1957

I'm busy with the Holy Ghost. He is going to be a waterstain—very obvious but the only thing possible. I also have a fine visitor for Asbury to liven him up slightly. I'm highly obliged for your thoughts on this ["The Enduring Chill"] and I am making the most of them. When I get this finished I'd like you to see it again because it is already much improved—but I notice my stories get longer and longer and I'm afraid this one may be too long. If I've finished with it, I'd like to send it to the Cheneys for a Christmas card and will hope that you might have time to look at it there. If not, I'll send it to you after Christmas . . .

I had counted on getting to the Cheneys for the weekend of the 20th, but I have lately been getting dizzy because I am taking a new medicine and have got an overdose of it. So I figure I'll do my staggering around at home. It takes some time for the dose to get regulated. Every time something new is invented I get in on the ground floor with it. There have been five improvements in the medicine in the 7 years I've had the lupus, and they are all great improvements.

A friend of mine at Wesleyan, a Dr. [Thomas] Gossett, wrote me that he and his wife had just come from the Modern Language Asso. convention in Knoxville or somewhere and had heard Willard Thorpe read a paper on the grotesque in Southern literature. He (Thorpe) allowed as how the roots of it were in antebellum Southern writings but that the grotesque you met with in Southern writing today was something else and has serious implications which the other didn't approach. He said he had no satisfactory explanation for the change. The Gossetts decided the reason he didn't was because he doesn't know enough theology. I seem to remember that he wrote one of the better reviews of *The Malefactors*, but I may be mixed up on the name.

You are more sanguine about this pilgrimage than I am. It's not that I'd rather be a tourist; I'd rather stay at home. You are good to ask us to stop by Princeton, but knowing the difficulties of getting anywhere, I doubt we could engineer it. I envy you that energy you have. I wish you would come to see us. We have a lovely place—as evidenced by my reluctance to leave it for 17 days of Holy Culture & Pious Exhaustion. Pray that the Lord will (gently) improve my attitude so I can at least endure it.

Cheers, thanks, love and Merry Christmas to you & Allen.

⤝ Gordon and Tate spent Christmas that year in Smyrna, Tennessee, with the Cheneys—one more attempt at reconciliation. O'Connor missed the gathering but sent the latest draft of "The Enduring Chill." Her friends read the story aloud in her absence and telephoned O'Connor on Christmas Day. The advice that follows summarizes their discussion at Christmas. O'Connor would share the letters critiquing "The Enduring Chill" with Betty Hester the following year, saying, "I think that if you study these you may learn as much as I have learned writing this story. I have learned more on this one than on any in a long time, merely because she has had patience with me. I have a few instincts but she has a few more plus thirty more years of experience."

Caroline Gordon to Flannery O'Connor

Undated [December 1957]
Comment on original and first revision:
(1) The talk between Asbury and the negroes struck everybody as brilliant . . . They all thought it was a shade longer than it needed be . . . that being prolonged as it was smacked of virtuosity . . . the consensus of opinion was that the cutting of one exchange—and only one—would be a good thing.

(2) The folks didn't know whether Asbury was going to live or die. They were unanimous on this, so I guess this revision you've done was necessary. I think the revision makes it plain that he is going to live, with the enduring chill, instead of the fiery death he has looked forward to.

(First revision subsequent to conversation via phone on Xmas day . . . . to take care of criticism from AT [Allen Tate] that there was no mention of the HG [Holy Ghost] in the beginning of the story . . . and to clear some confusion over whether Asbury was to live or die. First revision is considered above and as follows.)

(3) I find that it is the common practise of the masters to support the structure of a story by, as it were, three pillars. That is, the theme is stated at the beginning of the story, stated again in the middle and again at the end.

In this revision you state your theme but too abruptly, I think. We are not prepared for Asbury to talk about the Holy Ghost. I think that here you ought to state your theme in such a way that the reader will take it unconsciously . . . as Hemingway does in *A Farewell to Arms*: "The leaves fell early that year" . . . ergo . . . my love died young. Or as I did without in the least realizing what I was doing in "The Last Day in the Field": "That was the year when the leaves stayed green so long"; it is the story of an old man whose spirit for adventure outlived his bodily capacity for it.

In the hope of getting over my point I shall be specific here. I think that the sentence "The Holy Spirit was at last going to descend on the old lady but with ice instead of fire" is not only too abrupt but in this case is too overt. We can't take it in. I think what you need is what [Ford Madox] Ford called a *progression d'effet*. That is, this idea ought to be introduced but in some form of variation so that we won't recognize till the *effet* has progressed a little further [than] just what we've been handed. On the other hand, we ought to recognize sub-consciously that we've been handed something. This means, I think, that you'll have to take more time on this.

And here I can only say what I'd do if it were my story—I don't think I'd have the nerve to tackle it—but if I were tackling it I'd do something like this:

His mother, at the age of sixty, was going to be introduced to reality and he supposed that if the experience didn't kill her it would assist her in the process of growing up. He stepped down and greeted her. (I think 'gleeful leer' is too violent here.)

Here I want to remind you of something. Anything that's important usually belongs in a sentence by itself. He greeted her. She kissed him, gripping his elbow possessively. His irritation returned tenfold. You have too many things in one sentence here. I'd split them up into several sentences.

I'd also split up the first *progression d'effet*. The first step would be his thinking that at the age of sixty she was going to be introduced to reality. I'm not sure where the next step would come but I'm not sure either that you can get away with shifting your viewpoint to the mother before you can have the son's viewpoint firmly established. That rather jolts me each time I read it. Anyhow, soon after Asbury is established in the car I think he ought to go into the second step of the *progression d'effet*. He ought perhaps to have some mental image which is a preparation for the introduction of the HG and I think his clinical observation of his own imaginative processes will also be a part of the preparation. If you go at this preparation slowly enough the reader will unconsciously realize that something is being prepared for and will be curious to know what it is.

I think that on page 26 you have an opportunity to insert the "middle pillar" which will support your fictional structure.

The HG is introduced here in the middle of a paragraph. When you introduce something important you blur its effect unless you end a paragraph with it. (Same principle as putting important things into a 'periodic' instead of a 'loose' sentence.)

Suppose you broke this paragraph up and ended it with: "Ask God to send the Holy Ghost."

I think that Asbury ought to respond in some way here to mention the HG even if it's only repeating what the priest has said: "The Holy Ghost?" I'm in rather deep waters here but what I'm trying to say is that this paragraph ought to go more like this:

Priest: . . . . .
Asbury: . . . . .
Priest: . . . . .
Asbury: . . . . .

instead of having the priest say it all in such a rush that we can't take it in.

I think this "middle pillar" is very important in the structure of the story. Asbury ought to make some kind of response here which will prepare us for his recognition of the HG upon him.

I come now to the end which you have certainly improved. But I have a few more remarks to make on that.

"He sat up and stared around him and saw that the room was the same."

You have established his viewpoint. When you say that he "saw" that the room was the same you interpose a veil between the spectator and the event. Why not record the fact that the room was the same? Or rather, specify so that the reader will conclude that it is the same: "the dresser still stood between the two west windows . . ." I think that here you handle too many ideas in one sentence . . . several times. I'd say, "Instead of dying, knowing he was going to live, knowing nothing." Anything as tremendous as that realization does not belong in a subordinate clause. It needs a sentence to itself.

Every time I read the sentence "with ice instead of fire" I have the same reaction. I do not like it. I think it is because the phrase is too vague. As I said in my other letter, how is the HG going to bring this ice—in a bucket to chill champagne or as the surface of a pond? I think you have got to say the same thing some other way. "A warm ripple across a deeper sea of cold" seems to me on the right track. Perhaps you could develop that notion further. The chill creeping up but I do not believe you can get away with the flat-footed statement that the HG is coming with ice instead of fire. Could there be a *progression d'effet* here? That is, could he have a sort of vision of the HG (not named but foreshadowed) as whirling down with flames in the beginning of the story, and in the conversation with the doctor a re-evocation of this image (with some change) and finally, at the end, the dramatization of the flames giving way to the enduring chill.

Here is another idea that has popped into my head . . . May be nothing to it. This story, in a way, lacked in its first version a "peripety," the walking around, the adventitious happening, unforeseen by the characters which often resolves a situation. The priest furnishes this peripety but it may be that he has to be prepared for, too. Suppose Asbury has a friend in New York who has said the same thing to him that the priest is going to say . . . in different terms, but terms that will prepare us for what the priest says.

A [Allen Tate] thinks that your stuff is terrific but he says that he thinks that you are sometimes "too flat-footed" in going about getting your

effects. He thinks that this is the case here. In this story you ought to cap-
ture the ineffable. Ergo, the fact that the HG is ineffable ought to be foreshadowed in the beginning of the story.

~ O'Connor sent a revision of "The Enduring Chill" to the Cheneys; Lon
forwarded the new pages to Gordon. Gordon's response seems to be a contin-
uation of her previous letter—the ellipses that begin the letter are Gordon's.

Caroline Gordon to Flannery O'Connor

[21 January 1958]
    Comment and analysis 2nd revision . . . written 1–21–58 . . . and that
brings me to a subject that has been much on my mind: your story. To
begin with, I feel like a fool when I criticize your stories. I think you are a
genius . . . I might as well come out with it. I also think you are one of the
most original writers now practicing. It really seems presumptuous for me
to offer you suggestions. But you have asked for them and since you have
more talent and more humility than most of the young people who ask for
my criticism I shall just set forth my notions as they come into my head.
    A [Allen] has compressed into one sentence everything I can offer in crit-
icism of this story. He said it was "too flat-footed." Perhaps the best thing I
can do is to try to amplify what he says. It is that old business of the far blue
peaks of Helicon always being visible on the horizon. That, Logan Pearsall
Smith says, is the secret of a fine prose style. [T. S.] Eliot says: "Stetson,
Stetson, you who were with me in the ships at Mylae." Stetson is a fellow
who to the unperceptive eye is not at all heroic. "Stetson" is a flat-footed
name. Fellow might be from Texas. All right, but he is spiritually of the
company of heroes. The lesson you, I think, need to learn as a prose stylist,
is contained in Eliot's *Sweeney Agonistes*, "Ape-neck Sweeney" a man who
is seemingly not far removed from the ape. The scene is a low café. Among
the people present are two prostitutes. One of them tries to solicit a man,
"a man who is not much above Sweeney," a "silent vertebrate in brown," he
says, in effect, nothing doing to the prostitute, "declines the gambit, pleads
fatigue" then goes outside and looks back in the room through the window: "branches of wisteria circumscribe a golden grin." The poem begins
with a hero who is as low as you can find them, but, since it is to conclude
with the identification of this creature with the Greek hero Agamemnon,

there is a gradual sort of climbing up in the elevation of the style. "Branches of wisteria circumscribe a golden grin" is one of those intermediate passages. The use of the Latin derived word "circumscribed" elevates the style a little in preparation for the magnificent climax. Eliot keeps bringing the section back to its low level, too: "The person in the Spanish cape yawns and sits on Sweeney's knees." Then comes another intermediary passage which again elevates: "The landlord converses with someone indistinct, apart" is a preparation for a sudden upward climbing up: "The nightingales are singing in the convent of the Sacred Heart" . . . . then comes the magnificent climax which identifying this scene in a low café, says, in effect, that human nature is always and ever has been the same: "And sang within the bloody wood when Agamemnon cried aloud, And let their liquid siftings fall to stain the stiff dishonored shroud."

You will note how he links the hero, Agamemnon, with the ape-like Sweeney and the prostitutes, by the emphasis on nature. The nightingales are singing now and sang then. As [Gerard Manley] Hopkins says, "for all this, Nature is never spent . . ." But the thing I want you to concentrate on is Eliot's see-sawing back and forth between the low and the elevated. On his horizons the far blue peaks of Helicon . . . the Greeks thought the Gods lived there. . . . Always visible.

We come—blunderingly—to a consideration of your immediate problem. You have two chief difficulties, I think. The first (how many times have I said this?) is that being the age you are [you] did not have the kind of education—a classical education—which would best serve your talents. The second is that you're doing something that hasn't been done before, something so new, so original that you have to cut your own way through the underbrush.

If I read your work aright you are viewing the rural South through the eyes of Roman Catholicism. Nobody else has done this. It is a tremendous feat and God knows you are doing the thing that most needs to be done.

But you are at times in danger of succumbing to what [poet and literary critic] Yvor Winters calls "The Fallacy of Imitative Form." You'll find what he says quoted in my last book (HTRAN) [How to Read a Novel]. The artist's task is to impose form on matter. Even if he is dealing with the formless, his work must not reflect formlessness.

People confuse your work with that of Carson McCullers, Truman Capote, Tenn. Wms., et al. because I think these writers portray

characters who are grotesque, misshapen, perverted . . . perhaps because they themselves are perverted. But your people are grotesque,
misshapen, perverted and also flat-footed because, I take it, they have
been deprived of the blood of Christ for so long. Your subject is men in
contact or in pursuit of the ineffable—notably in this last story. But your
style lacks a dimension necessary for the handling of such a subject. You
go out with nets to catch the wind but you go forth too flat-footedly
and your net doesn't have enough silken fibres. The thing you want slips
through if the net is too coarse.

Another way of saying it may be that you are too modest. You have
learned well the lesson that the author must keep himself . . . off the scene if
his characters are to have free play but we must remember that the characters in a story don't always know what is going on. You try to tell Asbury's
adventures with the HG entirely through Asbury's consciousness but in
a story like this a superior intelligence to his ought to be guiding, maneu-
vering the reader to the place where he, the reader, will see what you, the
author want him to see.

Consider the way Faulkner handles this problem, unconsciously, I feel
sure. He is not an avowed Christian. In fact, A Fable fails I think because
of his ignorance of theology . . . a fiction writer isn't bound to use theology
but if he does he's got to be sound on it, just as much as if he were dealing
with the intricacies of plumbing or molecular physics. But you've heard
me say that before. Back to F . . .

Faulkner's characters are rural like yours, talk the same way. (Your ear is
perhaps a little subtler than his.) But you both render faithfully the common speech. But almost any paragraph that Faulkner writes has a dimension which your work (in general) lacks. Take this passage [from Spotted
Horses]:

"That's a fact," Ratliff said. "A fellow can dodge a Snopes if he just starts lively
enough. In fact, I don't believe he would have to pass more than two folks before he would have another victim intervened betwixt them. You folks ain't
going [to buy] them things sho enough, are you?" Nobody answered. They
sat on the steps, their backs against the veranda posts, or on the railing itself.
Only Ratliff and Quick sat in chairs, so that to them the others were black sil-
houettes against the dreaming lambence of the moonlight beyond the veranda.
The peach tree across the road opposite was now in full and frosty bloom,
the twigs and branches springing not outward from the limbs but standing

motionless and perpendicular above the horizontal boughs like the separate
and upstreaming hair of a drowned woman, sleeping upon the uttermost floor
of the windless and tideless sea. ———end of quote.

That passage is, perhaps, a thought over-written. Faulkner, who doesn't
know with his conscious mind what you were brought up knowing, that
there is only one plot; the Scheme of Redemption, and every other plot
that is worth a damn is a splinter off of it. Faulkner, who doesn't apprehend
this, the basic fact of fiction, consciously, yet knows it unconsciously, and
continually puts it into practice. (Any great fiction writer has apprehended
the Christian archetypal symbol, whether he knows them by name or
not—witness James.) Faulkner, not knowing consciously what you know
consciously, is inclined to beat his breast and howl and moan a bit—his
superior intelligence is one who directs us with screams and yells at times.
But he is nevertheless always on the job. Almost every paragraph he writes
emphasizes the fact that man is both animal and spiritual. The paragraph
I've quoted starts off mighty flat-footed but climbs pretty high—in fact to
the archetypal—by the time he's got to the end.

Notice, too, how he takes time to make his high-falutin effect. You,
where such an effect is needed, sometimes squeeze out one sentence that
is in a higher key than the rest and let it go at that. As a rule, one sentence
won't do the trick. It isn't enough to establish a mood.

"'He must have drunk some unpasteurized milk up there,' his mother
said softly" is fine, but it ought to be followed by something that contrasts
with it, a paragraph that reminds us that man—even if he has undulant
fever—also has an immortal soul. Asbury, about to face the HG, is as flat-
footed as his mother. You say that "the red sun was about to slip behind
the tree line as if it had temporary business in the woods." Even the sun,
powerful and mysterious symbol of Christ, goes about its business flat-
footedly. When you ascribe to it concerns like those of a human being you,
as it were, cut it down to human size and lose its value as a symbol. Also
you give this effect one sentence. It isn't enough. Asbury ought to stare out
on something pretty terrific before he turns back to face his ceiling and the
HG descending from that particular ceiling.

But the note of the ineffable, the symbolic, can't be struck suddenly at
the end. It ought to be prepared for from the beginning. This note of the
archetypal, ineffable—call it what you will—ought to be what Ford called

un progression d'effet. That is, it ought to have its own progression through the story, ought to be twined into the action like one of the threads that makes up the whole strand and, therefore, ought to have its own progression or progress.

You do the same thing at the beginning of the story that you do at the end. One grudging sentence that indicates a mention of other than the consciousness of Asbury: "The sky was a chill grey and a placid looking sun was rising beyond the black woods that surrounded Timberboro." Fine—so far as it goes, but it takes more than that to make the reader feel what you want him to feel.

Do you *have* to start your story with a subordinate clause? I do so dislike that. Why not "Asbury's train stopped so that he could get off . . ."?

There is one thing that I am certain. Ober Tuttle will not do. We have enough flatfooted characters in this story now. Another one is the last thing that's needed. I think you want a young man who contrasts with Asbury's background, who is everything that Mary George and the people around home are not. Somebody who pleases Asbury by the very fact that he is exotic. New York, God knows, is full of such young men. I wish you knew a Fr. Wiegel whom Allen admires very much. Fr. W., evidently sound in the faith, is yet an expert on Zen Buddhism, Hindu philosophies and what have you and what have you. One of my students at the New School complained that a certain teacher's course was just a course in Zen Buddhism, said teacher being hipped on it at present. My old friend Estlen Cummings [E. E. Cummings], maintains that he is a Taoist, a follower of Lao-Tse. Even in my pre-Christian days I used to wonder how he went about practising his religion. But there actually are in these benighted parts temples to strange gods—in New Brunswick a Buddhist temple was opened not too long ago with appropriated ceremonies. Wystan Auden used to fool around with this sort of thing before he reformed. Aldous Huxley still does.

God knows I don't want to poke my nose into your story any more than I already have but I'd be glad to help any way I could with research. The New York telephone book has an imposing list of temples to strange gods which I'll gladly copy in case one of them might be of use.

Every Monday when I lecture at the New School I ride up in the elevator with sari-clad females, bearded types who, I feel sure, lecture on Yoga or Vedanta—you can find every kind of person in that elevator.

And here I am going to do something that is dangerous but since I am doing it with good will, let us hope no ill will come of it. Here I plunge in where angels fear to tread—right into the action of your story.

Suppose that Asbury had a friend with a more glamorous name than Ober Tuttle, one of those young men who work in banks or department stores or GE offices by day and take courses at the New School by night. All my students are of this type. Suppose Asbury's friend attended a course on Yoga and Vedanta philosophy, taught by somebody with a name like Sechim Majumdar. (Beware: that's a real name.) Suppose that Asbury's friend is possessed of a certain amount of missionary zeal and one evening pays four dollars and a half (that's what a single session costs) so that Asbury may have a chance to hear Sechim What's His Name on The Vedanta.

I think you need in this story what Aristotle called "a peripety," the un-foreseen incident which brings about a solution and yet springs out of what has gone before. Suppose that, as very well might be, one of the students in this class is a sort of Fr. Wiegel, a young priest whose superiors have al-lowed him to take this course. They do this thing all the time—I had a col-ored Franciscan monk taking my novel course at Columbia. Suppose this priest were dark and saturnine—in short, Asbury's idea of what a Jesuit should be. Suppose—as happened the other night in my class—the stu-dents repaired to somebody's apartment and had a bull session. The priest would certainly maintain a certain reserve since he knows something that the lecturer doesn't know. Asbury, misinterpreting this reserve, might call for a Jesuit—and get one who seems very different but who, in the end, is the same kind of fellow. You would then have a perfectly credible and operative peripety.

There might well be at this gathering—perhaps at his friend's apart-ment—the other people who, in a way, would stress the note of the exotic. I dined the other night with a little Indian girl who I think I'd shove in this story if it were mine. She did not want to marry the young man her family wanted her to so she wrote to every college in the United States and finally got a scholarship to Gustavus Adolphus College in Minnesota whither she repaired with her saris and sashes—had to wear storm boots all winter and was glad to flee Gustavus Adolphus for New York. She works in the Oriental department at Macy's—or did she work there and now has a job at the United Nations? Anyhow, she is the most aggressive, pushing vulgar young woman I ever encountered. You should have seen Allen's face when she forced on him a scrap book containing not only pictures of herself, in sari and storm boots, but also some of her poems! Her name is Sita Something and she calls my friend who is her reluctant hostess here in Princeton on weekends "Mom" and her husband "Pop." Pop is a far flung business man and her father is one of his clients is how she came into their lives. She speaks English fluently and a half other dozen languages as I recall. The point I am trying to make is that New York and other places are full of people fooling around the fringes of religion. It seems to me that if Asbury got in with such a group you'd have a better preparation for his final encounter with the Jesuit.

If I were doing it I'd have Fr. Whatever His Name in New York main-tain a courteous impenetrability that would appeal to Asbury as sort of defining the limits of the kind of world he always thought he belonged in. Fr. Whatever His name might answer questions as if from a book, always courteously, but being a trifle remote—a remoteness which comes from not taking this course the way the others do.

. . . . *finis pertinencies* in 2nd epistle.

⌇ Gordon received the next draft of "The Enduring Chill" and wrote again to O'Connor. Gordon defends the "martial spirit" of this critique by telling O'Connor in the following letter, "If you were less stout-hearted and less talented I wouldn't dare to say the things I am saying to you."

Caroline Gordon to Flannery O'Connor

26 January 1958

Comment and analysis 3rd revision:

What facility you have! I'm amazed at the way you've taken my suggestion and built it up into a convincing scene. I think that bringing people of this kind into the action does a lot for the story structurally. Association with people who are not like the people at home helps to explain his horror of dying at home.

The priest seems fine, too—a splendid contrast for Fr. Finn, just what Fr. Finn needed to bring him out in all his full bloom!

And now I come up with another admonishment, being, as you know, never satisfied. This is, really, a comment on your prose style in general but I will try to show what I mean by using some sentences from this story as examples.

I suppose that in common with everybody of your generation, you were brought up to feel that any concern you might have with grammar took place long ago and is now no concern of yours. But I think reflection on the parts of speech and their function is helpful for any of us at any time.

Do you, for instance, ever reflect on the respective nature of the "loose" and the "periodic" sentences and the differences in their functions?

In a strong prose style the periodic sentence—the sentence which saves its punch for the end—predominates. There is a psychological basis for this. You put the thing you want the reader to remember last.

"While Goets had listened, enthralled . . . strictly reserved interest" is a "loose" sentence—it trails off. The important thing, the fact that Asbury's gaze had rested on a priest, is buried in the middle of the sentence. The reader, the laziest and stupidest of God's creatures, is not going to dig it out but will carry a blurred impression away from the reading. If I were writing this sentence I'd automatically end it on the word "priest."

You make this mistake several times in the story, and make another mistake which is allied to it. Anything that is important ought to have a sentence all to itself. Asbury's approaching death is the most important thing in this story. You introduce it in a subordinate clause. It ought to have a sentence all to itself.

I think that the passage you have interpolated in the first paragraph helps a lot but I think you have crowded your effects too much here. If I were writing this passage I would emphasize its importance by breaking it up into several—perhaps three—sentences instead of crowding a lot of ideas into one sentence.

I would beware of the word "such." It is trivial.

"Single block of one story brick and wooden shacks" *sounds* ugly. (Of course they *are* ugly.) You are crowding things here again. The important thing is that the sun casts a strange light on these structures. If you try to crowd information you want the reader to have—that the town consisted of a single block—into this sentence you run the risk of minimizing the importance of your strange light. You cannot handle but one idea in a sentence. That idea ought to be presented in the joining of the subject and the predicate. Anything else in that sentence ought to be subordinated— in the form of subordinate clauses.

I'd break this passage up into several sentences: "Asbury felt that he was about to witness a majestic transformation. The flat wooden roofs might at any moment turn into the mounting peaks of some exotic temple." I'm not crazy about "mounting peaks." Can a temple have peaks?

Similarly, he "gazed after the aluminum speck disappearing into the woods. It seemed to him that his last connection with a larger world was vanishing forever" would be better, I think, when putting it all into one sentence.

I'd break "The real world was behind him now . . . a death by torture" into three sentences. Each idea here is important enough to have a sentence to itself.

This sounds awfully elementary but since people are no longer forced to learn these things in infancy—by the perusal of Caesar's *Gallic Wars* or Xenophon's *Anabasis*, etc.—they don't always learn them.

Ernest Hemingway has won a good deal of fame and fortune by a complete mastery of the principle I have been setting forth. His style is founded on it. He cannot write the long complicated sentence which is the glory of Joyce's style, but he never has two ideas fighting each other in one sentence. The structure of his style is relatively simple. When he needs a complicated sentence he forms it by joining two of his short periodic sentences together. It works—for him. He doesn't tackle any very compli- cated or elevated theme. His style is suited to his subject matter.

I suspect you are unconsciously following his example of late. You have got to the point where the flatfooted simple sentence won't always serve. Instead of writing another kind of sentence you take several of your flat- footed sentences and link them up. You do that quite often in this story.

But you are after bigger game than Ernest, the biggest game there is in this particular story. There ought, in this story, to be some sentences, indeed passages, which show forth the grandeur of your theme and the height of your aspirations. The structure of your story ought to be antiph- onal. We ought to have throughout a contrast between Asbury's present situation and his imminent fate—a fate which is pretty grand, for all his horror of it. To have the HG descend upon you in any form makes a hero of you. Asbury is just a boy from Georgia, but he is made in the image of God and will shortly confront eternity. If the HG is to descend upon him—in whatever form—in the end that fact ought to be foreshadowed in the beginning. We will sympathize with his sufferings more keenly if his heroism is foreshadowed from the start.

In the first version, as I recall, you foreshadowed the fact that his spirit had a wider horizon than his mother's or his sister's by one grudging sentence about a red sun. One sentence! You can't turn around on a dime. One sentence like that won't create the effect that is needed here. You have improved the story enormously in your revisions. Enormously.

What I have to say further is about your style in general. This takes me back to first principles—principles which I can name outright to you but which I have to approach cautiously with my secular pupils. There is only one plot, The Scheme of Redemption. All other plots, if they are any good, are splinters off this basic plot. There is only one author: The HG. If He condescends to speak at times through a well-constructed detective story, which I think he does, he certainly will condescend to speak often through FO'C. Your chief weakness as a writer seems to be a failure to admit the august nature of your inspiration. You speak almost always like FO'C. That is fine. You have the best ear of anybody in the trade for the rhythms of colloquial speech. In this particular story what the negroes say in their last conversation with Asbury is exquisitely rendered. I don't know anybody else who could have brought that off. Red [Robert Penn] Warren couldn't. Andrew Lytle couldn't. Their ears are not delicately enough attuned and they are always forcing things, too. But you have this enormous advantage: what Yeats called the primitive ear. He had it, too and got a lot out of it.

But you have another kind of ear, one that is attuned to—shall we say the music of the spheres? It is attuned to that music or you would not choose the subjects you choose. The nature of your subject—its immensity, its infinity—ought to be reflected in your style—antiphonally. Asbury, conversing with his mother, his sister, the negro hands, ought to speak down to earth, flat sentences. But he ought to take a more elevated tone when communing with his soul—in which presumably God may dwell. If he did you would have a wonderful contrast in tones—an antiphonal effect—which would reinforce our dramatic effects.

[Edwin] Muir, who is himself a considerable stylist, gives an illustration of what I am trying to say in his translation of Kafka's "[The] Hunter

Gracchus." The action of the story is recounted in flat down to earth narrative. The denouement is, however, foreshadowed in the first paragraph which is like a painting by a primitive painter . . . a window seems to open into the blue distance of infinity. The heroism of which the human soul is capable is implied by the fact that a hero is flourishing a sword on high on a monument—still flourishing it even if a man uses the monument only to rest in its shadow while he reads a newspaper. Everything is kept keyed down to the concrete till the last sentence which carries the notion of infinity in its very cadence: "My ship has no rudder, and is driven by the wind that blows in the undermost regions of death."

Every time I read your last sentence in your story I balk. I balk on the phrase "with ice, instead of fire." It is vague, inexact. This magnificent climax to which you have built up so well is not the place for careless inexact phrasing. You cannot say that the HG is coming with ice instead of fire. The phrase is colloquial . . . If I am having a party and don't have enough ice cubes I can say properly, "The Johnsons are coming, with ice" but you are talking about the HG and your diction and the construction of your sentences ought to reflect, as far as is humanly possible, the enormity of his presence. Couldn't you say "enveloped in ice instead of flames"? And couldn't you give Asbury and the HG each a sentence to himself? "He blanched in recognition. But the HG, enveloped in ice instead of fire, continued, implacable, to descend."

I am very grateful for the word "implacable" and for the hard cutting off sound in the word "descend." They do a lot to get the idea across. I think it is fine to end on the word "descend." Your instinct is certainly right here. It betrays you only in allowing you to use careless, almost colloquial phrasing at a high moment.

In my day we diagrammed sentences. This is what we call a compound sentence: a sentence made up of two or more equal and coordinate clauses.

The sun rose with power and the fog dispersed

is what [John] Nesfield gives as an example of a compound sentence. I don't think that a compound sentence is what you need here. Asbury's blanching and the HG's descending are not ideas of equal importance. Asbury's blanching in recognition of the presence is our chief concern in this story but the descent of the HG is what [Honoré de] Balzac called the "constation," the summing up, the appeal from the particular to the general. Each ought to have a sentence to itself.

If you were less stout-hearted and less talented I wouldn't dare to say the things I am saying to you but I expect you to do not only better than any of your compeers but better than has been done heretofore. In this martial spirit I shall comment on your last paragraph even further.

It seems to me that it is fine as far as "his hand shot out and closed over it and returned it to his pocket" or indeed as far as "He glanced across the room into the small oval-framed mirror."

You say, "A dazed looking youth stared back at him."

I think that this statement is too general, at the very place where you need to know what he saw. The eyes he stares into will, in a few seconds, witness, as it were, the descent of the HG. This witnessing of an ineffable sight ought to be prepared for in this very sentence. He's got to see more than just a dazed-looking youth. He's got to see eyes that are about to mirror infinity.

Have you ever read a story of mine about André Gide called "Emmanuele! Emmanuele!"? In the climax of this story a young man looks into eyes that are, in turn, contemplating an eternity of torment. The action of the whole story is sunk in those eyes.

Anyhow, suppose you made his eyes mirrors of infinity or about to become mirrors of infinity. He shudders, naturally, and rather than contemplate his own soul, looks out of the window. What does he see? You don't feel like putting your extraordinary imagination to work on this passage so you write—carelessly and inexactly—". . . over the treeline." An awkward phrase to begin with. If you are going to use those trees give them a chance. Really put them in there. The trees that lined the whatever it was or surrounded the so and so were so and so. The sun that heralds the descent of the HG ought to have a sentence to itself. The next sentence, which ought to be one of the strongest, is weak and poorly constructed. "Like some magnificent herald" and "as if it were preparing for the descent of an unspeakable presence" are really repetitious of the same idea. Similes are dangerous, anyhow. It is usually better to show how something looked and then say that it was like something else rather than try to convey the notion of what it is by telling us what it is like. You ought to make us really see this sun and in order to do that you've got to create it. I'd leave out the word "aghast." The fact that the boy fell back on his pillow and stared at the ceiling conveys the fact that he *was* aghast.

I think that you are going to have to elevate the tone a little here. You keep on being flatfooted till the end, but it won't do. The tone should be gradually rising all the way to the denouement.

Here I can only say what I'd do or try in this case. I think that after he falls back on his pillow and stares at the ceiling that I'd have a passage about his body, a passage which would do two things at once, prepare for the enduring chill and also engage the reader's sympathies by reminding him that this is the frail body of a young doomed creature. Oh, something like "His limbs, which in the past weeks had been racked alternatively by fever and by chill now seemed to have no feeling in them. It was then that he felt . . ." Oh hell, it would take me days, perhaps weeks to do it. I see that going the way I'm going I'd get into "chill" too fast. What I'm saying so poorly is that this passage must be elevated in tone, but so gradually that the reader doesn't know what's happening. You can't go straight into the Presence talking Georgia. There must be a moment in which Asbury—being a hero—must stand for all mankind, as Liharev does in Chekhov's "On the Road," as Gabriel Conroy does in [James Joyce's] "The Dead." Words, indeed, phrases, consonant with the hero's high calling must be used in your denouement.

Allen taught me this in one lesson. He read the last scenes in *Green Centuries* and said they would not do. I had been working on a deadline for months and I burst into howls and tears and said, "All right then. I can't write it. You will have to finish the book." Not caring for hysterics, he said he would finish it in the morning and in the morning, standing behind my chair, he calmly directed the operation he wanted me to perform. He said that I could not use "Warn'ts" and "ain'ts" in portraying the death of Cassy, that such colloquialisms or vulgarisms marred the tragic effect I wanted. The scene was rendered from her husband's viewpoint. He was an illiterate frontiersman and I had been rendering his speech as faithfully as I could. Allen said I must paraphrase his feelings, taking a more dignified tone than he himself would take. The tone of the style must begin rising—imperceptibly—at a certain point and continue till it had reached a considerable height. "If you can work in a classical allusion, so much the better," he said, and damned if I didn't get one in, about Diana.

Your concluding passage ought to reflect Asbury's status as a hero by a gradual elevation of the style. This can be done partly by identifying Asbury with all mankind, partly by using words that may not even be in his vocabulary, words or phrases such as a really omniscient and hence all-compassionate observer might use. And I come up with another objection: the phrase "The fierce bird with the icicle in its beak" worries me the same way "with ice instead of fire" worries me. If I were doing it I'd say something like "The fierce bird that during the long nights had seemed to his feverish fancy to hold an icicle in its beak now appeared to be in motion." That's corny. I'd have to revise it a dozen times, but still I'd start out working in that direction. The bird, with an icicle in its beak, is an awkward construction. Do get rid of it.

〜 During the time O'Connor was revising "The Enduring Chill," she received an unusual request: Susan Jenkins Brown wrote to ask if she might adapt one of O'Connor's stories—or her new novel—for the stage. Though Brown never completed a dramatization of O'Connor's work, the two women corresponded for a year and a half before abandoning the project.

In April 1958, Gordon and O'Connor briefly saw one another in New York, before O'Connor traveled to Lourdes and Rome with her mother and Sally Fitzgerald. On her return, O'Connor brought Gordon water from the spring at Lourdes.

That summer, Gordon was invited to address a symposium, "The Catholic Contribution to American Intellectual Life," held in River Forest, Illinois. CBS's Catholic Broadcast Hour would televise the program August 17. Gordon wrote to O'Connor about the experience, but only an excerpt of the letter survives.

Caroline Gordon to Flannery O'Connor

Undated [July 1958]

I was on a panel with Fr. Gardiner and a young novelist named Charles Bracelen Flood at CBS yesterday. We were taped then and will be broadcast by National Catholic Men on the last Sunday in August at ten o'clock if that's any comfort to you. If I don't appear like a fiend in a human guise I'll be surprised. Seldom have I been testier. Before we went on our panel we were taken into the viewing room to view Carson McCullers and a couple of play-writes maundering about the drama. They mentioned spiritual things quite often. They all agreed on one thing, that spiritual things were really quite spiritual and in the end right important. They thought that Tennessee Williams was perhaps the most "spiritual" writer in the USA these days. It took them so long to arrive at these conclusions that I got up and walked out. Fr. Gardiner came after me and suggested that he and I and the young novelist "go into a huddle" about what we would say. He agreed that Carson and her gang were pretty corny and drew from out of his black Jesuitical sleeve something of C.S Lewis which he said he thought he could start off with. I was deeply pained then and am still pained to hear myself saying, "Fr. Gardiner, I am tired of C.S. Lewis." I fear that I went on to say that it was a very very hot day and that I was missing my train for Princeton in order to be on that panel and that there was one thing that I wanted to say and that I would be obliged if he would let me say it. He gave ground but it went hard with him. By the way, I don't see why somebody doesn't slip the mantle from Bishop Sheen's shoulders and drape it over Fr. G. He's perfect for television. Awfully handsome. Right at his peak now. He was the only one of us who got any make up. A young man ran over and ran a powder puff over his high and somewhat shining forehead—just to take a little of the lustre away.

≈ O'Connor didn't own a television and was unable to see Gordon's appearance on CBS. She told Betty Hester, "A little boy here in town who comes out on Wednesday saw Caroline and the Rev. G. [...] He said they did nothing but agree with each other and that Caroline did most of the talking."

That fall, Tate and Gordon again lived apart. Gordon taught, and she revised *The House of Fiction* for a second edition. Gordon was only sixty-three, but the ongoing strain and exhaustion were taking a toll: biographer Nancylee Novell Jonza described how Gordon "gave the wrong lecture to one of her classes and feared she would be fired for incompetence." Gordon also made significant errors in an essay she wrote about O'Connor's *Wise Blood* for *Critique*. O'Connor appreciated Gordon's efforts but struggled to navigate her response to Gordon's mistakes. "It was news to me that Sabbath was the blind man's mistress or that she was fiercely maternal," O'Connor told Betty Hester, "and every detail that she could get wrong, she did. [...] You can't criticize Caroline. That is the one thing she won't take. I wrote her and thanked her for it and suggested that there were a few details that were a little mixed up, but that was all I could do." Gordon's inaccuracies presented additional problems—Gordon had offered to write an introduction to the French edition of *Wise Blood*.

Without consulting O'Connor, Hester contacted Gordon directly about the mistakes. O'Connor worried that Hester had overstepped, but more urgent were the reports that Gordon seemed near a breakdown: "She is about half-mad right now with Allen who is off on one of his periodic flings and she thinks is about to go out of the Church. [...] Pray for Caroline. She is really in a bad way."

To Hester, O'Connor expressed her frustrations freely: "Caroline is an old lady. I can't point out any more of her errors to her." With Gordon, however, O'Connor would always reserve a diplomatic tone.

Flannery O'Connor to Caroline Gordon

16 November 1958

I guess they sent you a copy of CRITIQUE. It helped to have you say something good about the novel [*Wise Blood*] since Brother Louis D. Rubin didn't exactly get it. On reading it over, I have discovered what is wrong in the name of the Church as you have it. I knew something was wrong but I have only just realized what it is. Haze's church is always called simply The Church Without Christ, never the Church of Christ Without Christ. That one comes in with Hoover Shoates and is further lengthened to the Holy Church of Christ Without Christ by Onnie Jay Holy. This doesn't make any difference in the CRITIQUE but you will want to correct it in the introduction or the book will contradict what you say. Also another detail I noted is that Haze reads the sign about Leora Watts' friendly bed in the train station, not on the train. M. Coindreau probably isn't through with the translation. I mean to write him and ask him to visit us when he comes South.

I gather Lon is very disappointed over the reception his book [*This Is Adam*] has met with. McDowell didn't get the review copies out in time; also they surely didn't proofread the book. And this is a shame because it is a good book.

Big news for me. The doctor says my hip bone is recalcifying. He is letting me walk around the room and for short spaces without the crutches.

If it continues to improve, I may be off of them in a year or so. Maybe this is Lourdes. Anyway, it's something to be thankful to the same Source for.

⌖ Allen Tate filed for divorce in November. When Hester continued to criticize Gordon in letters, O'Connor agreed—"Caroline is wildly mixed up"—but she defended Gordon once again: "The harshness with which you speak of Caroline is not justified."

Caroline Gordon to Flannery O'Connor and Brainard and Frances Cheney

First Sunday in Advent, 1958 [November 30]
Flannery, I have been sort of walking on air, myself, over your latest news. I can't tell you how happy I am about it. By the way, did you hang on to that half of a letter from Mother Mary Magdalen of Jesus Christ Crucified (yep, that's her name in religion) that I gave you just before you went to Lourdes? I, myself, feel sure that Mother Mary Magdalen has been in on this affair. I was lounging at "the Turn" over at the Carmel, chatting with the sister in charge the day before I last saw you in New York. She told me what I had not known before—that Mother Mary M. had been taken to Lourdes at the age of nineteen, supposedly dying of tuberculosis and that as she went down into the water she promised the Virgin that if she were cured she would become a Carmelite nun. She lived forty-five more years and founded four Carmels. A Catholic (cradle) friend of mine is always asking intercession of Bd. Martin Porres, because, he says, Bd. Martin is "gunning for sainthood" and a saint, in such a situation, *he* says (shocking the way these cradle Catholics talk!), *he* says that at such a time a saint is very accessible. Mother Mary M. already has what looks like one miracle to her credit. A Mrs. William Wright here in Princeton had one of those exploratory operations for cancer and the doctors said she was too far gone to even operate—ten years ago. Mother Mary Ma. heard about her and asked her to come see her and prayed for her and the woman is going about her business today in apparent perfect health. Her husband was so grateful that he wanted to have dozens of quarts of milk delivered to the Carmel each morning, but the Rev. Mother said no—that their Mother Theresa would not have liked that. It would have been all right with them if

he had brought a few quarts up each day, himself. Mrs. Wright was talking to Mother Mary M. once and she said, "Mother, I think you are a saint. I know another person I think is a saint. Jacques Maritain. I want you to meet him." There was silence from behind the grill then Mother Mary M. said, "Has he got any money?"

And now, speaking of prayers still, I want to ask you, my three dear friends, to pray hard for me and to pray hard and in a special way for Allen.

I gave you a pretty bad time when you were here, Lon, and I am sorry. I was just overcome with rage—and fright. But I am calm as any cucumber now. This is the sixth of these seizures of Allen's that I've gone through but I never had the Church to help me until a few years ago.

Christmas plays a strange part in Allen's life. We had our first quarrel at Christmas time thirty-four years ago. I said, "Darling, I think you are drinking too much. Don't you think you ought to cut down a little." I said nothing else. Allen said I had "drenched him with vituperation" and abandoned me shortly after Nancy's conception. You and Lon, Fannie, will remember that I spent Christmas of 1945 with the Starrs, waiting for a divorce, which Allen said we must get "so we can get married again."

That affair cost around fourteen thousand dollars. His brother, Ben, let him sell Benfolly for six thousand dollars and it certainly was worth twenty thousand. It also cost him his job at Sewanee. I knew when he gave me a certain smile last Christmas and told me that I need not be afraid to go to Sewanee, that everybody there had forgiven me for the awful things I'd done, that A. was off his rocker again and I up and had convulsions in the Ten Cent Store and in the car going home—I just did not feel equal to going through one of those seizures again and I tried to convince myself that I imagined it. But the symptoms piled up relentlessly and his paranoia is now in full bloom—in time for the season of good will and peace on earth.

He has started divorce proceedings in Minnesota, hoping to get a divorce on grounds of mental cruelty. I have consulted three priests and they all say unhesitatingly that it is my duty to actively oppose a divorce. I, myself, think that it would be a prelude to Allen's getting out of the Church and if he does that he is a goner. However, I don't have to worry my brain over what I ought to do. My spiritual advisers speak so plainly and firmly that all I have do is obey as best I can.

I am appalled, though, at the prospect. Loss of the job is also a part of the pattern of one of these seizures. A contested divorce action is not going to do Allen any good in Minnesota, where he already has a reputation for considerable eccentricity—the students call the poor darling "Moon." He said he wondered why they did!

We have been separated for three years now, by Allen's wish, and on the suggestion of Dr. Bernhardt, the Jungian psychiatrist we had in Rome. Allen is now bitter against her—he used to revere her. He says she did not do him any good because she never pointed out what was right and what was wrong, just presented the picture and left it up to him.

Allen has not been getting better in the last few years. He has rather retrogressed considerably. His confessor (who naturally lives in Washington while his penitent is either in Minnesota or flying around the world) his confessor is a wonderful man, a holy man, I think, but he was in a retirement in a mental institution for a year and a half—the diagnosis was schizophrenia. He has been spiritual adviser to a lot of famous people and his mania took the form of delusions of grandeur. Allen also seeks the society of other disturbed people. For years his eccentric behaviour was directed mostly at me—very few people knew that there was anything wrong. But now that I play such a small part in his life his eccentricity is becoming common knowledge. All the editors who have had dealings with him speak frankly of him as irresponsible. The cleavage in his life is becoming apparent to the world. In a way, this frenzied desire for a divorce may be a sign of health—bringing his situation out in the open in Minnesota.

We have moved every two years since we were married. When we went to Minnesota we had the first financial security we had ever had but it was quickly dissipated. Allen fell into his mother's pattern—she moved four times a year. She lived in an apartment hotel. He lives in an apartment hotel. No matter how weary he is in the summer he will slip in an extra teaching chore—to keep the sacred number of four. When I got back from Rome he said that we would have to move into an apartment hotel—and also continue to pay rent on our apartment!

Allen himself says that when he has one of his seizures he feels as if an evil spirit has taken possession of him. He uses words and phrases when this spirit is in possession of him that he does not use at any [other] time. But the spirit is infernally clever. One of the first things I learned in my long and agonizing effort to get help for Allen is that the psychosis seems to have a separate life of its own and runs, like a fox, from cover to cover. Allen's demon is not making new earths in which it can take refuge.

Two years ago he flew off to India, leaving me with no money at all—and no job. He had worked for three years, I now discover, to alienate my daughter from me. She has come near having a nervous breakdown as a result—and now has a psychosomatic loss of her voice which recurs every now and then. It has Percy scared.

Two years ago Allen got drunk and reeled all over New York, Paris, Rome, Bombay, Florence, Calcutta, or whatever city we tax payers paid his way to, denouncing me. I know this because Vivienne Koch had no more sense than to, as it were, put on a record one of his drunken evenings. His demon has decided that that is poor policy. He is being scrupulous about money matters, and other practical matters and from every side I get reports of how "nicely he speaks" of me these days.

Francis Fergusson says that he first had an inkling of Allen's condition when he told him some things that he knew were not true. Francis says that he thinks that Allen, as he roams the world, tells each person he meets the half-truth or lie that he thinks will best go down. I am certain that when you and he had that conversation in Cambridge, Lon, that he was not telling the truth.

When we were young, poverty was an anchor for Allen. That was when he did his best work, the work for which people still admire him. But now that he can get a Fulbright at the drop of a hat he whirls about the world like an autumn leaf.

Something happened the other day, however, which heartens me considerably. Berthe Marti, a Bryn Mawr prof whom we knew in Rome, told me about a gathering of old Rome hands in New York this week end. When they parted everybody was sending their love to Allen by a painter who is going abroad. Berthe said that she could not send Allen her love, that her affection for him has been altered by his cruel treatment of his wife and daughter.

Lon, you told me that you and Fannie remonstrated with Allen in 1945 and I'm sure you did. But none of us knew as much about these cases then as we do now. I think this event is important in poor Allen's life. It is the first time anybody had protested publicly and in words that will reach another continent against his misconduct. And this protest comes from a woman who admired him about as much as you can admire a person.

The Fulbright business has had me in despair. There seemed little hope of his ever facing reality when he could keep whirling about the globe, but the Lord can shrink the globe, of course, if He thinks it best to do so.

I come finally to my point. (My poor Lon—to have to hear all this over and over!) But I feel not about Allen the way St. Thomas More felt about his son-in-law when he got "fantastical heretical notions" and More said, "Son Will, I have responded with thee and I have talked with thee and I have argued with thee but I am going to give all that over and get me to God and pray for thee."

I am going to pray for him as hard as I can but I am pretty wicked—and a little crazy, myself—and then, too, my resentment against his cruel treatment sometimes overcomes me and gets in the way of my prayers. But you three are all good people and, I believe, powerful in prayer. Pray hard for him, please. His soul is in great peril.

The chaplain at the Carmel made a remark which astounded me as much as it will astound you. He has spent forty years in China, in solitude and is a holy man. He has refused to let me become a Carmelite tertiary because of my marital status which gives too much occasion for sin, but one day after long contemplation he said, "Madame, your husband hates you because of your love, your charity, and your patience." I said, "Father, I love my husband but it is evidently in the wrong way. I am woefully lacking charity and notoriously impatient." He said, "Nevertheless, even a grain of charity or love or patience will inspire hatred in a person who is possessed by an evil spirit."

I think that Allen really is possessed now by an evil spirit. He thinks so too—when he is himself. The letter I had announcing his plans for a divorce were not only frenetic but full of heretical statements, according to the priests who have seen it. I think his rage was provoked by my referring in my last letter to marriage as a sacrament. He holds—at present—that it is a "wholly interiour experience."

Lon, I *am* sorry I gave you such a bad time when you were here. But even in my dim-witted state I got a glimpse of your plans for your next two books and am very excited over them. I think you've got quite a lot there.

Love for all three of you. I am sorry to write about such sad affairs but Allen needs your help. We have tried God knows how many psychiatrists. I am convinced that his enemy is supernatural and that only supernatural help can save Allen.

[postscript]

Lon, in the midst of all these horrors, it has been a comfort and pleasure to me to reflect that during the coming months you will, as it were, have your intellect and imagination at your own disposal—to put it at the Lord's disposal. You have got important things to say and I see that you are going to be able to say them. I will pray for your intentions every day.

〜 "The letter from Caroline today was pretty bad," O'Connor told the Cheneys after reading this letter. "It doesn't look like you can do anything for them but pray."

O'Connor remained uneasy about Gordon's offer to write an introduction to Gallimard's edition of *Wise Blood*, and sought to extract herself from the arrangement. A draft of a letter O'Connor wrote follows.

Flannery O'Connor to Caroline Gordon

Undated Letter Draft [1958]

I know that worried as you are about Allen you don't have time to bother with trifles like this. Nevertheless this has come up and so I want to let you know about it. I have some French friends who have been here & I was telling them about having an introduction to the French W.B. [*Wise Blood*]. They were horrified and said whatever I did not to have an introduction to it for the French that this would only irritate them and that the book ought to stand on its own. On thinking it over, I believe myself that it would be better to leave off the introduction & just let it go on its own. It is somehow more the way a first book ought to be when it has a living author and since the piece has been published in *Critique*, that done its good here. Grateful as I am for it I believe it would be pretentious for me to have an introduction. It smacks of me having too good an opinion of myself & makes me uncomfortable. I know you don't have time to fool with it & you may not see M. Coindreau and as I want to write him an invite to visit us, I will just ask him to leave it off.

I looked up the letter of Mother M.M. I hope she had a hand in it. Somebody did.

≈ O'Connor never sent that letter. Before Christmas, O'Connor reported to Hester, "I took the introduction that Caroline had written and knocked it down to two pages, cut out all the explication of WB, cut out Truman, cut out Faulkner, cut out Camus, and left Henry James, the elder. I then mailed this to her and said what about it. Haven't heard from her yet. I hope this won't be the straw that broke the camel's back. It's every word hers but she may not want to put her name to such a truncation. We shall see."

Gordon's introduction, ultimately, would not appear in the French edition of *Wise Blood*. In January, Gordon told O'Connor about receiving Betty Hester's letter: "Your admirer, Miss Somebody or other, feels that anybody who makes as many mistakes as I did is not capable of grasping your work. I am keeping her letter—to show anybody who is ever fool enough to ask me to write another preface. Show 'em I can't do it." Maurice Coindreau, the translator, wrote to O'Connor at the end of January and told her not to worry about Gordon's introduction; he hoped to write an essay that would provide context to the European reader.

O'Connor finished a draft of *The Violent Bear It Away* and delivered it to Gordon. A month later, O'Connor told Hester, "It would have done your heart good to see all the marks on the copy, everything commented upon, doodles, exclamation points, cheers, growls."* But this time, O'Connor thought Gordon's support rang false. She asked others (the Fitzgeralds and Catherine Carver) for some much-needed feedback. O'Connor thanked Carver that April: "You have done me an immense favor that nobody else could have or would have done. Caroline read it but her strictures always run to matters of style. She swallows a good many camels while she is swatting the flies—though what she has taught me has been invaluable and I can never thank her enough. Or you . . ."

In February 1959, O'Connor received a Ford Foundation grant of $8,000. Fellow recipients included Katherine Anne Porter and Robert Fitzgerald. Spring took her to lecture at Wesleyan and Vanderbilt.

---

* In 1979, Sally Fitzgerald told Gordon that her letters about this novel were among the "missing" and asked Gordon if she had copies. Fitzgerald never located Gordon's letters. See SF to CG, 14 December 1979, SFEU.

Flannery O'Connor to Caroline Gordon

10 May 1959

You heard the subterranean note in [Robert Lowell's] voice correctly, I guess. Bob Giroux spent last Monday and Tuesday with us and said Cal hospitalized himself before the party. He thought it a good sign that he did it himself and didn't have to be forced to. Giroux had just been to Gethsemane. He stopped over in Atlanta and visited the Trappist monastery in Conyers, which he said was much better looking than the one in Kentucky, or at least will be when they complete it. All the people in the outlying areas go to look at the monks—like going to the zoo.

I'm glad you have set out on The Air of the Country. With all the other things you do I don't see how you find time for it but I suppose after teaching it is a real relief to do it. It will be a big treat for me to see it.

I read at Wesleyan last week—"A Good Man is Hard to Find." After the reading, I went to one of their classes to answer questions. There were several young teachers in there and one began by saying, "Miss O'Connor, why is the Misfit's hat *black*?" I said most countrymen in Georgia wore black hats. He looked quite disappointed. Then he said, "Miss O'Connor, the Misfit represents Christ, does he not?" "He does not," says I. He really looked hurt at that. Finally he said, "Well Miss O'Connor, what IS the significance of the Misfit's hat?" "To cover his head," I said. He looked crushed then and left me alone.

I am doing the whole middle section of the novel over. The beginning and the end suit me, but that middle is bad. It isn't dramatic enough. I telescoped that middle section so as to get on with the end, but now that I've got the end, I see there isn't enough middle.

I don't reckon I saw many Fugitives at Vanderbilt. The Kreigers asked for you. He read a paper which was over my head, but was very nice when he wasn't reading a paper. The Mabrys came down from Guthrie and I was glad to meet them. While I was at the Cheneys' I read part of Ashley's thesis, the chapter on *The Malefactors*. Ashley ought to get to work on that book and publish it. I think it's the best thing I've read on *The Malefactors*. If you would give him a verbal shove, he might get on with it. He is leaving Santa Barbara after this term but I don't know where he will go.

We were real pleased to hear your word about M. Coindreau. I guess he has gone by now. I have some clippings for him about evangelistic goings-on. One ad says, "Thrill to the Music, Message and Magic of this team!"

≈ Relatively few letters between O'Connor and Gordon have been found from 1959 to 1962. The women often received updates from mutual friends Ashley Brown and the Cheneys.

On May 12, Gordon told the Cheneys about a hopeful development, which they shared with O'Connor. Gordon wrote, "I was lying in bed with a bad hangover and I said to myself that I was not as young as I once was and it behooves me to take care of myself and I decided I would just stay in bed all morning. Unfortunately I had put the typewriter on the night table. As I recall, I sort of turned over in bed—and the first thing I knew I had eight pages of The Narrow Heart written. Had another whack at it later and I now have twelve pages, so I'm committed. The gaff, as my father would say, has been slipped home."

In June 1959, O'Connor wrote to Susan Jenkins Brown about divorce proceedings between Tate and Gordon: "I haven't heard from Caroline in a couple of weeks but I hope the news is no more doleful than it was then. She did say she had started on a novel which I should think would be the best place for her mind to be set right now." But by the end of the summer, O'Connor reported to the Cheneys that Caroline "was in a terrible condition."

The Tates divorced August 18 in Minneapolis. In another stunning blow to Caroline, Allen Tate remarried on August 27, to Isabella Gardner.

In October, Gordon contacted O'Connor. Now, eight years after writing her first letter to Flannery, Caroline planned a visit to Andalusia, after Ashley Brown suggested she accompany him. "I've been dying to visit Flannery for years," Gordon said, "and this way of going about it furnishes the needed impetus." Gordon and Brown traveled at the end of October to see the O'Connors.

O'Connor described the visit to Betty Hester as follows:

Last weekend Ashley brought Caroline down for Saturday and Sunday. She flew to Columbia and he drove her over. This was her first visit here. It was somewhat nerve-racking keeping her and my mother's personalities from meeting headlong with a crash. We went for a ride and Caroline saw a dog on the highway that she decided was lost and she wanted to pick up. Of course Regina was not ABOUT to pick up any dog, so Caroline prevailed upon Ashley when we got back to take her

out in his car to look for the dog. She told him the dog could stay in his care overnight. He later told Regina that he was not ABOUT to have that dog spend the
night in his car. Anyway, he took her and they didn't find the dog. She is terribly
silly about animals. Oh the poor doggy, etc. There was also another near collision
about artificial breeding. She was quite shocked that we use it. Apparently she fails
to take in the difference between man and animal. Sunday morning she gave me
a valuable two hour lecture on the subject of my prose. When she is doing something like that she is most nearly herself. When the weekend was over my mother's comment was that she understood "why that man would want to divorce her."

O'Connor heard from Gordon in November; Gordon was "more or less
cheerful," O'Connor said. That month, she sent Gordon "The Comforts of
Home." Gordon wrote Ashley Brown, "Just got a new story from Flannery
which I would be reading this morning if I weren't stealing the time to paint."
Uncharacteristically, Gordon simply told O'Connor that the story was "fine."

O'Connor's novel *The Violent Bear It Away* was published in January 1960.
"The back jacket is devoted to a quote from Caroline's piece in *Critique* [on *Wise
Blood*]," O'Connor told Betty Hester, "which will be like waving the red flag in
front of several bulls."

Caroline Gordon, back cover copy from *The Violent Bear It Away*, by Flannery O'Connor (Farrar, Straus, and Cudahy, 1960)

The talent of Flannery O'Connor, one of the most original among
younger American writers, was recognized soon after the publication of
her first short stories. . . . Miss O'Connor's work, however, has a characteristic which does not occur in the work of any of her contemporaries.
Its presence in everything she writes, coupled with her extraordinary talent, makes her, I suspect, one of the most important writers of our age.
. . . In Miss O'Connor's vision of modern man—a vision not limited to
Southern rural humanity—all her characters are 'displaced persons.' They
are 'off center,' out of place, because they are victims of a rejection of the
Scheme of Redemption. They are lost in that abyss which opens for man
when he sets up as God. This theological framework is never explicit in
Miss O'Connor's fiction. It is so much a part of her direct gaze at human
conduct that she seems herself to be scarcely aware of it. I believe that this
accounts to a great extent for her power. It is a Blakean vision, not through

symbol as such but through the actuality of human behavior; and it has Blake's explosive honesty.

⌒ Gordon finished revising the anthology *The House of Fiction*, and a second edition was issued in 1960. For this edition, Gordon included O'Connor's "A Good Man Is Hard to Find." Scholar Frederick Asals proposed that this inclusion marked a turning point in making the story a "favorite of anthologizers" and in generating "serious criticism" of it.

Spring and summer passed. Gordon visited Andalusia again in September 1960. O'Connor wrote to the Cheneys, "I had a call from Mrs. Gordon Tate Herself from Princeton saying her aunt in Chattanooga had summoned her and she would like to come see us on her way back. She said she would come on the following Tuesday but arrived instead on Monday. She stayed until Wednesday and we haven't heard from her since she left. However, the people over at Wesleyan are having one of those Arts Festivals that no college can now do without and have invited her to be on the panel (me too) and she wrote the man she would come down as she would be glad to continue her visit with us. So it appears we are to be honored again."

The October 1960 Wesleyan Arts Festival featured O'Connor and Gordon alongside Katherine Anne Porter and Madison Jones, all "paid (well) to swap clichés about Southern culture." Lon Cheney—who didn't attend the conference—told O'Connor that he'd heard Gordon was "embattled against the world." Biographer Nancylee Novell Jonza wrote, "Age had not mellowed Caroline: if anything it made her all the more fierce."

After the conference, Gordon and Porter visited Andalusia. Gordon read a draft of *A Memoir of Mary Ann*, written by the Dominican sisters at Our Lady of Perpetual Help Free Cancer Home. O'Connor had agreed to edit and write an introduction for the book. Gordon admired the work and urged O'Connor to find a secular publisher.

The long weekend exhausted O'Connor, who told a friend, "I have been recuperating from [. . .] an Arts Festival at Wesleyan attended also by Caroline and Miss K. A. Porter. Caroline spent the weekend here after it and she is a strenuous woman and one night of it, we had the lot of them to supper." Nonetheless, O'Connor seemed able to compartmentalize her complicated feelings about Gordon: she might articulate her frustrations to close friends, yet she continued to solicit criticism and selectively apply Gordon's suggestions. When O'Connor received Gordon's critique of her introduction to *A Memoir of Mary Ann*, for example, O'Connor decided, "I have no intention of changing the opening, but I will do the smaller things she suggests. I feel that the opening is all right. I think she is right about putting myself in too much."

News of O'Connor's decline in health reached Gordon after Christmas. "I am awfully worried about Flannery," she wrote to Ashley Brown. "The news I've had lately is not good. I'm afraid that lupus has attacked her jaw." Brown didn't have any updates on O'Connor's health when he responded, but mentioned that O'Connor had sent him "The Partridge Festival." "I am really worried about Flannery," Gordon wrote back. (She didn't mention whether she had read the story.) "I wish you'd manage to find out how she is, one way or another. I'm afraid this is the most serious yet."

In April 1961, O'Connor sent Gordon her new story, "Everything That Rises Must Converge." If Gordon critiqued it, no evidence survives.

Summer arrived; Gordon planned another visit with Ashley Brown to Andalusia in mid-July. "Ashley's task was to keep Mrs. O'Connor occupied," wrote biographer Brad Gooch, "while Caroline and Flannery went off to discuss theology and literature." During this visit, O'Connor shared her story "The Lame Shall Enter First." The story wasn't dramatic enough, Gordon said. O'Connor was writing too many essays and it was affecting her style, Gordon thought. O'Connor agreed with Gordon's analysis. There were "a million other things that I could have seen myself if I had had the energy," O'Connor said. "So much of my trouble is laziness, not physical laziness so much as mental, not taking the trouble to think how a thing ought to be dramatized." One change during this visit: Gordon had stopped drinking—not even a glass of sherry. O'Connor thought that Gordon seemed much improved. Still, she found, "Ashley and Caroline were strenuous, as usual."

Flannery O'Connor to Caroline Gordon

16 November 1961

Yesterday we went to the [Conyers] monastery for dinner and I met your friend Fr. Charles.* We took two of our Protestant friends and as a surprise the Abbot invited my cousin, Msgr. [Patrick] O'Connor. I hadn't

---

* Jack English, ordained Father Charles, O.C.S.O., resided at the Holy Ghost Monastery and was formerly one of Dorothy Day's Catholic Workers.

seen him in thirty years. He was an actor before he became a priest and afterward taught Sacred Oratory at the Catholic University for many years. It was quite a gathering. Afterwards we went to see the Church—which is unbelievable—and there was Fr. Charles. Apparently all the young monks are very excited about those records you are getting for them. He said you couldn't imagine how much it meant to them. He was eager to talk of course but didn't get too much of a chance. He said he heard a lot from Walker Percy, and that your letters meant a great deal to him. Fr. Paul was away getting a kiln. They are going to start doing pottery.

I have just got back from Marillac, the college for all nuns. About as lively a bunch as I have come across. They all said they understood Tarwater perfectly because they had had the same experience he had.

I have about finished that story ["The Lame Shall Enter First"] you saw a first draft of when you were here and I think you would approve of it now, but I am not going to afflict you with it because I know you have a million things to do.

We have decided that my swans are Polish swans because they have such even dispositions. I will be able to tell when they hatch (IF). If they are Polish, they will be white; if mute, grey.

You said you wanted a picture of me and I enclose same. I had to have these taken. All teeth and spectacles.

Tell Jim hello.

Caroline Gordon to Father Charles, Flannery O'Connor, and Ashley Brown

St. Catherine's Day, 1961 [November 25]

(I had a friend years ago who developed a habit of writing all her letters in triplicate or quadruplicate. All of thus addressed felt that this was pretty awful of her. But then, none of us were very charitable. I appeal to all three of you to bear with my barbarous means of communication—there are things I want to say to each one of you and I do not seem to have a moment's leisure these days. I do not believe that it is entirely because of my unskillful apportioning of my time. I work the way I have always worked, as hard as *I* (who am naturally slothful) can, but I never get out from under the burden of "the evil of the day." I swear I believe the Devil has got some new tricks up his invisible sleeve!)

I want, however, to call first upon your charity in another way. Will you please extend the great charity you have shown to me and pray for my little granddaughters, Caroline and Amy? I am inclined to ask that you pray for them specifically: that they will be sent to the school which the Sisters of the Sacred Heart will open here soon? The writing of novels was, for me, for years, a substitute for the art of prayer—I did not know till I was middle aged that art was practiced by anybody! When you get to be as old as I am, however, and have spent as many years contemplating patterns of human behaviour, you are apt to feel—or fancy—that you sometimes get a glimpse of the Lord's operations. I have been working, whenever I get the chance, on the last novel that I will write, in all probability. One of its themes, strands of narrative—whatever you want to call it—is a consideration of the kind of education women get nowadays. It seems to me that it's all wrong. The girls get out of the colleges thinking they know everything—because in their "survey" courses they have got a smattering of many things. Most of them, the ones who come my way, at least, feel that since they know practically everything they don't need to do any more studying. Actually, the best educated women I have ever known did not go to college. The education St. Thomas More gave his daughters seems to me a model for the education of women and I have been much impressed by the way the foundress of the Sacred Heart came by her learning. I gather that her older brother taught her everything he learned—for sheer love of learning or teaching. And she actually acquired a fund of knowledge before she had any idea what she was to do with it. I am convinced that there is no "career" possible for any women, without sacrificing some part of her womanhood—except in the Church.

My older granddaughter, Caroline, is very bright and does well at school. I think that she has already undergone a serious religious crisis—one that has actually affected her health. She and her two brothers and her mother and father have all been baptized in the Church but her parents have lapsed and are now trying to be Episcopalians. They went at it rather half-heartedly until Caroline demanded that she be allowed to go to some church. So now the whole family gets up early and the two little girls go to the Episcopalian Sunday School. (The two boys are off at school.) The youngest child, Amy, has never been baptized. She is frail in health and until recently was more like little Pearl in *The Scarlet Letter* than any child I

have ever known. She is less perverse now but is—to me, at least—alarm-
ingly precocious.

I have never discussed religion with my daughter or her husband.
Circumstances seem to make it best not to. But I gather that they are
faced with a family crisis. My daughter longs to practice her religion but
has given it up in obedience to her husband's wishes. He, I feel sure, will
be a wonderful Christian in time but right now he is in confusion and has
led his whole family away from the Church. Caroline speaks sometimes
of ".... if we ever get Amy baptized" and I am sure that my daughter and
her husband face a terrible problem. They have insisted that Caroline become an Episcopalian and she keeps asking why Amy is not baptized in
that church and they, so far, it seems, haven't so far been able to face that
kind of baptism for Amy....... That's enough about this. But you can see
that it's a situation that calls for fervent prayers.

Father Charles, I make such a fool of myself so often when I talk that I
often find myself thinking that I should follow closer in the foot-steps of
the Trappists—and then I think what a poor contribution I've made so
far to those Trappist tapes! Those conversations that seemed so easy to
arrange when we first got the idea! I believe, though, that I am on the point
of getting a dialogue taped that will be of great interest—to anybody who
uses and loves the English language.

Ashley, I think you will be interested in this. A friend of my daughter's,
head of the English department of a preparatory school, came here to dinner the other night. This young man has been going around the country
at a great rate, attending conferences held by linguists on a new grammar
they have devised. It is called "structured grammar." The linguists who are
in the front of this movement hold that "traditional" grammar was "im-
posed" upon us in the eighteenth century by scholars whom they sometimes refer to as "Nazis."

My friend Jack [Myers], who seems to have been pretty well indoc-
trinated, said that "positioned as he was, he did not feel that 'traditional
grammar' was structured to meet the demands of his students." Why, he
asked, should a noun be the name of anything? He said that he would
not feel "honest" if one of his pupils asked him why a noun should be
the name of anything and he was not able to justify this label to said
pupil.

Yes, Ashley, this is what he said, condensed—because, after all, we are all busy people. He took till two o'clock in the morning to say it, but this is what he said. Since then I have done a little investigating and I find that he is on the verge of joining the ranks of the "structural grammarians." I have even read a bit in one of these grammars. It is called *English 2600* and is "programmed" so that the student is put through what they call "frames" (a little the way laboratory rats are propelled from cage to cage, it seemed to me). There is another book called *Poetry 230.** It is all part of what Charles Carpenter Fries, one of their leaders, calls "the measurement movement in education." C.P. Snow was in Philadelphia this weekend for a conference of these structural workers. He seems to be the moving spirit in England.

Jack first made me conscious of this movement which I consider a new Communist movement deeper underground than they have yet gone, when he remarked casually a few months ago that "Literature is a dialect of Linguistics."

John Farrelly, who took a "First" at Cambridge, groaned the loudest when Jack spoke of how he was "positioned." I thought I'd try to get Jack Myers and John Farrelly to talk on this subject for our tapes. (I am working at them, you see—but so slowly!)

Flannery, I think that Mary Ann's memoir is even more imposing in print—as things often are. The narrative reads even better than it did in manuscript. And I have heard several people express admiration of your ingenious and telling use of the passages from Hawthorne. I remember how you suffered over the preface but it certainly was worth doing. Don't you feel that now?

Herbert Read and I seem to have traded girls for a while. I wrote him months ago, sending him a translation of one of Callimachus's poems that Carol Johnson made. I've been sending copies to several of my elderly friends. She's got some beautiful lines: "the god who gave tablet in his youth will not desert the poet when he greys". . . . (That's not it exactly. Quoting from memory. Another line I keep well in memory: ". . . feed the victim fat, the poet slender . . .") Herbert finally wrote and said

---

* *English 2600: A Scientific Program in Grammar and Usage* by Joseph C. Blumenthal (New York: Harcourt, Brace, and Company, 1960) was the original "programmed learning" text designed to teach grammar and usage without a teacher. Such programmed textbooks—*Poetry 230* was another book in the series—purported to conserve an English teacher's valuable energy.

he wasn't sure what I wanted him to do about this young woman. He also revealed the fact that his daughter, Sophie, is in New York, with a temporary job at the Bollingen Foundation. I told him to have Carol to lunch and look at some of her poems and invited Sophie down for the week end. She has Herbert's sort of mask-like Saxon face (they live three miles from the ancient church where his Saxon ancestors are buried in the crypt; he's a dalesman of pretty pure stock). Sophie, whom I last saw when she was fifteen, still has "a fringe" as she calls it, black hair falling to her shoulders, lovely blue eyes and the poise of a convent-bred *jeune fille*. It was the week end of the Yale game. I met her at the bus and took her straight from there to a big pre-game luncheon and later in the day took her out to a party Joe and Marion Kelleher were giving at their re-modelled, towered, all-but moated barn. Everybody was enchanted by her. What got me was that she has at times an expression exactly like little Caroline's.

Flannery, Jim MacLeod came out a week or so ago, pretty irritated because his "worship professor" had defined worship as "spiritual togetherness." He was so annoyed that he had jumped into what seems to me another frying pan. Just sat down and wrote him a short story. It was my painful duty to reveal to him the depressing fact that no matter how strongly we are impelled to write stories we must somehow contrive that the reader is just as strongly impelled to read them. This was naturally a blow to him but he certainly took it on the chin. He is certainly very intelligent. Whether he ever becomes a fiction writer or remains a Presbyterian—well, I'll be interested to see. He has been a great help to me. The other night he told me something about Calvin that I have been trying to find out for two years.

Ashley, I haven't as yet had the decency to thank you for reminding me that the words "the region cloud" are in that sonnet of Shakespeare's, whence, it seems to me, they are most likely to have filtered into [Percy] Lubbock's imagination. Haven't got my piece on that finished yet. I hope to get it out of the way in the Christmas holidays.

Father Charles, the quotation from Gabriel Marcel is so apt in the work I am now doing as to be startling. He had sort of got off my list of things I must read right away. Thanks for the tip. I'm glad your health is better. Once in a while modern science comes across with something worth while. I'm glad you liked *The Malefactors*. It has an "Invention" in it which ought to be of service to other novelists: the extension of the dimensions of many of the scenes by having on the stage characters who are not subject to ordinary mortal disturbances, a saint, a dead poet, a dead painter, and a madman. Dorothy [Day], who, I suppose served as a model for the saint—she is one of the two or is it three characters whom I have drawn straight from life—Dorothy, I started to say, didn't like the book—chiefly, because she feared that it might be prejudicial to her work, I gather. Jacques Maritain liked it, however, and wrote me a letter in which he registered his reaction to my "invention." Needless to say I was very pleased to have such a reader.

He was here for a month this Fall. This time last year he said he planned to come back to Princeton every Fall. I think that most of us wondered whether he'd ever make it—he looked so frail and spent. He told me then that he found it almost impossible to work [because he] missed Raïssa so. But he seemed much improved in health and spirit this visit. Everybody remarked on that. And everybody was fascinated with his style of dress which, I imagine, reflects his changed condition. He told me: "I am no longer Monsieur Maritain, I am Jacques." He has always worn a scarf around his neck—expressing the French aversion to *current d'air*, no doubt. But he wore no scarf this time and wore a jacket such as only the French can produce, a kind of cross between what they call "a sporting" and a sailor's pea-jacket. His shoes were of undressed leather, of an odd shade of brown and fearfully and wonderfully laced. He went from here to Notre Dame to confer with the people who run the Maritain Institute there. He has done something that delights me more than any public gesture made in my time: he has bequeathed (that seems the right word in spite of the linguists) he has bequeathed his heart to Notre Dame!

This seems to me a gesture in the grand manner and certainly it is traditional. Wasn't it the custom for kings and other important personages to bequeath their hearts to monasteries? (I was always horrified and, at the same time, pleased to read that the boatman who was conveying Madame de Montespan's heart to her sister's priory let it fall into the river! The poor man probably felt unconsciously that that was the best place for it!) But this gesture of Jacques' seems to me not only poetic in the deepest sense but also an act of the imagination which few people of our own day seem capable of making. I am speaking, of course, of laymen and lay women.

Dorothy is the only lay person I know who has performed the same kind of heroic act of the imagination. But of course any professional religious starts out with the effort, doesn't he?

There is a book called *The Orphic Voice* (much obliged, Ashley, for recommending it to me). It ought to be in the monastery library. If you don't get a copy I'll send you mine as soon as I get through with it. But I'll be using it for some months. It is by Elizabeth Sewell, Yale Press.

I must get back to work. We start on *The Eumenides* this week in my class at the New School. This class has come near killing me—it has meant so much extra reading and a more careful preparation of lectures than I have ever made before. But it has been worth it. And it seems to be going over. At least it has the largest enrollment I have ever had.

I began this letter with a request for prayers and find that I must close it with another request for prayers—for the soul of my old friend, Vivienne Koch, who was buried in the Rabbi Stephen Wise Cemetery last Friday. Her funeral services were held in "The Universal Chapel" at Fifty Second and Lexington and was a painful ordeal, I suspect, for everybody present. She was quite gifted, a good critic and had written three books. The service was conducted by a "divine" from Harvard who put on a black skull cap and read some verses in Hebrew at the beginning and end of the service. The rest of the service was a detailed account of poor Vivienne's professional activities, a little like a review of an author's book worse than any he could imagine. A tribute to her spirit, which was spontaneous and generous, came through his babble but I think that almost everybody there felt as if he had been put through a sort of emotional wringer. It was better in the cemetery which is a beautiful and impressive spot. On a mound overlooking woods and water. We were each given a flower to throw on the heap of flowers that rested on the "pall" and the "divine" had us repeat after him the lines of that beautiful prayer for the souls of the dead. Is it called Kaddish? I am going to find out.

Vivienne's father died seven years ago. She and her brother and sister each had some sort of visionary experience connected with his death. She was only forty-seven years old. If she had lived longer I think she would have joined the Church. I reproach myself because I made so few gestures of affection toward her in her last illness, but she died in a few weeks after she became ill and I kept putting off going to see her, partly because I was so busy and partly because I was afraid of intruding. I ask

your prayers, Father Charles, and the prayers of the other brothers for
her soul.

With many thanks for all your past favours, and with love in Christ and
Our Lady—

[postscript]

I am excited to hear about the pottery project. I trust that before
long a few figurines—I am modest in my demands—a few small statues, statuettes, representing saints (and the beasts who embody their
attributes) will come from the monastery studio. Do you realize that it
is hardly possible to purchase a statue portraying a sacred object that
one can bear to look upon? I mean one made by a contemporary artist?

I have been making the figures for years, out of terra cotta when I have
time to get them fired, out of "Hugo's Moist Clay" when I haven't time to
do things properly. My older granddaughter, Caroline, has helped me. The
other day I decided that it was time to discard a rather blobby figure of
the Virgin which she executed in Hugo's Moist when she was four. But I
was still reluctant to put it in the trash can and it landed on the windowsill
where it stayed for a week or so. Amy, who, at five, is in the grip of "sibling
rivalry," looked at the figure one morning and remarked sourly: "Mary
looks real ugly this morning—Caroline's work."

My Baptist cleaning woman felt differently, however, and asked if she
might have the figurine. I was so touched that I felt that I had to give her
the Mary and Joseph I have used now for several years, terra cotta and fired
properly so that they will last. But that necessitated my snatching a whole
morning from other duties and modelling another Mary and Joseph out of
Hugo's Moist. Caroline executed a lovely Bambino—but he broke before
he got time to harden. So now we have to do another one. . . . I do hope
that pottery will produce some proper images of the Holy Family! And I
am sure a lot of other people will feel the same way.

≈ In February 1962, Caroline contacted Robert Giroux, telling him that "I
have just sent on to Flannery a note from one of her fans—a fellow named
Maritain. [. . .] He says: ' . . . La plume de paon de tres belle, et je suis content
qu'elle vienne de chez Flannery O'Connor, vous savez que j'ai une faible pour
elle . . . .'* I have been much pleased to observe how Mary Anne [*A Memoir of*

---

* "A very beautiful woman's peacock feather, and I am quite happy that it has come from Flannery
O'Connor, you know that I love her."

Mary Ann] goes forward. I felt sorry for Flannery while she was struggling with that task but it was certainly well worth doing."

For O'Connor, the next year was filled with travel, lectures, and work on a new novel, "Why Do the Heathen Rage?" "I have been writing every day but I don't know what as the brew has not begun to thicken yet," she told an acquaintance.

Gordon, meanwhile, took a position as writer-in-residence at University of California–Davis in the fall of 1962. She worked on a novel, *A Narrow Heart*, and a chapbook about her mentor, Ford Madox Ford. That Thanksgiving weekend, O'Connor gave the Cheneys an update on Gordon, who "seems to have taken a new lease on life in California. She's painting up a storm and having a grand time."

Flannery O'Connor to Caroline Gordon

12 December 1962

I survived my trip which included two jet flights, one which almost didn't get down, but as least we met no whistling swans. They, you know, were responsible for bagging 17 people in that United plane outside Washington. The paper said they hit it like two soft cannon balls.

I met Walker Percy, his wife, daughter and Cynthia Smith in New Orleans and certainly did like them a lot. I had a pretty good audience at Loyola. The others weren't so hot. Once I get shet of these commitments that I have somehow got myself into, I ain't going nowhere else but am going to stay at home and tend to my proper bidnis. I am sick of going but I have got myself into going to Sweet Briar in March. M. Coindreau will be there so except for the weather and having to write a paper for it, it ought to be all right. They are having a symposium on Religion and the Arts and I am the novel person. The gent who is running it says we are to conceive religion broadly as ultimate concern. Maybe I told you this already.

We had a visit from Ashley week end before last and also a visit from a young Italian critic named Claudio Gorlier who will be at Berkeley in February and will probably get in touch with you as he is doing a paper on Southern literature, or maybe it's a book. Anyway, he's a very nice young man and doubtless needs enlightenment of the kind you could give him.

All our pipes are frozen and I am just limber enough to be able to wish you a Merry Christmas.

Part 4

Revelation
(January 1963–August 1964)

~

Let me sum up my own Credo, in the hope that
I can make what I am trying to say clear. A novel, any novel,
in the first place, must be about love. There is no other subject.
—Caroline Gordon to Walker Percy, Undated [January 1952]

Fiction is the concrete expression of mystery—mystery that is lived.
Catholics believe that all creation is good and that evil is the wrong use of
good and that without Grace we use it wrong most of the time.
—Flannery O'Connor to Eileen Hall, 10 March 1956

～ In one of her repeated lectures, "The Shape of the River," Caroline Gordon described a letter Ford Madox Ford wrote to Joseph Conrad comparing a writer's efforts to a boat "on an immense river, in impenetrable fog. And you row and row and never, never will you see a mark on the invisible banks that will tell you if you are going upstream of if the current bears you along." Gordon wasn't simply highlighting "the uncertainty of the voyager." She seemed most attuned to "the voyager's loneliness."

Gordon and O'Connor each progressed slowly on their novels in 1963. Gordon wrote to a friend, "[I]f anybody had pointed out to me how much harder fiction is than the other arts, I am not sure that I'd have had the nerve to go ahead."

Scribner's reissued a collection of Gordon's writing that year, *Old Red and Other Stories*. Kirkus Reviews described the stories as "scrupulous, almost standard examples of naturalism" and, with one exception (the story "Emmanuele! Emmanuele!"), "a smashing score."

Meanwhile, O'Connor's successes and challenges mirrored Gordon's. In 1962, the New American Library had reissued two novels and a short-story collection under the title *Three by Flannery O'Connor*. "Everything That Rises Must Converge" received the 1963 O. Henry Prize. But in 1963, O'Connor was frustrated by her progress as she worked on "Why Do the Heathen Rage?" O'Connor told Sister Mariella Gable, "I've been writing 18 years and I've reached the point where I can't do again what I know I can do well, and the larger things that I need to do now, I doubt my capacity for doing." To John Hawkes, she said, "I have been working all summer just like a squirril on a treadmill . . . I think this is maybe not my material (don't like that word) but anyway I am committed to it for a spell at least." To Cecil Dawkins, O'Connor wrote, "I've just been going on about my fictional bidnis this summer, staying doggedly on

the wrong track I think, but I suppose you have to pursue the wrong road long
enough to be able to identify it and then you can get and keep off it."

Caroline Gordon to Flannery O'Connor

Undated [1963]
[California]

I spent my "inter-term" vacation on the orange ranch of an old friend,
Howard Baker, whom I last knew in Paris one thousand years ago.* He
took a Guggenheim fellowship and bought an orange ranch with it and
now he is a president of an olive co-op and an orange co-op—and writes
when he feels like it. He felt like writing the enclosed review of Robert
Fitzgerald's translation of *The Odyssey* for *The Sewanee Review*. I thought
maybe Robert would like to see the review now as I don't know which
issue Andrew plans to publish it in. I had a card from the Fitzgeralds at
Christmas but I don't know their address.

Would you forward said review to Robert?

I am working away on my novel—in the few days left between terms. I
feel as if I had seen about as much of this country as I can take in. Couldn't
have done any better if I had brought my own car. Howard drove me way
up in the high Sierras to a place where he used to camp when he was a boy.
Lord, the redwoods. You have to see them to believe them—and then you
can't believe they're real. The odd thing is they have such short, stubby
branches and the tip of almost every one is stubby, too—blunted against
the stars one is tempted to believe.

Will write more at length later. Love and all good wishes for you and
Regina and all your beasts. I have just painted what seems to me an accu-
rate portrayal of the burial of St. Paul of Thebes—by two lions, you may
remember.

≈ Gordon finished teaching at the University of California–Davis in the
spring, and then accepted another one-year position at Purdue, which precip-
itated another move. That fall, in addition to teaching, she delivered four lectures (including "The Shape of the River") at St. Mary's College of Notre Dame

* Howard Baker, a poet, dramatist, and literary critic who lived with American expatriates in Paris
after World War I, taught at Harvard in the 1940s and later taught at the University of California,
in Berkeley and Davis.

University. At least one of Gordon's performances, O'Connor heard from Lon Cheney, was "very unbuttoned." The following spring, however, Gordon would have breakfast with Eudora Welty, who "marveled" at Gordon's energy with her students at Purdue.

Throughout 1963, O'Connor maintained a vigorous schedule of lectures and readings: Sweet Briar, University of Georgia, Troy State, Smith, Georgetown, Hollins, and more. At Georgetown, O'Connor met Gordon's longtime friend Ward Dorrance and began a correspondence with him. (Dorrance once encouraged Gordon, "You would go on writing novels if you had to strike matches in a cave to do it.") O'Connor's long year of speaking engagements did yield two positive effects: she returned with "enough money to float me through the next six or eight months" and a revitalized spirit: "I come home raring to write."

In November 1963, O'Connor finished a draft of "Revelation" and sent the story to Betty Hester and Catherine Carver. Carver thought the story to be O'Connor's "blackest," called her character Ruby "evil," and suggested that O'Connor remove the final scene. "I am not going to leave it out," O'Connor told Hester. "I am going to deepen it so that there'll be no mistaking Ruby is not just an Evil Glad Annie."

O'Connor fainted just before Christmas and remained in bed through the New Year; doctors believed she suffered from severe anemia. Nonetheless, she was determined to address Carver's criticism and rework the story's tricky final scene. "I've really been battling this problem all my writing days," she said.

This "problem" was hard for O'Connor to articulate. Synthesizing the multiple planes of her highly complex stories into the powerfully dramatic conclusions found in her best work often took painstaking revision, informed by the critiques of her most trusted readers. Caroline Gordon, more than any other, could assess the technical elements of O'Connor's fiction—narrative viewpoint, scenic rendition, and structural components—while understanding O'Connor's deepest artistic intentions. Gordon first addressed the issue in her 1951 letter critiquing *Wise Blood*: "Henry James says that at the beginning of every book 'a stout stake' must be driven in for the current of the action to swirl against. This stout stake is a preparation for what is to come." Gordon's analysis was so effective, however, because her theory was continually bolstered with concrete direction: "You begin and end the book with his [Haze Motes's] eyes. This is one of those places that mustn't be hurried over." Gordon offered similarly insightful and specific advice on "The Displaced Person," "The Artificial

Nigger," and "The Enduring Chill," about which she wrote, "[T]he note of the
ineffable, the symbolic, can't be struck suddenly at the end. It ought to be prepared for from the beginning."

After Christmas, O'Connor sent "Revelation" to Gordon and received a
lengthy response. "I had thought I wouldn't send this one to Caroline because
I hadn't heard from her in a long time and I thought I might be in her black
book; however I heard from her, so I sent it," O'Connor wrote to a friend. "She
liked the story all but a couple of sentences which she proceeded to analyze
grammatically insofar as it was analysable. She is a great hand at grammar. She
wrote me six pages about grammar and another six about her Christmas vacation, which was all on broken-down trains and planes that didn't fly and mis-
connected busses—from Lafayette to Chattanooga to Princeton to Lafayette.
What that woman has is Vitality."

Although O'Connor seemed to write dismissively about Gordon's critique,
Gordon's letter did encompass far more than grammar, and O'Connor did ultimately make the revisions Gordon suggested.

Caroline Gordon to Flannery O'Connor

8 January 1964
[West Lafayette, IN]

I don't think of you as a "writer." . . . Well, that doesn't sound very nice,
does it? I mean one of those writers whose works I *have* to read. Reading
one of your stories is, for me, always an adventure and a delight, as you
must know. I have just got back from wanderings that were pretty fatiguing
and found your ms. on top of the pile of accumulated mail. I have read one
quarter of it so far. Took it in hand and dashed with it to my seminar in fiction which gathers at half past seven on Monday evenings. I explained that
I was taking the liberty of sharing this reading with them because Miss
O'C. has the humility of the true artist and, I felt, wouldn't mind sharing.
I, myself, don't yet know what you are up to and I suspect that you are
working in this story a kind of magic (wrong word, *that!*) —anyhow, shall
we say you are using a technique you have used before in some of your
best stories? A technique which induces the reader to most willingly sus-
pend his disbelief. You do it by making him laugh his head almost off. My
students responded heartily. They laughed—till some of them had tears in

their eyes. Don't see how you could expect to accomplish more than that in six pages . . . More on this subject later.

I am awfully sorry to know that you had to take to your bed during the holidays. Do let me know how you get on. I can't help being anxious about you.

My aunt, who is eighty-six years old, announced that she was being hostess at her last Christmas dinner on this earth. I realized that this was a command performance, changed my reservations (made weeks ago), and set off on a *giro* that I egotistically believe would have daunted Odysseus. However, the Lord, as so many of the theologians point out, mercifully veils what is to come from our sight. I was afraid that I would not get to Chattanooga in time for the dinner so decided to go by train since planes so often can't take off this time of year. I embarked on the Monon, "Indiana's own railroad." I shared a day coach with three other passengers, the student rush away from Purdue not having begun. The conductor and, most of the time, the brakeman, sat opposite me and discoursed on the complexities of railroad travel. The conductor had had to assist on and off the train a lady who was travelling with a standing bird cage. Christmas present for her parrot. He had other tales of eccentricities of travelers. To all of them the brakeman responded, antiphonally: "I don't want to have nothing to do with folks."

The conductor pointed out that freight trains were frequently wrecked. The brakeman was not shaken in his conviction that it is best not to have nothing to do with folks. At Louisville, where I had a roommate engaged, I de-railed and was told that if everybody I consulted were me they would "run over to Track 3 and see if I could get on to 99." I checked my baggage through to Chattanooga and ran for 99. The conductor let me get on but he said that he would have to make me pay for the roomette he would give me as the baggage agent had unintentionally retained my Pullman reservations. I said all right and dosed down. Ninety nine detoured because of a wreck in which fifteen freight cars had piled up. I, myself, think that she got to enjoying her comparative freedom and detoured in a wider arc than was necessary. Anyway, we hove into Nashville at seven o'clock in the morning instead of the two o'clock we would have hove at had I not obeyed the injunctions to run and catch 99. I stayed in the Nashville station until five o'clock that evening, making hurried dashes out into that snow-covered city at intervals. Once, to buy a change of under wear, another time to get my hair shampooed and set. One of the times I was dashing about on Church Street my old friend, Isabelle Howell, archivist of the State of Tennessee, was struggling to her feet on said street, having just been knocked down by a Negro man who took her purse, containing forty dollars, and ran off with it. Isabelle rose to her doubtless heavily galoshed feet and, with admirable courage, sprinted after him. Failed to catch him and sprinted on, block after block after block till she came upon a policeman. I, alas, never encountered her.

We took off at five o'clock p.m. on the Dixie Flyer. It had been derailed a few hours before so had reason for being late. Anyhow, as the song says, it is not Ninety Seven so nobody could expect it to put into Chattanooga or Jacksonville, Florida on time. At Tullahoma, Tennessee, the birthplace of the uncle whom I aspired to dine with ultimately, we stopped two hours. Interestingly enough, opposite that wreck of freight cars which the conductor was referring to (if only prophetically). Fifteen of them in all, one mounted upon another, like Ossa upon Pelion. Wheels pointing towards the sky as if, granted Ruskin's "pathetic fallacy," they aspired to get to Heaven—to dine, say, with Jove. Dantesque lights played over the scene and dim figures moved about in the Stygian gloom.

I forgot to say that before reaching Tullahoma (you know, of course, that you pronounce it Tellahoma)—before we got to Tullahoma we stopped several aeons at the railroad center of Guthrie, Kentucky. It is the birth place of Red Warren and my own folks, those Meriwether Mights, settled three miles from the state line when they came out from Virginia to see if they could find some land to grow tobacco on (having exhausted the fertility of the soil in the Piedmont). I have been moving about that area for eight years now—in that novel I am writing—trying to crawl, fiction-wise, from Merry Mont, the farm I was born on, past Woodstock, the farm my grandmother was born on, up to Meriville, the fine brick house her great grandfather built, three miles from Guthrie when he decided he did not want to live in Scotland and came back to the land of the free and the home of the brave. I have also been crawling for some time now along the Natchez Trace, in company with Meriwether Lewis, who, we are told committed suicide at "Grinder's Station" while trying to get back to Washington to find out why the federal government had dishonoured two of his vouchers. He was, perhaps, the best marksman on this continent at that time and (history tells us) shot himself in the forehead twice and then stabbed himself ten or twelve times before he succeeded in departing this life. Thomas Jefferson, when called upon, had only time for one hurried comment— "suicide ran in the family." He was pretty busy about then wrapping up and dispatching to French countesses shrubs that Lewis and Clark had brought back to him from the far west. (They also brought back two live grizzly bears. He never bothered much with them. Sent to live in the private menagerie of a friend of his, where, I regret to say, one of them tore an arm off the keeper.)

But this kind of total recall is a bit grim in the day light and hardly bearable in the middle of the night. At least, in a railroad car that is unheated and unlighted.

I arrived at Chattanooga at four o'clock in the morning and attempted, taxicab-wise, to ascend Missionary Ridge. It was encased in ice. I forgot to tell the driver to go over the boulevard so he tried to creep up one of those side roads that depend, like Medusa's snaky locks, down all the sides of that mountain. When we skidded for the third time on the sharp curve of a very narrow road, I got out of the cab and made him slide down the hill and take the boulevard up to the Crest road. They were all glad to see me. The Christmas dinner was perfect. Absolutely perfect! The dessert was triple perfection: ambrosia, custard and coconut cake. The coloured retainers, of a family whose head has, so to speak, been long beatified, gathered, more for social life than for service. Their mother, "Darling Katie," died last year and the feast was held partly in her memory. It is a teetotal household. The only person who showed any signs of having had anything to drink was her only son, George, George, over six feet, still handsome, though grey haired, wobbled a bit as he handed things around. But everybody felt that was to be overlooked, for George was acknowledged to have suffered the heaviest bereavement. "Now I ain't got a friend in this world," George said as he left his mother's grave.

My cousin's husband, Frank Carden, spent his Christmas hauling black and white up that ice-encased mountain. Two of the grandchildren asked George what their father was like when he was little. "Fat," George said after a moment's reflection. "He et everything he could get his hands on. Drunk a lot of milk, too." To a similar query about what Paul's sister, Maggie, was like, George said, "Fine. She was just fine." This seemed reasonable to me. One of my fond memories is of George on the point of

leaving for his day off. He is holding Maggie's hand and bending down
from his great height to attend her goodbye. What she used to say was,
"Now, George, be a good girl!" I remember a letter that came to my uncle
once from George. In some jail in Georgia. "For vancre," he wrote.

To continue my saga, I stopped briefly in Princeton and in Middlebush,
seventeen miles away from Princeton. I could not tell Nancy when I would
arrive. She and Caroline were in New York, viewing the Nutcracker suite.
So I saw nobody but young Allen, who admitted that he was not doing
well at Webb's school, where he was sent last Fall. (The school he had been
attending up near Boston was reconciled to his leaving.) He said he didn't
know *what* it was with him and study. I pointed out to him that what it was
is that he doesn't know how to study, embraced him fervently and left him
to his Television. And the company of Jamie McAmy. Amy's Scottie. I do
think that's a good name, don't you?

The only other persons I saw were Winky Barr's research assistant,
Margaret Thorp, walking her fourth dachshund (she kills them, one by
one, by over-feeding) and my cleaning woman, Lucille. After years of effort, on her part and mine, she has proved that she was born, in North
Carolina, sixty-five years ago and receives thirty-two dollars a month from
her grateful government. She recounted woe after woe that beset her and I
dealt with each one as best I could. Finally she came out with what was *really* the matter with her: Kennedy's assassination. "It shuck me, Mrs. Tate
. . . It shuck me. That's all there is to it." She then got out the picture of him
which she preserves. It didn't look much like him, she said, but she kept it
to remember him. "I ain't got nothing and don't never hope to have nothing . . . but it shuck me, Mrs. Tate. It *shuck* me!"

When I reached my uncle's house, my cousin, Manny, warned me not to
mention Kennedy's name. My aunt doesn't like him much better than she
liked Roosevelt. Those members of my family have all turned Republican.
I always feel like saying, "But you haven't got enough *money* to turn
Republican." This time, I thought that maybe they had. Seemed to be doing well in that line. I suppose you feel an obligation to turn Republican if
you succeed in laying your hands on a certain amount of dough.

Northern New Jersey was also encased in ice, but—thank God—laid
down flat. I was astonished and pleased to find New York streets free from
snow the next day and the weather balmy. I plodded up and down Fifth

Avenue, doing my chores and had a pleasant lunch with Eric Langkjaer. I did not want to encounter Tom Walsh, my official editor at Scribner's, so asked Eric to meet me in [a] book store. We then repaired to one of my old time haunts just off Fifth Avenue, opposite the Time and Life building— where I used to sit and talk with Tommy Mabry.* One reason I am fond of it is because of a sight I saw there. The building has old fashioned iron balconies outside. Once, as Tommy and I sat gabbling, a huge tom-cat, a real alley cat, filthy dirty, mangy and with one ear torn off, swaggered by, holding in his mouth a pigeon he had just caught. It's a French restaurant, naturally. An upright American restauranteur would never let that tom cat set foot in his kitchen, much less swagger among his guests. Eric and I were a mite disconcerted when we sat down to note that in a near corner, Broadus Mitchell, now editor in chief at Scribner's, was eating a lonely lunch. However, we got along by using initials instead of certain names or words. Eric's grandmother, who went swimming last summer, has just had a stroke, at the age of eighty-eight. His mother has been nursing her until they got her into a nursing home.

I aspire to end my days with the Carmelites, so stayed over a day in order to trek over to the Madonna Residence in Brooklyn. It is a huge building, fronting on that imitation Place de la Concorde which was set up in hon-our of the Grand Army of the Republic. Opposite is the Brooklyn Public Library *and* the Brooklyn Art Museum. The sight of the place sharpened my desire to get in there but the sister who finally consented to see me was pretty discouraging. Still, she admitted, we *do* have vacancies . . . Yes, I thought, thanks to the Grim Reaper.

The air plane people, still patient over my changes of reservations, re-gretted that they simply could not get me a flight out of Chicago on Lake Central. When I set out on my travels, years ago, it seems, I kept in mind, the fifteen thousand students who would be rushing back to Purdue, plus the twenty thousand rushing to Indiana U. and foolishly thought that since it was only half an hour I could get back to Lafayette sooner or later. I finally saw the light, was about to set forth at half past nine at night on a Greyhound bus, reflected that there might not be any cabs meeting any busses at that

---

* Thomas Mabry, a native of Clarksville, Tennessee, and longtime friend of Gordon and Tate, wrote fiction and served as executive director of the Museum of Modern Art in New York City.

time of night, so dossed down in one of those hotels which, I then discovered, abound near any airport. Mine was the Holiday Inn. Divine! But I am told they all are. After all, practically all their guests are "displaced persons." I telephoned the Greyhound bus people next morning, was told that a bus left at half past nine, got a cab and set forth. When I landed at the bus station I was told that no busses entered "that area" during the day. A sympathetic strike had been called in the interim between the time I telephoned and the time I got to the station. People were piled up, like freight cars, like Ossa upon Pelion. The Information desk was closed and passengers were asked to refer all questions to the ticket agents. These putative saints said over and over and over out of the corners of their mouths while issuing tickets to long queues of people: "Sorry. I don't have any information on that." Special passenger agents and policemen moved about, soothing people. The newspapers reported that many a pocket was picked but I marveled at the patience and orderliness of the throngs. I can only hope that the Greyhound people took care of the travelers whose money ran out. But it seems to me they made quite a mistake in maintaining such a mystery about the strike. Nobody mentioned that word. I was so dull of wits that it took me some time to realize what had happened. Finally I got up the strength to telephone the Monon, Indiana's own railroad, on which I set out so long ago. They said they had a train at ten o'clock. I rushed over there, expecting to stand up all the way, but thinking, slyly, that maybe my grey hairs would get me a seat. To my astonishment, I reposed comfortably in a sparsely inhabited car. From time to time, when the train stopped—only fifteen minutes late, that train—I looked out upon platforms thronged with fresh, rosy, grinning adolescent faces. Thousands of students, all being taken care of by Indiana's own railroad! From time to time, the conductor would pause and chat with me about the running of railroads. The Monon, he said, rented seven extra cars, at the beginning and end of each academic vacation. "All it takes," he said, "is looking ahead." He didn't say a word about how hard it is to deal with folks. But then my first conductor didn't mind dealing with them, either, and I never met my brakeman of yesterday.

I recount my adventures and misadventures at such length, partly because I want my friends to share some part of my sufferings, and, also in the hope that being forced, as it were, to participate in mine, may help a little bit, even, to console you for having to be in bed during the holidays.

Being in bed is tough any time, but I must say that if I have to take to my bed, I would prefer to take it during the holidays. Two years ago I had the worst attack of flu I have had since I was sixteen. (It felt like the kind you had then. "Spanish Flu." Katherine Anne had it and it turned her hair grey.) I was put out of circulation by losing my voice. A man I was trying to talk to long distance finally said, "I wish you'd hang up. You sound like a bat trying to talk." I thereupon got into bed and had one of the happiest Christmases I ever had. But some of my friends in Princeton refer to that Yuletide as "that time you said you had the flu."

How did the Methodists take Ernest's balking at the door of the chapel?* No doubt they were polite about it but I bet my hat they had dark subterranean thoughts, such as what can you expect of a jackass raised by Papists. I am going to put him in Needlepoint yet. I had my Needlepoint and my *Divine Comedy*, plus Charles Williams' *Figure of Beatrice* along on my wanderings. If I hadn't had something to really occupy me I think I would have been locked up somewhere along the route.

I have almost finished a portrait of a Lhasa terrier by the name of Llew Llaw Gyffe. It *is* amusing how the imagination works! I had a chance to get L.L. to sit for his portrait and worked madly and, I think, succeeded in getting a real likeness. Talk went on, of course. I guess we must have talked at some time of nineteenth century poets. Anyhow, some lines ran in my head for several days: "I cannot tell what flowers are at my feet."† All along, I have intended to have cento fleurs at Llew Llaw's feet. Then somebody asked if I was going to sign the work and I found myself saying no, but that it was going to be a Needle Point. I had just realized that Llew Llaw cannot see the flowers I am going to put at his feet. The legend is that these dogs result from a cross between a lion and a monkey. I sometimes think that a bit of Old English Sheep Dog crept in. I have never felt that Llew Llaw could see anything, with all that hair hanging over his eyes.

I must get back to my mountain of real mail—mail that has to be answered. I'll be writing to you about "Revelation" later. I'm quite excited about it.

---

* Regina O'Connor's burro was invited to take part in the Hardwick Christian Church's Christmas pageant, and "when the big moment came and the church full of Methodists, he wouldn't put his foot inside the door." FO to Janet McKane, 31 December 1963, *HB*, 555.
† From John Keats, "Ode to a Nightingale."

Much love for you and Regina. Do let me have some news when you feel like writing. I know you wouldn't take to your bed without good reason but maybe you needed a rest in more ways than one. You've been working pretty hard, haven't you?

Caroline Gordon to Flannery O'Connor

Undated [January 1964]

Just finished reading the whole of "Revelation." To myself and to my seminar. The poor things realize, by this time, that when I call their attention to the work of a master that I do not want—and will not easily brook—criticism, it being my conviction that you can't learn anything from anybody if you are trying to teach him something at the same time. We therefore dwelt (in seminar) only on the architectural structure of your story and the felicities of your style. I was really pleased by the way they took holt of the story!

Old Dr. Gordon, of course, muttered at intervals in private, the way she does. I have recorded her mutterings on several other pages. I wish I had taken time to organize them and type them better. I'm afraid you'll get weary plodding through them.

However, the chief thing I want to say I'll say on this page, unmixed with mutterings. This is a fascinating story. One of your best. Perhaps your most profound so far.

As I say, I took the liberty of reading it to my class. They pleased me immensely by putting most of their fingers on what makes it so masterly. The structure. The *architecture*. You build it up, as solid, as inevitable and, finally as towering as a cathedral.

From the very first, every stroke, even the man who pretends to be asleep when Mrs. Turpin comes in, Mrs. Turpin's entrance, the dirty child, even the magazines on the table—every single stroke is a stone in the remarkable edifice. That takes doing! That is what we all try to do—and what so few of us succeed in doing.

Henry James used to say of a novel that pleased him by its prose style that it was "*written*." Your story is "*built*," it seems to me. Solid as a church.

You will have gathered by this time that I *like* this story! . . . Must get to work—on some stories I can't like as well. Many thanks for sending it to me. Do write when you can. Love and all good wishes for both of you, not to mention Ernest and his Ma. I can't help but think he showed sound sense by balking at the Methodist threshold. I have never quite been able to share Fr. Knox's enthusiasm for John Wesley.

[postscript]

"Wart hog from hell" are certainly *les mots justes*! Were you keeping in mind the fact that the sow is the animal sacred to the earth goddess, Demeter—indeed, I believe, in all mythologies? (think that the Mosaic prohibition against eating the flesh of swine was to keep the Jews from relapsing into the worship of the earth goddess.) At any rate, as Rufus Morey, Princeton's great iconographer, once said to me: "The hog is the most chthonic of animals." . . . I had an old cousin, a rich Yankee lady who got connected by marriage with the Meriwethers, who, after her husband died, used to amuse herself by buying up farms in our neighbourhood, putting them in perfect order and selling them for a slight profit. She was, in the local phrase, "hell on wheels to deal with," though. Robert, a coloured man, who, with his wife, looked after her household, and her, too, once confided to me how he went about managing Miss Lucy.

"Whenever she gits a little off," he said, "I tries to git her down to the hog-pen. Once she gits there, she gits all right in no time."

Will send ms. in a day or two.

[Notes attached]

Page 3   The pot is not gold. It is gold-coloured. Similarly, there is—or was in my youth—no such thing as a "tan cow," an orange sweater etc. But that was when *I* was young and in another country to boot.

It's "aren't" the stylish lady said.

The girl's face is "seared," not "seered." In this masterly story it is Mrs. Turpin, who, like a blind seer in a trance, seeing all her own mischance, drifts, not down to Camelot, but up that there ladder of humility, celebrated by the A.A. Dante Alighieri, St. Bernard of Clairvaux and Franz Kafka—if in reverse. (At least, as I see it.)

Page 7   When Bunny [Edmund] Wilson interviewed himself in *The New Yorker*—couldn't trust anybody else to do it—he asked himself, "Mr. Wilson, to what do you ascribe your success as a critic?"

"To my mastery of the periodic sentence," Mr. Wilson replied. The truest word, it seems to me, he ever spoke and one of the most profound.

There is nothing like the sentence that ends with the thing you want to sock home for socking things home. You can sock practically any notion home if [you] are master of that particular sentence.

Have you ever cast you refulgent eye on Izaac Walton's elegy on John Donne? (Quoted by Herbert Read in his invaluable *English Prose Style*.)

Sentence after sentence after sentence after sentence which *begins* with the important thing. As Maitre Wilson and other[s] of his vintage would say, "Loose sentence after loose sentence after loose sentence . . ." Three quarters of a page of loose sentences. Then the whole movement is brought up short, turned back on itself so violently that it leaves the surface of the prose and is hurled into the air. By one periodic sentence.

But I shall see it reanimated.

Walton's immediate preparation for these pyrotechnics is a muted periodic sentence, to the effect that John Donne, the man whose virtues he has just finished enumerating, is now only

a handful of Christian dust.

But I shall see it reanimated.*

Page 13 Mr. Wilson and me would say ". . . as buoyant as if she weighed one hundred and twenty-five pounds."

And neither of us would use a numerical figure in a sentence. Our mentors would have rapped our knuckles, had we done that. But Mr. Wilson will soon be a handful of un-Christian dust in a very few years, my prose will be unintelligible to even my limited audience, full, as it will then be, of archaisms. (I am sometimes wrong in my Rhadamanthine judgements but I kind of think Maitre Wilson will go first, on account of he has drunk even more whiskey than even me and has had even more tantrums, public as well as private). But Time will doubtless tell.

"Her eyes fixed like two drills on Mrs. Turpin's" seems to me too carelessly shaped a sentence to have its full dramatic impact. Indeed, the paragraph strikes me as not having enough body.

Similarly, I feel that the next paragraph needs another stroke, another sentence—for the requisite body. I'd put Mrs. Turpin's speech in a

---

* The last sentence of Izaac Walton's biography of John Donne, *The Life and Death of Dr. Donne* (1640), reads "He is now a handful of Chrisian dust, but I shall see it reanimated."

paragraph by itself. It's pretty important. Leaving white space around anything helps it seem important.

Again, if I were doing it, I'd break the mother's explanatory speech up a bit. Perhaps by gesture. I'd let "Mary Grace goes to Wellesley College" stand for a second, anyhow, as the pleasant lady's explanation of her daughter's eccentric behaviour. Then, as I see it, this admirable woman who, herself, has suffered so much from Wellesley College (nice bit of projection, that) will realize that her audience will not have any notion of what Wellesley College can do to disrupt family lives and will hasten to specify some of the results of going to Wellesley College—like reading all the time etc.

The fact that Mrs. T thinks the girl looks as if she would like to hurl them all through the plate glass window shows that Mrs. T gets the idea. Also serves as beautiful preparation for the approaching resolution.

In my classes I try to organize something called "Participles Anonymous." Some people can take participles. If you can't, I advise to leave them alone. It seems to me that the fact that Mrs. Turpin's stomach shook is [as] important as revealing her relationship with her husband. Maitre Wilson never puts any action that is dramatic within a participle.

Participles are like the rigging of a ship. All those lines are attached to the mast—or they wouldn't function. You can have as many pieces of rigging as the mast will carry but you will not weather many storms if you have a lot of rigging dangling. Dr. Johnson has somewhere—and I wish I could lay my hands on it again—a sentence that covers half a page, rigged as tightly as any master mariner could desire.

I would also prefer to have Mrs. Turpin's stomach shake *before* she speaks. More life like. She had that stomach long before she says, "He's a caution."

I know I sound damn didactic. The point I am trying to make is that a carelessly used participle is like the first drink to an alcoholic. You use one and you'll use another. Keep on using participles to convey action and your prose style will eventually suffer damage.

Is it "pain" or "pang" of joy on page 16?

I don't like the shape of the crucial sentence on page 16:

It struck almost at the same instant . . .

I feel that you are right in using the imperfect tense here. Makes the reader see it happening instead of perceiving that it happened, as we perforce do most of the time in fiction. This shifting to the imperfect in crises is an artful and effective device. And it certainly works here. It's the shape of the sentence that bothers me. Specifically, the clause "and before she could utter a sound." More specifically, it's that "and." Diagrammed it would be

[see figures 1 and 2 for the diagrams]

It's a compound sentence because it has two subjects and two predicates. The subjects are "It" and "face." The predicates are "struck" and "came," aren't they?

"Face" is modified by the adjective "raw."

"Came" is modified by the prepositional phrase "toward her" and also by the adverb "howling."

It seems to me that you ought to decide which is the thing you most want to emphasize in this sentence. Is it the fact that the face is howling or the fact that it is crashing towards her?

Diagramming the sentence (not very well, either) reveals to me, at least, why I don't like it. It is *not* shaped right. Has a structural flaw.

It is a complex sentence.

A complex sentence is a sentence which has a clause depending from a relative pronoun.

The man whom I considered the finest man I knew has run off with my money and blackened my reputation and had the nerve to ask me to lunch with him last Monday.

Here is a complex sentence that won't work. Why? Because, I think, I am using it to convey two kinds of action which are not incompatible but which operate on different levels: physical action and intellection.

Mrs. T's realization that the girl is about to hurl the book is an intellection (leave us not to go into psychology here). The face coming towards her is an action which takes place on the level of physical action. When you try to combine the two levels of action in one sentence you get an ill-shaped sentence. You further confuse the issue when you make your complex sentence basically a compound sentence.

The boy ran and shouted

is the basic form of the compound sentence.

I had been told that if I wanted a quiet place in which to converse with a friend I would do well to go the Café St. Germain on East Forty Seventh

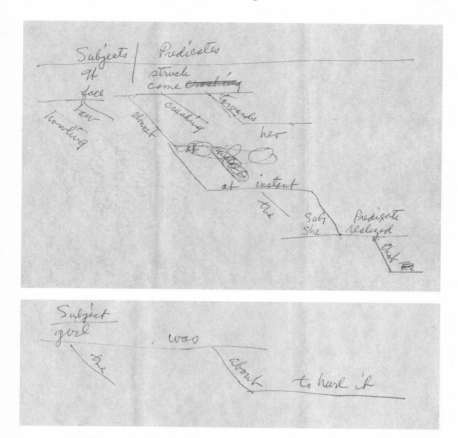

Figures 1 and 2. Caroline Gordon diagrams a passage from
Flannery O'Connor's "Revelation." Images courtesy of the Stuart A. Rose
Manuscript, Archives, and Rare Book Library, Emory University.
Used with permission of Caroline Wood Fallon.

Street. I accordingly walked over there with Eric Langkjaer. We had some
private business to discuss and I had asked him to meet me in the Scribner
Book Store because I did not want to go upstairs to the editorial offices;
I was afraid I might encounter So and So whom I would just as soon not
see; he edited my last book. Eric did not seem to mind meeting me down-
stairs. But when we got to the restaurant we were both a little taken aback
to see Scribner's new editor-in-chief sitting all by himself at a table over in
the corner.

A roughly written paragraph but I believe that it is grammatical. I don't say, "I believe it is grammatical." When you start leaving out the "that's" upon which those relative clauses depend, you get into trouble. You left out the "that" in your sentence.

The first sentence in my paragraph is a complex sentence. Involves hearsay and intellectual operations. The second sentence involves action and is, therefore, a simple sentence—that is, it has one sentence [subject] and one predicate. The third sentence is also a simple sentence, for all its dependent clauses. It's also a loose sentence; puts the predicate first. You also have an opportunity—rare in these days—of seeing two semi-colons used properly in this sentence. Quite a sight, isn't it? Like a bison of the plains, my semi-colons. Soon, soon, they will have gone down to dusty death— *Eheu*, as Maitre Wilson might allow himself to lament.

The last sentence in my rough-hewn paragraph is complex. The subject is "We," the predicate is "taken," modified by "a," "little" and "aback." "To see Scribner's editor-in-chief" (modified by "new") is an infinitive clause depending on "taken" and "sitting by himself" is a participial clause modified by "all," "by," "himself," "corner," "in," "a" and so on—God help us! The author has combined action and intellection in the last sentence, you will observe. One reason she did it without thinking about is because being taken aback and seeing the ed-in-chief seemed to her of equal importance. But you will also observe that she used that kind of sentence at the *end* of her paragraph. You go monkeying with a combination of the simple sentence and the compound sentence when you are portraying a train of action, you [are] going to get into trouble before you wind up your paragraph.

In the next sentence I take exception to the use of "floor" twice. I also object to the use of the word "astraddle." It comes straight from Mrs. Turpin's vocabulary. You have been using her vocabulary, for the most part, through the whole story, but Mrs. Turpin will soon have an experience which will transcend all her previous experiences. Language reflects experience, of course. But it is the common experience of the visionary to find his every day vocabulary inadequate for his transcendent experiences. St. Catherine of Siena—and how many other seers?—render their experience by "Aaa . . . aaah . . . aaah"?

"Astraddle" is too down to earth. "Astride" will do no harm to verisimilitude and will help lift the story to its new level of action. Allen taught me this when I was trying to finish *Green Centuries*. He made me at a certain point take out all the "ain'ts" and "hit wars" and begin preparing for the ultimate vision by elevating the tone of the narrative. As I recall, he suggested the introduction of a classical allusion. I'd say on page 16

> ... her heart which, it seemed to her—from side to side as if it were agitated in a great empty drum of flesh."

I would not say "*slapped.*"

"Agitates" is good. Lifts the tone.

It goes on mighty well—*mighty* well, it seems to me, until your concluding paragraph.

I know what a Hampshire White is but most folks don't these days. I'm not sure I'd choose that breed because of that black belt around the middle. Too hard to render pictorially. In fact, I know exactly the kind of pig I'd use if this were my story (said she, enviously). I am simply mad about this here landscape in this part of Indiana. Once when a Californian correspondent wanted to know why, I found myself saying, "I think it's the pigs." The houses in the country around here are all small, late Victorian jobs, with lots of scroll work and miniature cupolas and lots of fresh white paint. Each farm has a woodlot which looks, in autumn, like a bouquet of bronze and crimson field flowers and pigs are all over the field. Duroc-Jersey, Jersey Reds, white pigs and a profusion of spotted pigs. Tan or gold-coloured spots on black skin. "Maculate," like [T. S.] Eliot's giraffe. Not "Immaculate," like the BVM.

I intend eventually to embody some of those spotted pigs, along with Ernest, in a bit of needle-point. You might not respond to the sight of them as fervently as I do, though I rather think you would. But be that as it may, I believe we need to see your pigs a little more clearly—there where they are all settled in one corner around the old sow "who was" (so beautifully) "grunting softly."

It is from contemplating those pigs and the sow that Mrs. Turpin wins to her vision of the life (now and) hereafter, isn't it? Therefore, you ought to be vivid and exact at this stage of your "literal level."

I am going to make a few very tentative suggestions here. It seems to me that there ought to be a little more of the literal level—a little more action on Mrs. Turpin's part before she has her vision, or, rather a little more action interspersed in her vision. I'd put it in, I think, right after "abysmal life-giving knowledge." I'd have her make some movement right after that, one that was slow enough and hieratic enough not to break the flow of the vision. One that would rather reinforce the vision, the way the literal level which Dante so insists on, reinforces his visions by giving them a foundation—like that ledge which Dante reclines on, along with Virgil at the end of the First Day.

I puzzled for a while over "hoard." I even tried to recall the antics of the Nibelungs around that hoard of theirs which the dragon, Fafnir, guarded. I thought—I really thought—that you meant that a hoard of souls, which means to me a lot of souls hidden somewhere so nobody could get at them were rumbling towards Heaven. I was about to write you that the metaphor, whatever it was, seemed to me too violent and not well enough substantiated to work when one of my colleagues, a character of your vintage came along. I let him read the story. He is crazy about it! When I said I didn't think that "hoard" worked he said he thought it did. In the course of the conversation I discovered that for him, too, "hoard" and "horde" are synonymous. They aren't for me but

> I am old and you are young
> And so I speak a barbarous tongue. . . .*

I'd say that this "hoard" (horde) of souls were rumbling towards heaven. This is one of those places where the use of the imperfect is dramatic. Makes for immediacy.

One final objection. I do not believe that she *can* hear either the "hoard" (or "horde") of souls. She cannot hear any one of those souls any more than she can hear a hog or a railroad train or any object or person. She hears the *sound* emitted by the object or person.

You are making for the anagogical level. One doesn't use colloquialisms or idioms there—for the reason, I hazard, that there everybody understands everything anybody else says.

Allen has expressed astonishment at my story, "One Against Thebes." It is the stars in the final paragraph that puzzle him most. He says they "work" but he can't see why they work. The answer seems simple to me. Anybody—my nine year old girl, Mrs. Turpin—can look up and behold the same stars that Dante beheld as he emerged from Hell:

*From W. B. Yeats, "Two Years Later."

the beauteous burdens of the sky

Fletcher translates the line.*

Have you been reading *The Divine Comedy*? Or were you smarter than I am and read it years ago? I have just finished reading it for the first time, in what I begin to suspect, is a mis-spent life. Owe it to Ashley [Brown]. He kept going on about how I had learned this or that technique from Dante and I finally told him that, like so many of my contemporaries, I had read the *Inferno* all the way through but had progressed no further. He replied: "You'd better."

So I started in this Fall and, now that I have finished, I am going to pursue the plan I have followed for fifteen years with St. John of the Cross. Soon as I get through the whole works, I turn around and start in again at the beginning.

It seems to me that you—or I or any other fiction writer—can find any technique we can muster right there, used to perfection by Dante. All these things I keep trying to tell young people—he can show them to them better than I can ever hope to show them.

≈ That February, O'Connor learned she needed surgery: fibroid tumors were at the root of her severe anemia. Any surgery, however, risked triggering her disease from its remission. Proactively, O'Connor cancelled her upcoming lectures and travel. She told Robert Giroux before her surgery that she wanted to publish another collection of short stories.

By O'Connor's thirty-ninth birthday in March, biographer Brad Gooch wrote, Flannery realized "something was gravely wrong." O'Connor downplayed her fears about the resurgence of lupus: "I haven't had it active since 1951 and it is something renewing acquaintance with it," she said.

Gordon telephoned O'Connor from Purdue the first week of April. On a good day, Caroline learned, particularly following blood transfusions, Flannery might work up to an hour.

At the end of May, O'Connor returned to Piedmont Hospital in Atlanta. "I'm worried about Flannery," Gordon wrote once again to Ashley Brown. "[S]he definitely is getting worse. I've tried to telephone there several times but got nobody." Then, Gordon heard from O'Connor: "[S]he is not allowed to see

The Divine Comedy of Dante Alighieri, trans. Jefferson Butler Fletcher (New York: Macmillan, 1931).

anybody because the slightest effort brings on fatigue which causes repercussions [. . .] The monks at Our Lady of the Holy Ghost are annoyed with Regina for not letting Flannery see the abbot when he came to call but seems to me she's only following the doctor's orders. I guess the poor child is pretty sick."

Gordon flew to Georgia on May 29. O'Connor wrote to Brown, "Caroline breezed in one weekend. She visited Fr. Charles at the monastery and they came out to see me. She has dyed her hair the color of funnytoor polish. Startling effect." Gordon later described the visit in poignant detail:

> We were permitted to stay only twenty minutes. After the nurse had left the room, Flannery pulled a notebook out from under her pillow. "The doctor says I mustn't do any work. But he says it's all right for me to write a little fiction." She paused to grin at us, the kind of wry grin which a contemplation of the inordinate demands of his craft sometimes elicits from the fiction writer, and went on to confide that she hid the notebook under her pillow and wrote in it "whenever they aren't doing something to me." If the story she was working on turned out "all right" she planned to include it in the volume which we all knew by that time would have to be published posthumously.

Gordon wrote to O'Connor when she returned to Indiana.

Caroline Gordon to Flannery O'Connor

Undated [27 June 1964 postmark]
Tuesday, I am pretty sure!

Here I am, back in West Lafayette. I had intended to take off for Notre Dame this afternoon but have decided to stay over and approach that spot the way Allen said we must approach the Holy Roman Catholic Church: "slowly and intelligently."

The wisdom of said approach is more evident to me now than it was [the] day before yesterday. Seems to me we came near to meeting our Maker, Father William, two other priests and I as we sped towards the airport. Fr. William was driving more carefully than the Abbot drives but very doggedly. Keeping up a certain speed all the way. Packs of mongrel dogs were hunting in, on and around the highway and my backbone was already quivering with those near misses when an aged "red neck" suddenly drove out from his yard on to the road. He didn't glance in our direction because, we later found out, he couldn't turn his neck, being in a cast. Fr. William forewent his allotted speed but his brakes weren't all they should have been. With great skill he maneuvered us past the red neck's car and then, just as I decided that we would end in a red clay ditch—the car skidded fearfully—Fr. W. righted her in a brilliant zigzag and all would have been fine if another car hadn't suddenly appeared. Whereupon Fr. William zig zagged again but by this time he was so crowded he grazed the back of the red neck's car. No great damage done to their car, though fenders were bent and a door bashed in a bit. I only hope that Fr. William's brilliant manoeuverers didn't take too much out of him, nerve-wise, as we say. I have been a bit limp ever since. But then I am not made of as stern stuff as he is. But enough of this.

I can't tell you how glad I was to get a little visit with you in. I took what the doctor said seriously and wouldn't have tried to see you if the Abbot hadn't insisted. I am certainly glad he did. There was a rumor (promulgated by Brother Pius) that you were going home today or would it have been yesterday?

Brother Pius showed us some slides of the cloistered parts of the monastery the evening before I left. When I commented on the fact that they didn't have many people in their grave yard he dug me in the ribs with his elbow and said "If I was to die tonight they'd bury me just like this. No box, no coffin, just the way I am" and he fingered a fold of his habit with what seemed to me a bit of complacence. "What the well dressed man will wear at his funeral." I suspect that his satisfaction with his own appearance resulted from an encounter he had had half hour before. We were standing on the walk when three people came by. A middle aged man who looked all right. Sartorially, at least. He looked (in the face) as if he might be or have been a gangster or engaged in some illegal ventures. But he looked all right—on the surface. He was accompanied by a middle aged woman who looked all wrong. Something funny about her torso which was emphasized by the dress she wore and the way her hair was bleached and plastered on her skull. The man gave a young girl who was with them a shove when they came to us and said, "Go on. Ask him." She stepped up, chewing gum, and said to Br. Pius, "I want to ask you something . . . What makes you sleep in unheated dormitories?" "Because we're mortified monks," Br. P. said and added that they had plenty of blankets and actually liked that way of sleeping though it "was supposed" to mortify them. She ruminated over that then said, "What makes you keep silence?" He told her that that was because a whole refectory full of monks all talking at once would sound like the monkey cage at the zoo. She chewed a little more gum then said, "Well, why don't you eat meat?" "We just keep on trying to get mortified," says Br. Pius. She swaggered off after that. He looked after her, trying to identify the origin of her oddments of costume. "Those long grass ear rings look Mexican to me. . . . . Don't you think her sandals are Mexican, too? . . . Of course she could get those tight pants anywhere . . . Caroline, *where* do you think she got that sack?"

I told him I thought she got it out of George Catlin's paintings of the Indians of the northwestern plains. It was parti-coloured and open in the front and also on both sides. Fringed, too, as I recall. I may be wrong but it seemed to me that Brother Pius, as she looked after her, was a bit conscious of his own sartorial elegance, wearing as he did, just his habit, his white socks, his black shoes, his hearing aid and his spectacles.

I have got another 150 pages of Sr. Anne-Monica's thesis on Yeats to read before I leave here. Am going to tackle it under the hair dryer in a few minutes. It's most interesting but weighs a ton. We are going to try to see if we can't extract a book from it. She calls it *The Rogueries of William Butler Yeats*. I will know a lot more than I know now when I've finished it. She has tracked down the origin of almost every line Yeats wrote. She casts a cold (Catholic) eye on his life work. May be his own fault. He asked people or, at least, strangers to "cast a cold eye" on his tomb before they rode by. I find myself wondering whether it ever occurred to him that the cold eye would be a Catholic eye.

Must repair to the beauty parlor, along with Willy Yeats.
I go from here to stay with

Katherine Morgan
Rutgers University Press, New Brunswick, NJ

until June 19 when I go to the

Lakeview Hotel
Spring Lake, New Jersey

until July first when I rush back to the Red House [Princeton]. Don't pay any attention to my schedule. That sort of thing *is* work, as even a doctor would recognize.

Much love. I was glad to find you in good spirits, though, after all, good spirits are something you've never lacked. I'm glad, too, to know you sneak in a little "work." Will write again soon but don't bother to answer. *That's* work, writing letters is.

⮑ By July of that year, O'Connor had been in the hospital fifty days. "The wolf, I'm afraid, is inside tearing up the place," she said. O'Connor sent "Parker's Back," her final story, to Caroline Gordon and Betty Hester on July 11.

Flannery O'Connor to Caroline Gordon

11 July 1964

I finally got out of Piedmont [Hospital] after one month there. An old lady here wrote me that anyone who could survive a month at Piedmont had nothing to worry about as far as health was concerned. I've been home three weeks today, confined to two rooms, am not supposed to walk around, something about they want all the blood to go to the kidneys, but my momma arranged the table so I can get out of the bed right into the electric typewriter. Enclosed the result ["Parker's Back"]. Would you mind looking at it and letting me know what ails it or if you think it fits my collection? [It'll] be the usual *great* favor.

Did you find out how old swans have to be to lay? Mine do nothing but sit in their tub on the grass.

Never ride with the clergy if you are not immediately ready to meet your maker. They kindly offered to bring me home from the hospital but I declined even before your description of your ride to the airport. I hope Florida is doing Fr. Charles some good.

⮑ Gordon read "Parker's Back" and shared a detailed critique with O'Connor. Years later, Gordon said, "I did not realize or perhaps I was unwilling to admit to myself that she was so near death. At any rate, soon after I mailed my letter, I felt impelled to send her a telegram. I remember the wording: 'Congratulations on having succeeded where the great Flaubert failed.' [. . .] As time has gone on, it has seemed to me that I might have done better not to have written her about her story. What I said in my telegram better represents my whole-hearted reaction to the body of her work."

Caroline Gordon to Flannery O'Connor

Undated [July 1964]

[Princeton, NJ]

The story ["Parker's Back"] is certainly one of your good ones. Reading it, I am reminded of something one of my most talented pupils said some years ago. He said that he read *The Red Badge of Courage* and didn't really know what was going on until two days later, when, he said, "I gave a long shudder."

I imagine that you hardly know as yet what is in your own story. At least, that's the way it goes for most good writers, I think. But I, or rather old Dr. Gordon, sort of have to figure out what goes on on all levels if I am to be of any help in my comments.

The "action," of course, is what went on in Parker as regards his back. On the literal level. On the allegorical level the action, I take it, is the operation in the life of a man of supernatural grace coming into conflict with a certain heresy? The heresy is that Christ is all spirit. Let us leave the moral and anagogical levels to take care of themselves and consider the first two levels.

You fly pretty high on the allegorical level. It is therefore all the more essential that your literal level be firmly established. Dr. G. does not feel that the action is firmly enough located in space.

To begin with, she wonders why you have two houses. The one Parker met the girl in and the one on the high embankment under the pecan tree. Having to deal with two houses makes it harder for the reader. If he doesn't visualize each house clearly the story lacks that much credibility. What can't you have only one house? Couldn't the girl have inherited the house he first met her in? Couldn't it still be perched on that high embankment? I see it sitting there under that tree and I see Parker turning off the highway and bending over the hood and perhaps glancing up towards that house for whatever he needs and at the same time catching a glimpse of a moving object through the bushes. Then that old prickling in the back of his neck takes over. After an exchange or two I would have him ask her what she brought her broom along for. Is she going to sweep the highway? Then he is lammed by that terrible "claw." I think that she ought to use the same weapon for his final beating up. I have a notion that when he asks her if she is going to sweep the highway she makes a Biblical remark—well, I guess even Dr. G. could leave that one to you!

Similarly, I think the tree ought to be in at the start or rather be made more of at the start if he is to lean against it and cry at the finish. It seems more to me that this is implicit in your action. She accuses him of fornicating under every green tree.

If the house and the tree are stressed more you will get more unity. And the story will gain in stature. If you start a story with something and end it with the same thing (seen in different light), you get a structural unity that (geometrically) resembles a cathedral arch. Look at *The Idiot*. Starts with two men sitting opposite each other in a railway carriage, talking about a certain woman. Ends with the same two men sitting opposite each other, in the same attitude in a half dark room, with the dead body of the woman they were originally talking about lying beside their chairs in her coffin. That's what the Greeks mean by "unity of action." It's implicit in this story; but I think it needs to be brought out a little more.

I think that in the first paragraph of your story you go into Parker's consciousness too hurriedly. You have to convince the reader that a man exists before you can interest the reader in what goes on in his mind or heart or soul. It takes three "specifications" to do this. You give your reader one specification. Parker, so far a disembodied spirit, is "sitting on the step."

There are two ways of beginning a story, and, as far as old Dr. G. has discovered, only two. One is to start your story with "a long view" or "panorama." A panorama is what the word says: seeing all. It may be a rapid review or even summary of action or it may be a reflection of life in general. Like the first sentence of *Anna Karenina*: "The histories of all happy families are all alike" etc.

A prime example of such a panoramic opening is the first half of Mann's *Death in Venice*. Ostensibly it consists of reflections on the life of the artist—any artist. Actually, it is giving the reader the dope which will make him see why Gustave von Aschenbach met the peculiar death he met in Venice.

Scott Fitzgerald uses this form of opening (effectively if crudely) in *Gatsby*. He does not write as well as Mann so couldn't get his effect partly by tone, as Mann does.

Old Dr. G.'s "Tom Rivers" is another example of this way of beginning a story. It's done mostly with tone. As I recall, it goes: "I have never been able to understand it, though I think about it often, less and less, of course, as the years go by and his name is never mentioned. Still, in a large family connection such as ours . . ."

The tone is elegiac. All those "o's" and the three syllable Latin-derived words is what does it. It took our crotchety old friend around fifteen years to get to the point where she could pull *that* kind of effect off. Got a fan letter about it, I now recall. From Mrs. Herbert Croly,* who, after all, must have recognized good writing when she encountered it.

So much for one way of starting a story. Another tried and true way is to begin with action, the more violent the better.

"Hell," said the Duchess, "Take your hand off my knee!"

The old timers used to maintain that you had everything there, including snobbery and sex appeal.

Old G. would probably begin your story something like:

Parker's wife turned her head in his direction and said, "It's no reason you can't work for a man."

"You got to work for whoever asts you to work," Parker said.

"It don't have to be a woman," she said.

"Aw, shut your mouth for a change," Parker muttered.

They were sitting on the front porch of the house that Parker's wife had inherited from her mother. The house stood on a high embankment over-looking the highway, in the shade of a single pecan tree. Parker's wife said that the house had stood in a grove of pecan trees when her father and mother came there to live the year she was born. When his wife spoke of "the grove," Parker was likely to ask, "Who planted them trees?" When she did not answer, which was unusual, for she had a tongue "hung in the middle and going at both ends" most of every day, he might say, "Well, then, who cut 'em down? . . . And who sawed 'em up? . . ." or "What become of all the stumps?"

He was sitting now with his back against the wall of the house, his long legs, clad in ragged blue jeans, stretched out in front of him along the slanting floor boards. His wife sat on the second of the five rickety steps that led up to the porch. She had spread a newspaper on the top step and was "snapping" beans into it from the high tin bucket that stood beside her. When she had told him that he didn't need to work for a woman, Parker had kept his face immobile and had gazed past her, over the tops of the trees that bordered the highway to the (whatever the distant view is.

---

* Wife of Herbert Croly, cofounder of The New Republic.

Myself, I'd put a river there). But now he turned his own head so that, for
an instant, his eyes rested full on her face. She was plain. No denying that.
The skin of her face was. . . .

> Run on to end of paragraph.
> He was puzzled and ashamed of himself.

He shifted his gaze to the highway below. There was not much traffic
along here at this time of day. His wife customarily sat with her back half
turned to the highway but when a car came in sight she always veered
around long enough to look at it suspiciously before her eyes dropped to
her piles of beans. One of the things she did not approve of was automo-
biles . . . run on to end of paragraph.

> It was himself he could not understand.

I seem to have made a bit free with your beginning. But I am just sketch-
ing the action in, free hand, as it were, to try to give you an idea of the kind
of *shape* that it seems to me the action must have here. What I have written
is an example of the fictional principle I am citing.

I believe that you are violating one of the fundamental principles of craft
when you plunge straight into Parker's consciousness. Stephen Daedalus
is one of the most self-centered, indeed, one of the most Narcissistic heroes in all literature. But Joyce keeps the action completely objective for
fourteen pages. He does this, I feel sure, in order to prepare for the deep
plunge into Stephen's consciousness.

Most young writers are inclined to begin a story with a young man (or
woman) taking a walk alone and thinking about himself (or herself). You
skipped that stage. Lucky girl! You always present action objectively. Your
view point is objective. But some of the minor pit-falls still lie in wait. No
matter how objective a view you take of your hero, you have got to convince the reader of his existence before you can reveal any of the things
about him you want to reveal. The only way to convince the reader of the
existence of any character is to show him in action. Action (in fiction)
means being involved somehow with another human being. That's what
"stately, plump Buck Mulligan" is for—to convince us that Stephen exists.

Joyce lavishes all his skill on his preparation for the moment when
Stephen looks into the mirror. (Most young writers have the hero looking
into the mirror the first crack out of the box.) But Stephen (tired as I am of
him!) really *is* a hero. When he looks into the mirror, he sees not only his

own so dearly loved countenance but the face of Ireland. And Ireland in action. Ireland as servant to England, seeing herself in the "cracked looking glass of a servant." Being a hero, his apprehension transcends the immediate scene.

Parker is a hero, too!

This brings me to my second suggestion. I don't like your title. I don't think it is adequate. I suppose because it is too pedestrian. I think that it is a better story than "The Enduring Chill" but that is a better title. I think that maybe your title ought to come from the allegorical level. I keep thinking of "Green Tree . . ."

"Under a Green Tree?"

"Under Every Green Tree?"

I'm talking to myself here—or to you?

Maybe his back *is* the note that must be struck: "The eyes that were forever on his back were eyes to be obeyed."

I suspect that part of the trouble is with this sentence. I think you are rather pulling your punches here. Getting over the ground too fast. Suppose you broke this sentence up into say three sentences:

1. There *are* eyes emblazoned [on] his back. Fiery eyes . . . Lord knows what kind of eyes but the reader must be made to see them through their "attributes."
2. These eyes *could* look straight through you . . .
3. And they were there for *good*. They would *keep* on looking . . .

However, it goes, I believe you need three steps here.

One more suggestion. On page 17 you write ". . . A flat stone Byzantine Christ with all-demanding eyes."

The use of the word "Byzantine" there jars on me. It smacks of "author's comment." You haven't established the kind of omniscient view point which would allow you, the author, to interpolate this piece of information. I believe that the fact that the picture is Byzantine ought to be introduced in *action*. That is, Parker ought, perhaps, to find the kind of picture he wants under the heading "Byzantine." He might even ask the tattoo artist what in the hell that means and have the artist put him off with a vague generality. Maybe because the artist himself doesn't know? "Oh, it's one of the names. They have to have names. So you can find them in the book." Or something like that.

It seems to me that if Parker does not know that the eyes that are, as it were, boring into his back, are "Byzantine," that it is all the more dramatic. Also the *reader* will know that the Christ in Parker's back is Byzantine and have that agreeable sensation of knowing more than the hero knows.

On page 25 there is a crucial sentence: "and all at once he felt a light pouring through him, turning his spider web soul into a perfect arabesque of colors, a garden of trees and birds and beast."

I think that this sentence goes too fast. You have bitten off more than you or anybody can chew in one sentence. In my "seminars" I have been using *Alice in Wonderland* and *Through the Looking Glass* as textbooks in "fictional logic" for some years now.

Fictional Logic is opposed to the kind of Logic we live by. Perhaps because fiction is, after all, only a contrived illusion of life and not, as some ignoramuses think, "slices of life."

Since what we see in fiction is a reflection it is a "mirror image," or upside down. The best example I know of fictional logic is the Red Queen's asking Alice why she doesn't stand still if she wants to get there fast. Our natural impulse is to cover the ground fast when we get to something important in our stories. What we ought to do is to stand still or, at least, move very slowly. I think that this sentence ought to be broken up into several sentences. Same thing goes for a sentence above in which "a tree of light burst over the skyline." That is too sudden for us to take it in. Your tree doesn't quite "work" because you try to put it there too fast.

One last comment. I am wondering whether Ruth ought to have the last word? She could have the last word. One can always shift the view-point but it must be done in order to achieve a more dramatic effect, not to suit the author's convenience. It might be more effective to view the action through her eyes here but that fact must be established—dramatically.

I suspect that you suddenly begin to see things through Ruth's eyes here because you instinctively feel the need of another view point. I think that the view point you need is that of dat old Debbil, the Omniscient Narrator. Ruth probably won't serve. She thinks she knows everything but she actually doesn't know—or see—as much as she does.

I think that you weaken your *dénouement* on page 17 [27] when you comment on Parker's condition. I think that author's comment is out of place here. You are making the same mistake you made at the first of the story when you dived too suddenly into his consciousness.

If the action is to achieve the "cathedral arch" or Roman arch which is implicit in its structure, the comment is as out of place here as in the beginning. The reader ought to see what Parker does here. Any kind of comment should be reserved until the action is over. I'd say: "Parker sat there while she rained blows upon him with her broom. . ."

Oh, hell! Even Dr. G hesitates to trespass here. The point is that the reader ought to get a picture of what happened. Your comments: ". . . she had nearly knocked him senseless" serve only to get between the reader and what is going on. What you need is more stuff like ". . . large welts had formed on the face of the tattooed Christ." Again, though, you are working too fast to get the required dramatic impact. You ignore the mechanics of the effect. You give that Christ, who is all important to your action, only one specification: "large welts." Joyce, Flaubert, Ovid, Richardson, Fielding et al. would furnish four or five or six or even seven or eight.

Again, ". . . to get the taint of him off it" weakens the action. Action and comment, except under extraordinary circumstances, should not be handled in one sentence. This is one of the firmest bases of a serviceable prose style. A virtuoso occasionally puts action and comment in the same sentence but the comment comes nearly always at the last of the sentence and is always distinct from the action. You, succumbing to an evil prevalent in your time, incline to substitute comment for action. It never works. Just weakens your effect.

Here, at the last, I think that we ought to have a clear picture of both the woman and the man. I see him leaning against the tree. You ought to make me see her, too. Just see her. Leave her consciousness alone.

I have a feeling that the tone demands to be lifted to the plane of the omniscient narrator in the last sentence. Old Dr. G would show her clearly, looking out the window, and then show the reader what she sees. Something like this:

> ". . . and her eyes hardened. He was still standing there leaning against the tree. He had his arm up so that she could not see his face but she realized that he was crying. Obadiah Elihue Parker! Crying like a baby—or as if his heart were broken and broken so long ago that he did not know how that had come about and never would know now."

You will understand, I know, that when old Dr. G says that she would do it this way or that she is merely trying to give you, off-hand, an example of the kind of thing she feels ought to be done in a certain place. She could cite examples of the way other writers would do it but it is easier to cite herself.

However, you have examples of what I am talking about in, say Frank O'Connor's "Guests of the Nation." It starts off with a lot of the homely details that make a scene but throughout the first three paragraphs, if you examine them closely, you can find indications that, in the end, the scene will be enlarged—to the dimensions of eternity. The very word "dusk," for instance. Dusk is universal. If this story were to have a different kind of ending, O'Connor might have said: "Every afternoon, at 5 o'clock . . ." "Ashes" is another key note. Other notes foreshadowing the *dénouement* are the names of dances: "The Walls of Limerick," "The Siege of Ennis," and "The Waves of Tory." That "O" sound is very important.

He ends the story most artfully. The final paragraph is written in a style which is a cunning mingling of the omniscient narrator's tone and the tone of the man who tells the story, ". . . watching the stars and listening to the (damned) shrieking of the birds. It is so strange what you feel at such moments and not to be written afterwards . . . and the old woman and the birds and the (bloody) stars were all far away, and I was somehow very small and very lonely." And the last sentence, while it is written in the narrator's spoken idiom, nevertheless, has the effect of the omniscient viewpoint: "And anything that ever happened to me after I never felt the same about again."

I—or rather that old Dr. G—have been writing to you as if you were in the pink of health. But your doctor may have discovered, by this time, that there is a bit of work involved in the writing of fiction and may have forbidden you such effort. In view of this possibility, I am going to summarize my suggestions I have written at such length and so ramblingly because, in a way, I have been trying to talk this out with you. But if you aren't up to such conversations, why don't you concentrate on this shorter version which I will append, for your convenience.

As usual, I hope I am not giving you a bum steer but you are used to taking such risks, so I won't worry about that!

A letter from Fr. Charles reports that he is back at the Abbey "a changed man." I think that maybe his fling "in the world" may have changed him some. It's a mighty trying place. That monastery would seem a green oasis to me—after some of the places I've been in lately. Of course, getting up in the middle of the night to say those hours is tough. But then a lot of folks wake up in the middle of the night and have to take pills to get back to sleep . . . Not that I am minimizing the monks' mortifications. Still, it seems to me that if Fr. Charles wants to get any writing done he's got what amounts to a perpetual Guggenheim. I did point that out to him.

I have gone in for "false topiary work"—in a modest way. And now have the outline of a topiary peacock mounted on cunningly twisted wire legs over a clay pot. The idea is to make the sculptural shapes out of aluminum wire, which is soft and bends easily and cuts like butter. Then you plant vines in the pot and train them along the wires. I'm trying grape ivy because I can get that free out of Nancy's garden but the vines incline to wither. However, I'm sure I can get some rooted in time. After all, I've had this notion working like madness in my brain for years—ever since somebody sent me an issue of the Brooklyn Botanical Garden publications devoted to garden sculpture.

I know you must be glad to be back home. Love to you both, and congratulations on the story. It's one of your best. Grows on you.
[attached notes]
SHORTER VERSION OF SUGGESTIONS—Read this if you don't have energy for the longer version.

I think that the "geometry" of the story is that of the "cathedral" or Roman arch. Such architecture calls for a vivid, well rounded scene at the beginning and the same kind of scene at the end.

A standard example is *The Idiot* which begins with two young men sitting opposite each other in a railway carriage and ends with the same young men sitting opposite each other in [a] half darkened room with the dead body of the young woman they were talking about lying in its coffin beside them.

I think that you go into Parker's consciousness too suddenly before you have convinced the reader that he exists. The only way you can convince the reader that a character exists is to show him in action—that is, involved with another human being. To effect this you must give the reader enough "specifications" to enable him to visualize the character. You give the reader one specification for Parker: he is sitting. Tolstoy, Dostoevsky,

Flaubert et al. would have given the reader four of five or six or seven or more specifications thereby emphasizing the fact that he is a leading character. What I say applies also to his wife.

The same technique ought to be used in your final scene. That is we ought, first of all to see what the man and woman are doing before we are asked to grasp its significance. One can use fewer specifications in the closing scene because the ones that have already been used will now have a cumulative effect. But the final scene must have the same "weight" as the beginning scene—if the structure is to stand firm.

Your closing scene is marred by the fact that in several places you substitute comment for action: "Parker was too stunned to resist . . ." and ". . . to get the taint of him off it . . ." are examples.

This, as I see it, is your chief fault as a fiction writer. Here are other examples:

The eyes that were forever on his back were eyes to be obeyed.

You mix the literal and allegorical levels here. A virtuoso does this on rare occasions in order to achieve a certain effect. You do it to get over the ground fast. It never works.

You ought to have more steps in this effect:

1. The eyes *are* on his back. Those eyes (and by this time you ought to have made us see them) those eyes *are* fixed on his back. That's your literal level.

2. His belief that those eyes must be obeyed operates on the allegorical level (the level that says something other, something more than what has been said on the literal level).

Another example of this technical flaw is on page 25:

> ". . . and all at once he felt a light pouring through him, turning his spider web soul into a perfect arabesque of colours, a garden of trees and birds and beasts."

Again, you go so fast you blur your effect.

The remedy for this kind of technical imperfection is to resort to the kind of Logic which is used in *Alice in Wonderland* and *Through the Looking Glass*. The Red Queen asks Alice why she doesn't stand still if she is in such a hurry to get there.

This is an outstanding example of the "Logic of Fiction." Our natural inclination is to hurry when we get to a crucial scene. We ought, however, to go against our natural inclination at this point and stand still or move very slowly—in order to give the reader time to take in what is happening. (The movies use this technique all the time but it is hard to get fiction writers to see it. "The cursed craft," as Sean O'Faolain* calls it . . .)

The practical thing to do is to split these sentences I am speaking of into two or three sentences:

1. He feels a light pouring through. All right.
2. What kind of light?
3. What does it do to him? Turns his soul into an "arabesque of colours." (I'm not sure about that. The word "arabesque" connotes line not colour.) Anyhow, it turns his soul into something.
4. How do we know it does? Because you furnish the "specifications" which will convince the reader: Trees, beasts, birds, flowers, etc.

I think that your use of "Byzantine" smacks of author's comment. The reader needs to know that the eyes are Byzantine in order to picture them but I think that that fact ought to be introduced in action. Couldn't Parker ask the tattoo artist what in the hell "Byzantine" means?

Your title seems too pedestrian to me. I keep thinking of "Tree." She accuses him of fornicating under every green tree. "Under a Green Tree"?

I think you make a mistake in having two houses. The story suffers now from not being firmly located enough in space. Why not just one house? Couldn't Parker and his wife be living in the same house she was living in when he first met her? Having two houses is confusing; I hope I have made it plain that I think in the beginning of the story Parker and his wife ought to be seen clearly by the reader, doing whatever they are doing. In her case, "snapping" beans. In his case brooding. But you have to create a man before the reader is interested in his broodings. And the only way to convince the reader that a person exists is to show him in action—that is, involved with another person. [James] Joyce takes fourteen pages to convince us, through the antics of "stately, plump Buck Mulligan," that Stephen exists before he lets him start brooding.

(In the longer version of this letter I have sketched out my idea of the shape two of these crucial scenes ought to have: the first scene and the last scene in the story.)

---

* Irish short-story writer who lectured at Princeton in 1953–54.

≈ O'Connor received Gordon's letter. One week later, O'Connor wrote to Betty Hester, "Caroline gave me a lot of advice about the story but most of it [I'm] ignoring. She thinks every story must be built according to the pattern of the Roman arch and she would enlarge the beginning and the end, but I'm letting it lay. I did well to write it at all."

Flannery O'Connor to Caroline Gordon

21 July 1964
Milledgeville
    I do thank you for the remarks [on "Parker's Back"]. I read both versions and hope to do a little something about it all but I don't know how much as the lid has been just put back on me. I go to the hospital tomorrow for another transfusion. The blood count just won't hold. Anyway maybe I'll learn something for the next set of stories. You were good to take the time.
    One of the sisters at the Cancer Home wrote me that the Rev. Fr. (I presume she meant the Abbot) had had a siege of being in the hospital. She said he had some torn ligaments in his arm but didn't say what had happened to him. I'm glad Fr. Charles is better. Cheers to you and pray for me.
    Love,
    Flannery

≈ Before she was hospitalized on Wednesday, July 29, O'Connor learned that "Revelation" had won the 1964 O. Henry Prize.
    This time, this hospital stay, she was not strong enough to hide an unfinished manuscript under her pillow. Her kidneys were failing, and she entered a coma.
    Flannery O'Connor died in the early morning hours on August 3, 1964. The funeral mass was held the next morning, August 4, at Sacred Heart Church in Milledgeville.

Part 5

Postscript
(September 1964–April 1981)

All the rivers come from that one River and go back to it like it was the
ocean sea and if you believe, you can lay your pain in that River and get rid
of it because that's the River that was made to carry sin. It's a River full of
pain itself, pain itself, moving toward the Kingdom of Christ, to be washed
away, slow, you people, slow as this here old red water river round my feet.
—Flannery O'Connor, "The River"

The young man or woman who aspires to write fiction professionally
has a hard and dangerous voyage before him, as every one who precedes
him on this voyage can testify. It seems to me that if he has been properly
instructed in the Catholic faith he has an advantage over navigators
who have to discover the shape of the river for themselves. [. . .] This
knowledge—the knowledge of the *shape* of the river, by day or night, in
fog, in mist, going up the river or coming down, will stand him in better
stead on this voyage than any other knowledge he can acquire.
—Caroline Gordon, "The Shape of the River"

In *The Art of Fiction*, John Gardner challenged writers to exercise empathy—what he called "sanity." The writer who "never cheats in his writing," Gardner said, is one who "never forgets that he is writing about people, so that to turn characters to cartoons, or treat his characters as innately inferior to himself, to forget their reasons for being as they are, to treat them as brutes, is bad art."

Throughout her critiques of O'Connor's work, Gordon continually guided O'Connor away from "bad art," which was not merely a function of ungrammatical construction, inconsistent point-of-view, or ill-placed colloquialism. Art, at its essence, emerges from compassion. *Caritas.*

Others might call her characters from *Wise Blood* "grotesque denizens," but Gordon reminded O'Connor, "[H]ere are three young people trying to do as best they can what they feel that they ought to do. Sabbath wants to get married. Enoch wants to live a normal human life. Haze, who is a poet and a prophet, wants to live his life out on a higher level." And as for Sabbath, Gordon suggested, "I think it would be more dramatic if you were a little more compassionate towards her."

Gordon's critiques, filled with didactic analysis, sometimes obscure this *caritas*, her deepest artistic virtue. While O'Connor was revising "The Displaced Person," Gordon wrote, "Mrs. Shortley may be a poor white woman but she is in the act of dying and therefore is bound for one of three states of awful dignity: she will either be received as one of the Brides of Christ in a few seconds or she will go to Purgatory or she will be cast into outer darkness. Anyway, this is no time to call her 'Mama.' And no time to call the old man 'Papa.' 'Their mother' and 'their father' is the least you can give them at this moment."

After O'Connor's death, when Gordon was first asked to write a tribute for her friend, she struggled to find words. "Perhaps an attempt to appraise her peculiar and novel achievement is the greatest tribute her admirers can pay her,"

225

Gordon wrote in *Esprit*. "It seems to me that her chief distinction lies in the fact that almost alone among her contemporaries, she succeeded in wedding a revolutionary technique to its appropriate subject matter."

Her letters to others were less analytical, more searching, and tinged with some regret.

Caroline Gordon to Ashley Brown

5 September 1964

I have been wanting to write you ever since Flannery's death, but "the pressures" have been unremitting and more savage than usual. I think you are right in saying that she had "a moral assurance" that other young writers of her generation lack. It came straight from the horse's mouth, it seems to me. Actually, every word she wrote was a testimony to her faith. If she hadn't had that faith she couldn't have written good stories.

Fr. Charles summoned me down to the Trappist monastery in May to consult with him about his writing and the Abbott drove us at break neck speed over to Atlanta to visit Flannery in the Piedmont hospital. I thought then that she [was] "on the home stretch" as one of the monks put it. She looked like a very young girl, for one thing. I am awfully glad we had that visit with her. She seemed to appreciate our coming. She told me with a grin that it was all right for her "to do a little writing." She was keeping a note-book under her pillow and trying to finish a story to include in the volume which will doubtless soon be published. She had seven stories but wanted eight. She finished it and sent it to me several weeks before it [*sic*] died. It had her usual fault, a fault which, I fear was growing on her, a tendency to rely on statement rather than rendition, also lack of preparation for interior monologue. Nevertheless, I think it was one of her best stories. And I was able to telegraph her that I thought she had succeeded in a job Flaubert failed at: the dramatization of the workings of a heresy. Whichever heresy it is that maintains that Christ had no body. She called it "Parker's Back," a bad title, I think. But it is one of her good stories and, thank the Lord, I got it read and sent Old Dr. Gordon's few carpings on to her two or three weeks before she died, together with some heart-felt praise.

I didn't go to Georgia [for the funeral]. Couldn't make it. [. . .]

I had a mass said for Flannery at Sinclair Lewis' old homestead which is now a Carmelite monastery. They couldn't say a requiem Mass as it was the feast day of one of their special saints. St. Albert (not Magnus.) He is a patron of the lame. I thought that the coincidence would amuse Flannery. [. . .]

Caroline Gordon to Robert Giroux

12 September 1964

I have thought of you frequently in the weeks that have elapsed since our dear Flannery's death. I was down at Conyers this spring and the Abbot drove Fr. Charles and me in to see her at the Piedmont hospital. I thought then that she was not long for this world. She looked like a very young girl! I believe the monks had the same feeling. We were all so glad to have had that last visit with her.

She told me, with a grin, that the doctor had forbidden her to do any work but had said that "it was all right to write a little fiction" so she was keeping a note-book under her pillow and trying to finish that last story, "Parker's Back." She did finish it and sent it to me. She had been "letting me off the hook," as she put it for the past few years, but this year she sent me two stories and I have thought that she did so because she realized that she didn't have long to live.

My *alter ego*, that old curmudgeon, "Dr. Gordon," had a few suggestions (minor) as to how she might improve her story but I was able to telegraph her that I felt it was one of her best and felt, too, that she had succeeded in doing something Flaubert tried to do and failed at. Dramatizing a heresy is the only way I can describe it.

Now, I have got to write a piece about her for *Critique*, one of those little literary magazines which try and doubtless do keep certain torches that might otherwise go out burning. Nowadays it is hard for an aging author to get his or her own writing done, there are so many books being written *about* authors! I have on my desk queries about Stark Young, Ford Madox Ford, Thomas Wolfe, Max Perkins, Katherine Anne Porter, Scott Fitzgerald—and even poor Zelda Fitzgerald! The poor young professors have to write these books in order to get promotion . . . But I was just getting back to work on my current novel—I am only eight years over my deadline!—when this request came from *Critique*. I feel that Flannery had my tribute to her achievement when she was alive but I also feel that I can't decently refuse this request since the first issue of the magazine was devoted to my work and, as I recall, the second to Flannery and Jim Powers.

This recital of my trials is partly to elicit your sympathy and also, I hope, your help. I am pressed for time and my own files are in a state, as usual. I'd like to borrow from your files a bunch of reviews from which I might quote. I'll return them faithfully and *pronto*!

All the best to you, ever. It must be a satisfaction to be able to serve the cause of good letters and, at the same time, promote a kind of theological understanding which has been woefully absent from contemporary literature—until recently. I am astonished when I have time to pause and reflect on some of the changes that have come about since I began writing professionally. You have certainly had your share in bringing them about. Publishing Flannery's stories must have been a real joy.

Giroux replied to Gordon in early October. He reminded Gordon that he appreciated, as few others did, how Gordon helped O'Connor from her earliest days, when O'Connor was revising *Wise Blood*.

Gordon responded with her thanks. "There will be plenty of immediate tributes to Flannery," Caroline said, "but I feel that the best tribute I can pay her is a considered appraisal of her unique contribution to contemporary letters—and it will take time to write that. I'll send it to you when I finish it. I can say with you that her death brought out all sorts of things I was unaware of. I feel that I have new insights into her work and hope to get it into my piece."

O'Connor's final short-story collection, *Everything That Rises Must Converge*, was published on May 25, 1965. That same day, Regina O'Connor wrote to Gordon, telling Gordon that she had been reading Flannery's letters. Flannery had been grateful—as Regina was—for Caroline's teaching.

The next year, Gordon taught at Emory University in Atlanta. The 1966 Southern Literary Festival at the University of Alabama celebrated the memory of Flannery O'Connor. The featured conference speakers were Caroline Gordon and Robert Fitzgerald, the two Catholic writers who had powerfully endorsed a young Flannery O'Connor and her novel *Wise Blood* fifteen years earlier. In Gordon's April 22 keynote lecture, she opened with this story:

A few weeks ago I drove with some friends to Milledgeville, Georgia, to visit Flannery O'Connor's mother. We had a wonderful Sunday dinner. After dinner we sat on the porch in these fine old rockers that we have down here, and talked. We are all world-conscious these days so we talked a little of the state of the world. . . . I won't go into *that* now! One aspect of world news that interested us was the fact that Mrs. O'Connor has been kept busy lately signing contracts for her daughter's work to be translated into Italian, German, Swedish—I believe the last contract she mentioned signing was with a Japanese publisher. One of [our] companions shook his head when he heard that and said, "I wonder what *they'll* make of Flannery's stories!"

On our way back to Atlanta we stopped a little while at the O'Connor farm, "Andalusia." There was not a human being in sight but the beasts and the birds were all out enjoying the sunshine. There was a herd of Shetland ponies in one pasture. And in a pasture near the house, a young friend of mine, Ernest, a Sicilian burro, was grazing, surrounded by Muscovy ducks. Flannery's Chinese Geese practically mobbed our car and hissed at us the whole time we were there. I fancied, however, that the peacocks were gladder to see us than any of the others. I think they were glad to have a chance to show off. For peacocks, as you know, are very vain-glorious. At one time Flannery had a herd of about thirty. I remember her writing me that "Every one of those birds has a different way of showing off." On this Sunday afternoon they all showed off in their various ways. Some of them pretended we weren't there and just kept drifting over the lawn, with their tails spread out behind them and clearing the grass—like women who are wearing trains that they knew nobody would dare to step on. One pea-hen hid in a crape myrtle bush near the drive so that the last thing we saw as we drove off was a flash of blue and green and gold among the leaves. Another made his fan and then turned and strutted off haughtily as if we had hardly been worth the effort. Just before we left, one peacock sprang up on to the roof of the hen-house and perched there and uttered his shrill, discordant cry. I said idly, "I wonder what *he* thinks he's saying." That same witty fellow I quoted a minute ago said, "That's easy. He's explaining Flannery's stories to the Japanese!"

Caroline Gordon would outlive her younger friend by many years, continuing to write and teach prolifically before finally retiring with her family in Mexico. Her final novel, *The Glory of Hera*, was published in 1972. In the fall of 1973, just before her seventy-eighth birthday, Gordon moved to Irving, Texas, to teach at the University of Dallas, confirming, perhaps, O'Connor's quip that "What that woman has is Vitality."

Farrar, Straus, and Giroux released *The Collected Stories of Caroline Gordon* in March 1981. In his introduction to the book, Robert Penn Warren described Gordon's stories as "dramatic examples of man in contact with man, and man in contact with nature; of living sympathy; of a disciplined style as unpretentious and clear as running water, but shot through with glints of wit, humor, pity, and poetry." Reviewing Gordon's book in the *New York Times*, novelist Anne Tyler praised "Caroline's Gordon's crisp vitality and her constant alertness to the natural world." Despite some criticisms, Tyler concluded that "for the most part, Caroline Gordon writes with uncommon probity and assurance."

Caroline Gordon would never read Anne Tyler's review. She died in San Cristóbal de las Casas, Chiapas, Mexico on April 11, 1981, eight days before Tyler's review was published. Gordon was placed in a long purple dress and a casket filled with white roses. Throughout the night, her attendants said the Rosary. At her funeral, her son-in-law read Gerard Manley Hopkins's "The Windhover," one of Gordon's favorite poems.

≈

Caroline Gordon continued to champion Flannery O'Connor's legacy for the rest of her life. The year Flannery O'Connor died, Gordon delivered one of her favorite lectures, titled "The Shape of the River":

> The young man or woman who aspires to write fiction professionally has a hard and dangerous voyage before him, as every one who precedes him on this voyage can testify. It seems to me that if he has been properly instructed in the Catholic faith he has an advantage over navigators who have to discover the shape of the river for themselves. The Catholic writer has had the "general form of perfection" revealed to him in childhood. It may take him all his life and years in Purgatory to gain any understanding of what has been revealed but at least he has discerned its outline and, like Dante, can keep it in memory if he tries hard enough. This knowledge—the knowledge of the *shape* of the river, by day or night, in fog, in mist, going up the river or coming down, will stand him in better stead on this voyage than any other knowledge he can acquire.

A decade after O'Connor's death, while still living and teaching in Irving, Texas, Caroline Gordon received an invitation from Sarah Gordon, the editor of the *Flannery O'Connor Bulletin*, to speak at the first conference wholly devoted to scholarship of O'Connor at Georgia College, O'Connor's alma mater. A "delighted" Gordon accepted, writing to Sarah Gordon,

As for my relationship with Flannery, it is perhaps not fully understood. I feel that any established writer has an obligation to do what he can to help a younger writer, provided the young writer shows marked talent. I was convinced that Flannery had outstanding talent and when she asked me to advise her I did the best I could. I soon discovered that I had a genius on my hands. It is no light task to advise a genius! But my task was simplified by her great humility—the humility of a truly first rate artist.

Hurriedly, with all best wishes,

Caroline Gordon

Notes

Abbreviations

The following abbreviations are used in the endnotes.

PUBLISHED PRIMARY WORKS

CC   Ann Waldron, *Close Connections: Caroline Gordon and the Southern Renaissance*. New York: G. P. Putnam's Sons, 1987.

CG   Veronica Makowsky, *Caroline Gordon: A Biography*. New York and Oxford: Oxford University Press, 1989.

Con   *Conversations with Flannery O'Connor*. Edited by Rosemary M. Magee. Jackson and London: University Press of Mississippi, 1986.

Cor   *The Correspondence of Flannery O'Connor and the Brainard Cheneys*. Edited by C. Ralph Stephens. Jackson and London: University Press of Mississippi, 1986.

CW   *Flannery O'Connor: Collected Works*. Edited by Sally Fitzgerald. New York: Library of America, 1988.

EF   *Exiles and Fugitives: The Letters of Jacques and Raïssa Maritain, Allen Tate, and Caroline Gordon*. Edited by John M. Dunaway. Baton Rouge: Louisiana State University Press, 1992.

FAL   Brad Gooch, *Flannery: A Life of Flannery O'Connor*. New York: Little, Brown and Company, 2009.

HB   *The Habit of Being: Letters of Flannery O'Connor*. Edited by Sally Fitzgerald. New York: Farrar, Straus, and Giroux, 1979.

MM   *Flannery O'Connor, Mystery and Manners: Occasional Prose*. Selected and edited by Sally and Robert Fitzgerald. New York: Farrar, Straus, and Giroux, 1969.

US   Nancylee Novell Jonza, *The Underground Stream: The Life and Art of Caroline Gordon*. Athens and London: University of Georgia Press, 1995.

MANUSCRIPT COLLECTIONS

ABEU   Ashley Brown Papers. Stuart A. Rose Manuscript, Archive, and Rare Book Library, Emory University, Atlanta, Georgia.

ABPU   Ashley Brown Collection of Caroline Gordon. Manuscripts Division, Department of Rare Books and Special Collections, Firestone Library, Princeton University, Princeton, New Jersey.

BHEU   Flannery O'Connor, Letters to Betty Hester. Stuart A. Rose Manuscript, Archives, and Rare Book Library, Emory University, Atlanta, Georgia.

CGPU   Caroline Gordon Papers. Manuscripts Division, Department of Rare Books and Special Collections, Firestone Library, Princeton University, Princeton, New Jersey.

CPVU   Brainard and Frances Neel Cheney Papers. Vanderbilt University Special Collections and University Archives, Nashville, Tennessee.

FOCEU   Flannery O'Connor Collection. Stuart A. Rose Manuscript, Archive, and Rare Book Library, Emory University, Atlanta, Georgia.

FOGC   Flannery O'Connor Collection. Special Collections, Ina Dillard Russell Library, Georgia College and State University, Milledgeville, Georgia.

FOPEU   Flannery O'Connor Papers. Stuart A. Rose Manuscript, Archive, and Rare Book Library, Emory University, Atlanta, Georgia.

JCGC   Jean W. Cash Collection. Special Collections, Ina Dillard Russell Library, Georgia College and State University, Milledgeville, Georgia.

SFEU   Sally Fitzgerald Papers. Stuart A. Rose Manuscript, Archive, and Rare Book Library, Emory University, Atlanta, Georgia.

WDUNC   Ward Allison Dorrance Papers. Southern Historical Collection, The Wilson Library, University of North Carolina at Chapel Hill.

WPUNC   Walker Percy Papers. Southern Historical Collection, The Wilson Library, University of North Carolina at Chapel Hill.

PEOPLE

AB   Ashley Brown
AT   Allen Tate
BC   Brainard "Lon" Cheney
BH   Betty Hester
CC   Catherine Carver
CD   Cecil Dawkins
CG   Caroline Gordon
EM   Elizabeth McKee
FC   Frances "Fannie" Cheney

FO	Flannery O'Connor
JC	Jean Cash
JH	John Hawkes
JM	Jacques Maritain
MG	Sister Mariella Gable
MM	Mavis McIntosh
NTW	Nancy Tate Wood
RF	Robert Fitzgerald
RG	Robert Giroux
RL	Robert Lowell
RO	Regina O'Connor
SF	Sally Fitzgerald
SJB	Susan Jenkins Brown
WD	Ward Dorrance
WP	Walker Percy
WS	William Sessions

Introduction

1   "I'm glad you gave me": CG to RF, undated [May 1951], SFEU. A portion of this letter was also published in Sally Fitzgerald, "A Master Class: From the Correspondence of Caroline Gordon and Flannery O'Connor," *Georgia Review* 33.4 (Winter 1979): 827–46.

1   "Work with her" and "change the direction": Sally Fitzgerald, introduction to *HB*, xiii.

1   "I feel the objections," "slightly dim-witted Camp Fire Girl," and "if left to my fiendish care": FO to EM, 17 February 1949, *CW*, 880.

2   "So far as I am concerned": FO to EM, 10 March 1951, *HB*, 24.

2   "I'm still open to suggestions": FO to RG, 10 March 1951, *HB*, 23.

2   "The most shocking book": CG to WP, 11 December 1951, WPUNC.

2   "Someone, or more than one": Sally Fitzgerald, "Mansions of the South" (unpublished O'Connor biography), SFEU.

2–3 "she is already" and "a touch here and there": CG to RF, undated [May 1951], SFEU.

3   urged her to review Gordon's "extraordinary" suggestions: RG to FO, 7 June 1951, FOGC.

3   Gustave Flaubert, *Madame Bovary*, trans. Eleanor Marx Aveling (New York: Harper & Brothers, 1950).

3   "Carolyn approached her task": *US*, 36.

4   "took me by the scruff":   CG to Sally Wood, 21 January 1930, *The Southern Mandarins: Letters of Caroline Gordon to Sally Wood, 1924–1937*, ed. Sally Wood (Baton Rouge: Louisiana State University Press, 1984), 51.

4   "The best constructed novel":   Ford Madox Ford, "A Stage in American Literature," *Bookman* 74 (1931): 373.

4   they celebrated Thanksgiving: *US*, 75.

4   "One hand on the kitchen stove":   *US*, 182.

4   "It's like suddenly being given":   CG to WD, undated, WDUNC; also *US*, 271.

5   "I was converted":   CG to WD, undated, WDUNC; also *US*, 270–71.

5   "I do not believe":   Caroline Gordon, "To Ford Madox Ford," *Transatlantic Review* 3 (Spring 1960): 5–6.

6   wrote her first newspaper article: Mary Flannery O'Connor, "Officers Selected by Girls in Troop 7," *Savannah Morning News*, 14 October 1935.

6   Visiting poet Allen Tate: Allen Tate, in *Flannery O'Connor: A Memorial*, ed. J. J. Quinn (Scranton, Pa.: University of Scranton Press, 1995), 89.

6   "'Old Red' was the making of me":   FO to CG, undated [September 1953], FOPEU.

6   "reconcile her Catholic piety":   Paul Elie, "Pious Anxiety: Flannery O'Connor's Prayer Journal," *FSG Work in Progress*, 19 December 2014, https ://fsgworkinprogress.com/2014/12/pious-anxiety-flannery-oconnors -prayer-journal.

6   "Please let Christian principles":   Flannery O'Connor, *A Prayer Journal*, ed. William A. Sessions (New York: Farrar, Straus, and Giroux, 2013), 5.

6   "He gave me one of those":   FO to CG, undated [November 1951], SFEU; also Fitzgerald, "A Master Class," 845.

6   "What first stuns":   Flannery O'Connor, "The Writer and the Graduate School," *Alumnae Journal* 13.4 (Summer 1948): 4.

7   "There's a girl here":   RL to CG, undated [November 1948], *The Letters of Robert Lowell*, ed. Saskia Hamilton (New York: Farrar, Straus, and Giroux, 2005), 116.

7   "a thunderclap to O'Connor":   *FAL*, 156.

7   "Everything, sacred and profane, belongs":   Jacques Maritain, *Art and Scholasticism, with Other Essays*, trans. J. F. Scanlon (New York: Charles Scribner's Sons, 1930), 53.

7   "It has puzzled":   Alice Walker, "Beyond the Peacock: The Reconstruction of Flannery O'Connor," in *In Search of Our Mothers' Gardens* (New York: Harcourt Brace Jovanovich, 1983), 55.

7   "The novelist with Christian concerns":   Flannery O'Connor, "The Fiction Writer and His Country," *CW*, 805–6.

7 "doubly-difficult": Maritain, *Art and Scholasticism*, 53.
8 "people who don't have to spend": *US*, 299.
8 "The story, on the whole": CG to FO, undated [May 1953], SFEU.
8 "frees the storyteller": O'Connor, "The Fiction Writer and His Country," 804.
8 "[S]he dismisses the popular notion": Caroline Gordon, introduction to *Flannery O'Connor: Voice of The Peacock*, by Kathleen Feeley (New Brunswick, NJ: Rutgers University Press, 1972), xiii.
9 "defined by a set": Rosemary Magee, introduction to *Friendship and Sympathy: Communities of Southern Women Writers* (Jackson: University of Mississippi Press, 1992), xvi.
9 "[W]hile I am a woman": CG to WD, undated letter [1954–55], WDUNC.
9 "There is no one around here": FO to CG, undated [November 1951], SFEU.
10 "[E]ven college-educated women": Magee, introduction to *Friendship and Sympathy*, xxi.
10 "classical education": FO to BH, 24 March 1956, *CW*, 991.
10 "even write a complex sentence": FO to JH, 6 October 1959, *CW*, 1109.
10 "You can't go straight": CG to FO, 26 January 1958, SFEU.
10 "You may have a fondness": CG to FO, undated [November 1953], SFEU.
10 In a discussion of "The Enduring Chill": See CG to FO, undated [December 1957], 21 January 1958, and 26 January 1958 in this book.
10 "I know I sound damn didactic": CG to FO, undated [January 1964], SFEU.
10 "She takes great pains": FO to BH, 24 March 1956, *CW*, 991.
10 "taught me considerable": FO to JH, 6 October 1959, *CW*, 1109.
10 "I see anew her limitations": FO to BH, 4 March 1961, BHEU.
11 "You read it and then you have to sit back": FO to BH, 11 December 1956, *CW*, 1011–12.
11 "The Fitzgeralds have arrived": CG to FO, undated [October 1953], SFEU.
12 Sally remembered: Sally Fitzgerald, "Description of First Meeting of Sally Fitzgerald and Flannery O'Connor" (typescript, SFEU, 1979).
12 "adopted kin": FO to SF, 26 December 1954, *CW*, 927.
12 O'Connor saw a doctor: FO to RO, undated [24 May 1949], FOEU.
12 Regina O'Connor told Sally: Fitzgerald, "Mansions of the South."
12 "The preeminent O'Connor scholar" and "She made O'Connor": Elaine Woo, "Sally Fitzgerald: Flannery O'Connor's Friend, Editor, and Literary Steward" [obituary], *Los Angeles Times*, 14 July 2000, B6.
12 Fitzgerald and other correspondents: AB to JC, 21 June 1985, JCGC; SF to Joseph Childers, 9 August 1986, SFEU.

13   had been in Regina O'Connor's house: SF to CG, 4 January 1979, SFEU.
13   Publicly, Fitzgerald said: SF to CG, 25 March 1979, SFEU.
13   Privately, Fitzgerald expressed anger: SF to CG, 4 January 1979, SFEU; SF
       to CG, 25 March 1979, SFEU; SF to WS, unsent letter draft, 4 January 1980,
       SFEU.
13   Regina wrote to Gordon: RO to CG, 25 May 1965, CGPU.
13   Fitzgerald tried to explain: Sally Fitzgerald, notebook 25 (1978), SFEU.
13   Fitzgerald immediately published: Fitzgerald, "A Master Class," 827–46.
13   Fitzgerald then obtained permission: "Agreement to Permit Sally Fitzgerald
       to Publish the Letters of Caroline Gordon," 24 April 1979, SFEU.
14   "I think that this group":   CG to FO, undated [31 October 1953], SFEU.
14   "Revelation," she told O'Connor: CG to FO, undated [January 1964], SFEU.
14   "the most gifted":   CG to JM, 19 April 1956, *EF*, 57.
14   "I thank you the Lord knows":   FO to CG, 20 May 1953, SFEU.
14   "Whenever I finish":   FO to CD, 22 December 1957, *HB*, 260.
14   "You were good to take the time":   FO to CG, 21 July 1964, ABEU.

Part 1. Wise Blood (May 1951–February 1953)

17   CG to RF, undated [May 1951], SFEU. A portion of this letter was previously
       published in Fitzgerald, "A Master Class," 828–29.
21   advice she'd incorporated from Robert Giroux and Caroline Gordon: FO to
       MM, 1 September 1951, *CW*, 889.
21   "I think its a lot better":   FO to SF and RF, undated [1951], *CW*, 890.
21   "Opus Nauseous No. 1" and "was like spending the day":   FO to SF and RF,
       undated [1951], *CW*, 891.
21–22 Revising the opening chapter and "The business of a fiction writer":   *US*, 297.
22   CG to FO, undated [1951], SFEU.
23   "certainly increased my education": FO to SF and RF, undated [1951], *CW*,
       892.
23   CG to FO, St. Didacus' Day, 1951 [November 13], Fitzgerald, "A Master Class,"
       831–44.
34   FO to CG, undated [November 1951], SFEU. In the published version of this
       letter ("A Master Class," 845–46), Sally Fitzgerald omitted paragraph three.
       This letter as printed here is unabridged.
36   "They were all suggested by Caroline":   FO to RG, 23 January 1952, *HB*, 30.
36   "You will be interested to know":   FO to Robie Macauley, 2 May 1952, *HB*,
       35.
37   FO to CG, 17 April 1952, SFEU.
37   "I really do not think":   CG to NTW, undated [November 1951], CGPU.
37   Gordon believed that James's fiction: *US*, 300–301.

37   "The secret, I am convinced":   CG to NTW, undated [October 1952], CGPU.

37   Allen Tate had, at this time: *US*, 299–300.

38   "[W]e are anxious":   Caroline Gordon, "The Art and Mystery of Faith," *Newman Annual* [University of Minnesota] 1953, 55–56.

38   CG to FO, undated [April 1952], SFEU.

39   FO to CG, 2 May 1952, SFEU.

40   CG to FO, undated [May 1952], SFEU.

41   FO to CG, 12 May 1952, SFEU.

43   "I was more impressed":   Caroline Gordon, jacket copy from *Wise Blood*, by Flannery O'Connor (New York: Harcourt, Brace, 1952).

43   "Tennessee-Georgia dialect":   William Goyen, "Unending Vengeance," *New York Times Book Review*, 18 May 1952, 4.

43   "[A]ll too often it reads":   "Southern Dissonance," *Time*, 9 June 1952, 108, 110.

43   "a remarkably accomplished": John W. Simons, "A Case of Possession," *Commonweal* 56 (27 June 1952): 297–98.

43   Sally told Flannery: *FAL*, 213–15; Sally Fitzgerald, "Mansions."

43   O'Connor and Gordon met in person: FO to RO, undated [June 1952], FOPEU.

44   FO to CG, 11 September 1952, *CW*, 899–900.

44   CG to FO, 20 September 1952, SFEU.

47   "fits and starts":   *US*, 304.

47   "more Christian writers":   *CC*, 297.

48   "redeemed humanity" and "everything belongs to it":   Maritain, *Art and Scholasticism*, 54.

48   "Vague and ignorant piety":   Allen Tate, "Orthodoxy and the Standard of Literature," *New Republic* 128 (January 1953): 24.

48   FO to CG, 29 January 1953, SFEU.

49   It was a very good review: Brainard Cheney, review of *Wise Blood*, *Shenandoah* 3 (Autumn 1952): 55–60.

49   CG to FO, undated [February 1953], SFEU.

52   FO to CG, 22 February 1953, SFEU.

Part 2. A Good Man Is Hard to Find (March 1953–March 1955)

57   She earned $2,000:   *CC*, 298; "movie pay": See CG to FO, undated [May 1953], SFEU.

57   "I have enough energy":   FO to Elizabeth Hardwick and Robert Lowell, 17 March 1953, *CW*, 910.

58   CG to FO, undated [May 1953], SFEU.

62   FO to CG, 20 May 1953, SFEU.

64   CG to FO, 21 May 1953, SFEU.

68   FO to CG, 2 June 1953, SFEU.

69   "He says I am doing better":   FO to SF, undated [1953], *HB*, 61.

69   "I had a letter": FO to SF and RF, undated [September 1953], *HB*, 63.

69   CG to FO, 1 September 1953, SFEU.

72   FO to CG, undated [September 1953], FOPEU.

74   CG to FO, 22 September 1953, SFEU.

79   FO to CG, 2 October 1953, FOPEU.

81   CG to FO, undated [October 1953], SFEU.

83   FO to CG, 23 October 1953, FOPEU.

84   CG to FO, undated [31 October 1953], SFEU.

87   FO to CG, 8 November 1953, FOPEU.

88   CG to FO, undated [November 1953], SFEU.

92   FO to CG, 15 December 1953, FOPEU.

93   CG to FO, 26 December 1953, SFEU.

96   FO to CG, 10 January 1954, FOPEU.

97   CG to FO, undated [January 1954], FOCEU.

99   FO to CG, 8 February 1954, FOPEU.

101   "I send them all to Caroline":   FO to Elizabeth Hardwick and Robert Lowell,
      1 January 1953, *HB*, 65.

101   "There is too great a gap":   CG to FO, undated [6 November 1954], SFEU.

101   FO to CG, 27 October 1954, FOGC.

102   CG to FO, undated [6 November 1954], SFEU.

105   FO to CG, 14 November 1954, *CW*, 926–27.

106   CG to FO, undated [November 1954], SFEU.

107   Caroline Gordon, "The Use of Metaphor in Fiction," *Folio* 16.1 (November
      1950): 51–60.

111   CG to FO, undated [November 1954], SFEU.

112   Ran across this piece: Gordon, "The Use of Metaphor."

112   CG to FO, 19 February 1955, SFEU.

116   FO to CG and AT, 1 March 1955, FOPEU.

117   CG to FO, undated [March 1955], SFEU.

118   A recording of O'Connor's appearance on NBC's *Galleyproof* (May 1955) is in
      the Flannery O'Connor Collection at Georgia College and State University.

118   "mildly ghastly": FO to SF and RF, 10 June 1955, *CW*, 940.

118   "Dear old Van Wyke":   FO to SF and RF, 10 June 1955, *CW*, 940.

119   "It was interesting to see":   *CC*, 322.

119   "Flannery O'Connor spent":   CG to WP, 10 June 1955, WPUNC.

119   they also discussed the books: *CC*, 322.

119   "intense, erratic, and strange":   "Grave and Gay," *Times Literary Supplement*, 2 September 1955, 505.

119   "ten witheringly sarcastic stories":   "Such Nice People," *Time*, 6 June 1955, 114.

119   "profane, blasphemous, and outrageous": Walter Elder, "That Region," *Kenyon Review* 17 (1955): 664–70.

119   "characterized by precision, density":   Caroline Gordon, "With a Glitter of Evil," *New York Times Book Review*, 22 June 1955, 5.

Part 3. *The Enduring Chill (September 1955–December 1962)*

124   CG to FO, St. Jude's Day 1955 [28 October], SFEU.

128   Susan Jenkins Brown contacted O'Connor: SJB to FO, 19 December 1955, ABEU.

128   "all my usual admiration" and "It would be impertinent":   FO to Denver Lindley, 15 January 1956, *HB*, 129.

128   FO to CG, BC, and FC, 2 December 1955, *Cor*, 28–29.

129   "A sure sign":   *CC*, 320–21.

129   "[T]he two words not allowed":   FO to BH, 24 March 1956, *CW*, 991.

130   She wouldn't request Gordon's feedback: *CW*, 1251.

130   "I don't know anybody who has a greater respect":   FO to WS, 22 July 1956, *HB*, 167.

130   "one of those":   "Ode to the Expatriate Dead," *Time*, 12 March 1956, 124.

130   "They could not be expected":   FO to BH, 10 March 1956, *HB*, 145.

130   "tedious":   Review of *The Malefactors* by Caroline Gordon, *New Yorker*, 17 March 1956, 180.

130   "She is much concerned":   FO to BH, 9 May 1956, BHEU.

130   "For twenty-five years":   Arthur Mizener, "What Matters with Tom," *New York Times Book Review*, 4 March 1956, 4.

130   "the best woman novelist":   Vivienne Koch, "Companions in the Blood," *Sewanee Review* 64.4 (October–December 1956): 650.

130   "the sense of lovingkindness":   JM to CG, 28 March 1956, *EF*, 54.

130   "went all over Paris":   CG to JM, 19 April 1956, *EF*, 57.

131   Flannery O'Connor, review of *The Malefactors* by Caroline Gordon, *Bulletin*, 31 March 1956, in *The Presence of Grace and Other Book Reviews*, compiled by Leo J. Zuber, ed. Carter W. Martin (Athens: University of Georgia Press, 1983), 15–16.

132   Gordon joined Tate: *US*, 340.

132   She planned to visit O'Connor: FO to BC and FC, 21 June 1956, *Cor*, 37.

132   CG to FO, BC, and FC, undated [June 1956], CPVU.
136   CG to FO, undated [July 1956], CPVU.
137–38   Caroline Gordon, "How I Learned to Write Novels," *Books on Trial* 15.3
           (November 1956): 111–12, 160–63.
138   "Caroline has read the story":   FO to BH, 11 December 1956, *CW*, 1011.
138   "found herself facing":   *US*, 343.
138   "as promised" and "took every job offered her":   *US*, 344; see also *CC*, 341.
138   "I feel awfully sorry":   FO to BH, 29 November 1956, BHEU.
138   "Lord knows it creates":   FO to BH, 11 December 1956, *CW*, 1012.
139   Gordon taught four classes: CG to AT, undated [1957], CGPU.
139   "Does anybody ever hear":   FO to BC, 24 June 1957, *Cor*, 56.
139   "Whenever I finish":   FO to CD, 22 December 1957, *HB*, 260.
139   Flannery O'Connor, "*How to Read a Novel* by Caroline Gordon"
           [unpublished review, 1957], in *The Presence of Grace*, 47–48.
140   "I forsee":   FO to SF and RF, 4 November 1957, *CW*, 1048.
140   FO to CG, 10 December 1957, *CW*, 1054–55.
141   Gordon and Tate spent Christmas: *US*, 347.
141   "I think that if you study":   FO to BH, 7 March 1958, *HB*, 271.
141   CG to FO, undated [December 1957], SFEU.
145   O'Connor sent a revision: BC to FO, 2 January 1958, *Cor*, 64.
145   CG to FO, undated [21 January 1958], SFEU.
151   CG to FO, 26 January 1958, SFEU.
158   Susan Jenkins Brown wrote to ask: SJB to FO, 16 January 1958, ABEU.
           See also Ashley Brown, "An Unwritten Drama: Susan Jenkins Brown and
           Flannery O'Connor," *Southern Review* (Autumn 1986): 727–37.
158   Gordon and O'Connor briefly saw one another: FO to BH, 17 May 1958,
           HB, 282; *FAL*, 299.
158   O'Connor brought Gordon water: FO to WS, 15 May 1958, *CW*, 1071;
           FAL, 303.
158   CG to FO, undated [July 1958]. O'Connor retyped a portion of Gordon's
           letter in a letter written to Betty Hester dated 16 August 1958 (BHEU).
           Gordon's original letter does not survive.
159   "A little boy here":   FO to BH, 13 September 1958, BHEU.
159   "gave the wrong lecture":   *US*, 350.
159   in an essay she wrote: Caroline Gordon, "Flannery O'Connor's *Wise Blood*,"
           Critique 2 (Fall 1958): 3–10.
159   O'Connor appreciated Gordon's efforts: FO to BH, 11 October 1958, *HB*,
           299.
159   "It was news to me":   FO to BH, 25 October 1958, BHEU.

160	Hester contacted Gordon directly: FO to BH, 6 November 1958, BHEU;
	and FO to BH, undated, BHEU.
160	"She is about half-mad": FO to BH, 6 November 1958, BHEU.
160	"Caroline is an old lady": FO to BH, 8 November 1958, *CW*, 1077.
160	FO to CG, 16 November 1958, *CW*, 1081.
161	"Caroline is wildly mixed up" and "the harshness with which you speak": FO
	to BH, 22 November 1958, *CW*, 1082.
161	CG to FO, BC, and FC, First Sunday of Advent, 1958 [November 30], CPVU.
166	"The letter from Caroline": FO to BC and FC, 2 December 1958, *Cor*, 80.
166	FO to CG, undated letter draft [1958], FOPEU.
167	"I took the introduction": FO to BH, 20 December 1958, BHEU.
167	"Your admirer": FO to BH, 3 January 1959, *CW*, 1087.
167	Coindreau, the translator, wrote to O'Connor: FO to BH, 31 January 1959,
	BHEU.
167	O'Connor finished a draft: *CW*, 1251; FO to BH, 3 January 1959, *HB*, 316.
167	"It would have done your heart"; O'Connor thought Gordon's support: FO
	to BH, 28 February 1959, *CW*, 1088–89.
167	"You have done me": FO to CC, 18 April 1959, *CW*, 1094.
167	Ford Foundation grant: FO to BC and FC, 22 February 1959, *Cor*, 84.
168	FO to CG, 10 May 1959, SFEU. In the published version of this letter (*HB*,
	331–32), Sally Fitzgerald omitted paragraph three, as well as a portion of
	paragraph five. This letter as printed here is unabridged.
169	"I was lying in bed": BC to FO, 24 May 1959, *Cor*, 87.
169	"I haven't heard from": FO to SJB, 7 June 1959, ABEU.
169	Caroline "was in a terrible condition": FO to BC and FC, 5 August 1959,
	Cor, 94.
169	Caroline planned a visit to Andalusia: FO to CD, 31 October 1959, *HB*, 356;
	FAL, 317.
169	"I've been dying to visit Flannery": CG to AB, undated [September 1959],
	ABPU.
169	"Last weekend Ashley brought Caroline": FO to BH, 31 October 1959,
	BHEU. See also *HB*, 356.
170	"more or less cheerful": FO to BC, 9 November 1959, *Cor*, 105.
170	"Just got a new story": CG to AB, 25 November 1959, ABPU.
170	the story was "fine": FO to CD, 10 December 1959, *HB*, 361.
170	"The back jacket": FO to BH, 19 December 1959, *HB*, 363.
170	Back cover copy from Flannery O'Connor, *The Violent Bear It Away* (New
	York: Farrar, Straus, and Cudahy, 1960) is from Gordon, "Flannery O'Connor's
	Wise Blood."

171   a "favorite of anthologizers" and "serious criticism":   Frederick Asals, introduction to *"A Good Man Is Hard to Find"*: *Flannery O'Connor (Women Writers: Texts and Contexts)*, ed. Frederick Asals (New Brunswick, NJ: Rutgers University Press, 1993), 3, 9.

171   "I had a call":   FO to BC, 15 September 1960, *Cor*, 120.

171   "paid (well) to swap clichés":   FO to JH, 9 October 1960, *CW*, 1134.

171   "embattled against the world":   BC to FO, 24 November 1960, *Cor*, 123; see also *US*, 358.

171   "Age had not mellowed":   *US*, 359.

171   Gordon admired the work: FO to RG, 4 November 1960, *HB*, 415.

171   "I have been recuperating":   FO to CD, 8 November 1960, *CW*, 1135.

172   "I have no intention":   FO to BH, 25 November 1960, *CW*, 1138.

172   "I am awfully worried about Flannery":   CG to AB, undated [1961], ABPU.

172   Brown didn't have any updates: AB to CG, 14 March 1961, CGPU.

172   "I wish you'd manage":   CG to AB, Holy Saturday, 1961 [3 April], ABPU.

172   O'Connor sent Gordon her new story: CG to AB, undated [April 1961], ABPU.

172   Gordon planned another visit: AB to CG, 24 June 1961, ABPU.

172   "Ashley's task was to keep":   *FAL*, 338.

172   The story wasn't dramatic enough: *CW*, 1254.

172   "a million other things" and "So much of my trouble is":   FO to CD, 17 July 1961, *HB*, 445.

172   "Ashley and Caroline were strenuous":   FO to BH, 22 July 1961, BHEU; see also FO to BH, 22 July 1961, *HB*, 445–46; and FO to BC and FC, 23 July 1961, *Cor*, 138.

172   FO to CG, 16 November 1961, SFEU. In the published version of this letter (*HB*, 454), Sally Fitzgerald omitted paragraph two. This letter as printed here is unabridged.

173   CG to Father Charles, FO, and AB, St. Catherine's Day, 1961 [November 25], ABPU.

180   "I have just sent on to Flannery":   CG to RG, 27 February 1962, FOGC.

181   "I have been writing":   FO to Sister Julie, 17 June 1962, *CW*, 1167.

181   a chapbook: Caroline Gordon, *A Good Soldier: A Key to the Novels of Ford Madox Ford* (Davis: University of California Library, 1963).

181   "seems to have taken a new lease":   FO to BC, 24 November 1962, *Cor*, 160.

181   FO to CG, 12 December 1962, CGPU.

Part 4. Revelation (January 1963–August 1964)

185 "on an immense river":   Caroline Gordon, "The Shape of the River," typescript, CGPU.

185 "[I]f anybody had pointed out":   Caroline Gordon, "Letters to a Monk," *Ramparts* (December 1964): 4.

185 "scrupulous, almost standard examples":   Review of *Old Red and Other Stories*, by Caroline Gordon, *Bulletin from Virginia Kirkus' Service*, vol. 31, nos. 11–24 (1963): 814.

185 "I've been writing 18 years":   FO to MG, 4 May 1963, *CW*, 1184.

185 "I have been working all summer":   FO to JH, 10 September 1963, *HB*, 537.

185 "I've just been going on":   FO to CD, 16 September 1963, *HB*, 540.

186 CG to FO, undated [1963], SFEU.

187 "very unbuttoned":   BC to FO, 2 December 1963, *Cor*, 181.

187 Welty, who "marveled" at Gordon's energy: Ann Waldron, *Eudora Welty: A Writer's Life* (New York: Knopf Doubleday, 2010), 273.

187 O'Connor maintained a vigorous schedule: *FAL*, 352; FO to CD, 16 September 1963, *HB*, 540.

187 "You would go on writing novels": *US*, 253.

187 "enough money to float me" and "I come home":   FO to BH, 26 October 1963, *HB*, 543.

187 "blackest," "evil," and "I am not going to leave":   FO to BH, 25 December 1963, *HB*, 554.

187 O'Connor fainted: FO to Janet McKane, 31 December 1963, *HB*, 555.

187 "I've really been battling":   FO to BH, 25 December 1963, *HB*, 554.

187 "Henry James says" and "You begin and end":   CG to FO, St. Didacus' Day, 1951 [November 13], Fitzgerald, "A Master Class," 831–44.

188 "[T]he note of the ineffable":   CG to FO, undated [21 January 1958], SFEU.

188 "I had thought I wouldn't send":   FO to WD, 28 January 1964, FOGC.

188 CG to FO, 8 January 1964, SFEU.

196 CG to FO, undated [January 1964], SFEU.

205 "something was gravely wrong":   *FAL*, 358.

205 "I haven't had it":   FO to Louise and Tom Gossett, 12 May 1964, *HB*, 576.

205 Gordon telephoned O'Connor: FO to WD, 9 April 1964, DUNC.

205 "I'm worried about Flannery":   CG to AB, 30 April 1964, ABPU.

205 "[S]he is not allowed":   CG to AB, 13 May 1964, ABPU.

206 Gordon flew to Georgia: CG to AB, 13 May 1964, ABPU.

206 "Caroline breezed in":   FO to AB, 15 June 1964, *HB*, 584.

206 "We were permitted":   Caroline Gordon, "Heresy in Dixie," *Sewanee Review* 76.2 (Spring 1968): 265–66.

---

206 CG to FO, undated [27 June 1964 postmark], FOPEU.

209 in the hospital fifty days; "The wolf, I'm afraid": FO to MG, 5 July 1964, *HB*, 591; *FAL*, 366.

209 O'Connor sent "Parker's Back": *HB*, 592.

209 FO to CG, 11 July 1964, ABEU.

209 "I did not realize": Gordon, "Heresy in Dixie," 266.

210 CG to FO, undated [July 1964], SFEU.

221 "Caroline gave me": FO to BH, 25 July 1964, *CW*, 1218.

221 FO to CG, 21 July 1964, ABEU.

Part 5. Postscript (September 1964–April 1981)

225 The writer who "never cheats": John Gardner, *The Art of Fiction* (New York: Vintage, 1991), 201.

225 "grotesque denizens": Asals, introduction to *"A Good Man Is Hard to Find,"* 9.

225 "[H]ere are three young people" and "I think it would be more dramatic": CG to FO, St. Didacus' Day, 1951 [13 November], Fitzgerald, "A Master Class," 831–44.

225 "Mrs. Shortley may be a poor": CG to FO, undated [November 1953], SFEU.

225 "Perhaps an attempt to appraise": Caroline Gordon, "Flannery O'Connor—A Tribute," *Esprit* 8 (Flannery O'Connor Memorial Issue) (Winter 1964): 28.

226 CG to AB, 5 September 1964, ABPU.

227 CG to RG, 12 September 1964, FOGC.

228 "There will be plenty": CG to RG, 13 October 1964, FOGC.

228 Regina O'Connor wrote to Gordon: RO to CG, 25 May 1965, CGPU.

229 "A few weeks ago": Caroline Gordon, "An American Girl" [typescript], Southern Literary Festival, University of Alabama, 22 April 1966, CGPU.

230 Warren described Gordon's stories: Robert Penn Warren, introduction to *The Collected Stories of Caroline Gordon* (New York: Farrar, Straus, and Giroux, 1981), xi.

230 "Caroline Gordon's crisp vitality": Anne Tyler, "The South without the Scent of Lavender," *New York Times Book Review*, 19 April 1981, 6, 15.

230 Gordon was placed: NTW to SF, 30 July 1981, SFEU.

230 "The young man or woman": Gordon, "The Shape of the River."

231 "As for my relationship": CG to Sarah Gordon, 22 January 1974, CGPU.

Index